Literary Love

the role of passion in English poems and plays of
the seventeenth century

Literary Love

the role of passion in English poems
and plays of the seventeenth century

A.J. Smith

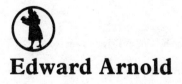

Edward Arnold

© A.J. Smith 1983

First published 1983 by
Edward Arnold (Publishers) Ltd
41 Bedford Square, London WC1B 3DQ

British Library Cataloguing in Publication Data

Smith, A. J.
  Literary love.
  1. English literature—History and criticism
  2. Love in literature
  I. Title
  820'.9'354   PR409.L67

  ISBN 0-7131-6388-7

Text set in 10/11pt Plantin Compugraphic by Colset Private Limited,
Singapore.
Printed and bound by Biddles Limited, Guildford, Surrey

Contents

Acknowledgements

The author acknowledges, with gratitude, the financial and academic support he has received from the following institutions: the Leverhulme Trust, the British Academy, the English Speaking Union, the Folger Shakespeare Library, the British Council, the University of Southampton, the University of Keele, the University College of Swansea.

Versions of material in this book appeared in *John Donne: the Songs and Sonets*, 1964; *Mermaid Critical Commentaries: John Webster*, ed. Brian Morris, 1970; *John Donne: Essays in Celebration*, 1972; *Contributi dell'Istituto di filologia moderna*, serie inglese, volume primo, ed. Sergio Rossi, Milano, 1974; *Thames Poetry*, July 1979. I am grateful for permission to draw on this earlier work.

Sense and Spirit

man, unlike all other living creatures upon earth,
is twofold. He is mortal by reason of his body;
he is immortal by reason of the Man of eternal substance.
He is immortal, and has all things in his power; yet
he suffers the lot of a mortal, being subject to
Destiny. He is exalted above the structure of the
heavens; yet he is born a slave of Destiny. He is
bisexual, as his Father is bisexual, and sleepless,
as his Father is sleepless; yet he is mastered by
carnal desire and by oblivion.

Hermetica, *Pimander*,
Lib.1, 14–15.

But there, where I have garner'd up my heart,
Where either I must live, or bear no life,

Othello IV, ii, 58–9

Had, having, and in quest to have, extreme;

Sonnet 129

To be absolute in a sexual attachment, and make a touchstone of the bond
with another person, is to put one's moral being in hazard to circumstance and the insecurities of human nature itself. When love is proved by
the sense it makes of life then the lover stands in jeopardy. Renderings of
love from St Bernard to Milton assume that amorous ardour may be a
means to final truth, yet they leave human lovers with a question. In a
universe impelled by pure spiritual love, what place has bodily fruition?
The heroic lovers of the thirteenth century, Cavalcanti and Dante, found
spiritual value in their devotion to a woman by pursuing an idea of her
beauty which might ultimately draw them to union with the divine
source of love itself. They escaped the limitations of the flesh by
transcending sense altogether.

In seventeenth-century plays and poems we find lovers who commit themselves to the bond of the body while they crave an attachment beyond the appeasement of sense; and they make themselves vulnerable to brute exigency. The heroic lovers now are those who will try to the limit the issue between their love and a timeserving world, or who resolutely direct their fervour in a higher service than sexual ease. We see them struggling to justify in the senses their assurance of a love that stands above change, and thereby to prove the integrity of a nature which intermingles flesh and spirit.

The studies in this book seek to bring out several straits of lovers in seventeenth-century English writing, such as reveal the times in the way that love drives its devotees to a metaphysical extremity. Shakespeare's very language commits him to the body as much as to the mind, putting our brave expectations of love in pawn to the frailties of sense. In *Troilus and Cressida*, *Othello*, and *Antony and Cleopatra*, Shakespeare gives dramatic immediacy to the conflict between love's absolutism and the claims of a world of change, a predicament which he shows to be no less a trial of the spirit when the lovers are pagans than when they inhabit a universe of grace. Donne's love lyrics express a lover who zestfully accommodates himself to the precariousness of sexual desire, but also claims that he and his mistress have found a condition of mutual love which altogether preserves them from alteration. Webster's *The White Devil* still more radically subjects love to an arbitrary world which exploits tenderness, undercuts loyalties, and mocks passion with sudden death. In following decades the true heroism seemed to lie in a better exercise of manhood and love than the bondage of sex allowed. Milton's Samson vindicates all those would-be regenerates who take the offer of solace in the world for a dire threat to their true vocation of love.

Sexual love looms so large in European writing from the twelfth century to the seventeenth century partly because it poses an acute form of a difficulty which inheres in ascetic Christianity. How may the life of the senses be reconciled with the aspirations of the spirit? The dilemma grew more vexing as human impulsions came to seem generally subject to natural laws. Writers for whom love furthers an organic process apprehend no less keenly than those who take it for a fortuitous concurrence of atoms the susceptibility to time and change of our most drastic human commitments. The spiritual crisis of the seventeenth century appears in the rendering of love, and defines itself there as a yearning for stability, such as committed some uncompromising souls to turn from secular ardours to an impassioned engagement with God. It was resolved for love poetry when love itself dwindled to a moral undertaking, or a quirk of sentiment. The true distinction of English writing about love between Shakespeare and Milton is that it takes love for a hunger of sense and spirit, which engages the intelligence no less than the feelings. In the tension between such divergent propensities of our nature is engendered a living metaphysic of love.

1

The Grammar of Love

since my soul, whose child love is,
Takes limbs of flesh, and else could nothing do,
  More subtle than the parent is
Love must not be, but take a body too,

Donne, 'Air and Angels'

It isn't only in the theatre that we mark the world of difference between a language which renders consciousness in direct impulse and gesture, and a language which just ruminates upon experience:

'Qu'attens-tu plus, hélas!
Antoine, hé! qui te fait différer ton trespas,
Puis que t'a la Fortune, à ton bien ennemie,
La seule cause osté de désirer la vie?'
Quand sa bouche en soupirs eut achevé ces mots,
Sa cuirasse il deslace, et se l'oste du dos:
Puis le corps désarmé va dire en ceste sorte:
  'Cléopâtre, mon cœur, la douleur que je porte
N'est pas d'estre privé de vos yeux, mon soleil,
Car bien tost nous serons ensemble en un cercueil:
Mais bien je suis dolent, qu'estant de tel estime
Tel empereur, je sois moins que vous magnanime.'
Il eut dict, et soudain Éros appelle à soy,
Éros son serviteur, le somme de sa foy
De l'occire au besoing: Éros a prins l'espée
Et s'en est à l'instant la poitrine frapée;
Il vomit sang et âme, et cheut à ses pieds mort.
  'Adoncques, dist Antoine, Éros, j'approuve fort
Cet acte généreux: ne m'ayant peu desfaire,
Tu as fait en ton corps ce qu'au mien je dois faire.'
A grand' peine avoit-il ce propos achevé,
Et le poignard sanglant de terre relevé,
Qu'il s'en perce le ventre, et lors une fontaine
De rouge sang jaillit, dont la chambre fut pleine.

Robert Garnier, *Marc-Antoine* (*c.* 1575) IV, 1586–1609

1

Unarm, Eros, the long day's task is done,
And we must sleep. . . . Off, pluck off,
The seven-fold shield of Ajax cannot keep
The battery from my heart. O, cleave, my sides!
Heart, once be stronger than thy continent,
Crack thy frail case! Apace, Eros, apace!
No more a soldier: bruised pieces, go,
You have been nobly borne. From me awhile.
I will o'ertake thee, Cleopatra, and
Weep for my pardon.

Antony and Cleopatra IV, xiv, 35–45

The change from narrated action to direct action brings more than a gain in vividness. It is plain that the shift of dramatic mode quite alters the value of the events:

J'ay veu (ô rare et miserable chose)
Ma Cleopatre en son royal habit
Et sa couronne, au long d'un riche lict
Peint et doré, blesme et morte couchee,
Sans qu'elle fust d'aucun glaive touchee,
Avecq' Eras, sa femme, à ses pieds morte,
Et Charmium vive, qu'en telle sorte
J'ay lors blamee; A, a! Charmium, est-ce
Noblement faict? Ouy, ouy, c'est de noblesse
De tant de Rois Egyptiens venue
Un tesmoignage. Et lors peu soustenue
En chancelant, et s'accrochant en vain,
Tombe à l'envers, restant un tronc humain,
Voila des trois la fin epouventable,
Voila des trois le destin lamentable:
L'amour ne peut separer les deux corps,
Qu'il avoit joints par longs et longs accords;
Le Ciel ne veut permettre toute chose,
Que bien souvent le courageux propose.

Etienne Jodelle, *Cleopatre Captive* (1552), V, 58–76

Give me my robe, put on my crown, I have
Immortal longings in me. Now no more
The juice of Egypt's grape shall moist this lip.
Yare, yare, good Iras; quick: methinks I hear
Antony call. I see him rouse himself
To praise my noble act. I hear him mock
The luck of Caesar, which the gods give men
To excuse their after wrath. Husband, I come:

Now to that name, my courage prove my title!
I am fire, and air: my other elements
I give to baser life. So, have you done?
Come then, and take the last warmth of my lips.

Antony and Cleopatra V, ii, 279–90

Shakespeare's language vividly realizes men and women who are acting out their minds before our eyes, as if they don't know from moment to moment where their thinking will take them. Antony and Cleopatra speak in the present tense, and their words make a series of imperatives which impel present action. Yet action intertwines with reflection. The images of physical events, and the bodily movements themselves, give us the sensible notation of an inner drama in which powerful ideas come to life and conflict with each other as the character thinks them through. The striking thing about Shakespeare's language is its fusion of gesture and idea, which gives a fullblooded stage action the consequence of a drama of the mind.

The half-dozen or so extant sixteenth-century plays about Antony and Cleopatra express a conception of dramatic speech, and of tragedy itself, which is quite unlike Shakespeare's.[1] They show another order of concern with the human material, which comes out notably in the way that these neo-Senecan dramatists concentrate the whole tragedy on a climactic moment of their protagonist's career, and exclude everything that might confuse the moral emblem. The contrast between this mode and Shakespeare's shows us why neoclassical critics made it such a backhanded recommendation of Shakespeare that he comprehends a world.

Shakespeare's immediacy, and spread, follow out a quite particular understanding of what it is to be human and to concern ourselves with exemplary lives. His interest in the affair of Antony and Cleopatra gives him far more in common with Plutarch than with other dramatists of the period, even Hans Sachs, who also essayed a panoramic version of the material: *Die Konigin Cleopatra mit Antonio dem Romer*, 1560.[2] It is a feature of Antony and Cleopatra that it gets in so much of Plutarch's commentary, and yet raises that mass of circumstance to a higher level of meaning in a coherent dramatic conceit. Shakespeare is exceptional among Renaissance dramatists not least in the scope and sheer sympathetic intelligence of his reading of his sources.

We feel at once the difference in dramatic syntax which sharply separates neoclassical drama from the writing for the English popular theatre:

[1] There is an excellent account of these versions, and of Shakespeare's play, in Marilyn L. Williamson, *Infinite Variety: Antony and Cleopatra in Renaissance Drama and Earlier Tradition*, Mystic, Connecticut, 1974.
[2] It is given in Hans Sachs, *Werke*, ed. A. von Keller and E. Goetze, Tubingen, 1892, xx, 187–233.

Cleopatra.   My face too lovely caus'd my wretched case.
My face hath so entrap'd, to cast us downe,
That for his conquest *Cæsar* may it thanke,
Causing that *Antonie* one army lost,
The other wholy did to *Cæsar* yeld.
For not induring (so his amorouse sprite
Was with my beautie fir'de) my shamefull flight,
Soone as he saw from ranke wherein he stoode
In hottest fight, my Gallies making saile:
Forgetfull of his charg (as if his soule
Unto his Ladies soule had beene enchain'd)
He left his men, who so couragiously
Did leave their lives to gaine him victorie,
And carelesse both of fame and armies losse
My oared Gallies follow'd with his ships,
Companion of my flight, by this parte
Blasting his former flourishing renowne.

Mary Sidney, *The Tragedy of Antonie* (1590), II, 430–46

These Senecan writers don't as much as seek opportunities of realizing intelligence in action, or of dramatic retrospect in which the exigencies of the moment might be imaginatively re-encountered. Incidents are presented so that they have no theatrical immediacy: and we find no dramatic equivalent of 'The nobleness of life is to do thus' or 'But I will be a bridegroom in my death', or 'I am dying Egypt, dying'. In Garnier's play Dircet simply reports to Caesar that Cleopatra and her women hauled Antony up to the monument, bringing out the pathos rather than the urgency of the incident: 'O! qu'il estoit perdu!' Garnier avoids even a narrated enactment of Antony's dying. In fact his Antony is already dead when he gets to the women who sustain him.

What does interest the Senecan dramatists is a completed action which affords striking examples, and calls for a categorical moral response. They put us in the position of godlike beholders, who stand beyond time and circumstance to judge an event which is distant enough for us to see it in its entirety, so that we may draw from it some truth of our condition; indeed they work on the assumption that all action in the end conforms to received general laws which simply subsume the quirks of individual nature, quality, will, and the local effects of manners and place. Their characters can do no more than follow out their hidden destinies to the end already resolved and settled, the fate we know them to have suffered. They are free only in the way they reconcile themselves to necessity, and endure it as nobly or pathetically as the decorum of their condition and their nature prescribes. The playwright's task is to exhibit them in ways which forcefully exemplify the general dispositions of human nature and affairs.

These playwrights make an art of resolving thought and action alike into settled moral attitudes which may be sententiously formulated. Their characters strike carefully composed postures, such as as articulate the images of the various dispositions we find in the handbooks of rhetoric, or personify truths which hold for our condition altogether and may be impersonally confirmed. A treatment of Antony and Cleopatra needs its Chorus of Roman soldiers, or Egyptian citizens,[3] to point the moral and pose the public issue:

> Shall ever civile bate
>   gnaw and devour our state?
>   shall never we this blade,
>   our bloud hath bloudy made,
>   lay downe? these armes downe lay
>   as robes we weare alway?
>   but as from age to age
>   so passe from rage to rage?

Mary Sidney, The Tragedy of Antonie IV, 1713–20

Readers untuned to the modes of declamatory rhetoric may suppose that the writing itself is the real focus of interest. We are often invited to pay as much attention to the decorous artistry of a performance as to the inward life of the speaker:

> *César:*   O dieux, quelle infortune! O pauvre Antoine, hélas!
>   As-tu si longuement porté ce coutelas
>   Contre les ennemis, pour le faire en fin estre
>   L'exécrable meurtrier de toy, son propre maistre?
>   O mort que je déplore, hélas! Nous avons mis
>   Tant de guerres à fin, estans frères, amis,
>   Compaignons et parens, égaux en mesme empire,
>   Et faut que maintenant je t'aye fait occire!
>
> *Agrippe:*   Pourquoy vous troublez-vous d'inutiles douleurs?
>   Pourquoy dessur Antoine espandez-vous ces pleurs?
>   Pourquoy ternissez-vous de dueil vostre victoire?
>   Il semble qu'enviez vous mesmes vostre gloire.
>   Entrons dedans la ville, et supplions aux dieux.

Garnier, Marc-Antoine IV, 1678–90

Rhetoric may not wholly merit its bad name, but this writing will strike us as a much more manipulative use of the language than a Webster's or a Middleton's, not to say a Shakespeare's or a Jonson's. The dramatist isn't so much thinking in words and images as managing formal devices, demonstrating his virtuosity in appropriate modes of elegance, or point,

[3] As in Samuel Daniel's *The Tragedie of Cleopatra*, 1594.

or dignity. He uses what scope for thought his language allows him to perfect his expression of settled attitudes. Such a mode has its artistic advantages, but it doesn't seek to admit that intense apprehension of present being which is the condition of metaphysical awareness.

Shakespeare's words imply or even impel gesture and movement. Their energy of syntax and rhythm articulates itself physically, no less in exposition than in action:

> Troy, yet upon his basis, had been down,
> And the great Hector's sword had lack'd a master,
> But for these instances:

Troilus and Cressida I, iii, 75–7

An actor who engages with the syntax will feel the simultaneous pull at his voice and muscles. Ben Kingsley well remarks that the energy of Shakespeare's words 'sometimes infects the body as well' in a way which the actor can't resist, as if the very rhythm of the language may 'make you use your body' and 'articulate a line with a movement'.[4] Yet the outward movement isn't the whole point. The language may have a physical life which is so vivid in itself that the actor who thinks his way through it can realize it in his voice, without need of large bodily gestures:

> And suddenly; where injury of chance
> Puts back leave-taking, justles roughly by
> All time of pause, rudely beguiles our lips
> Of all rejoindure, forcibly prevents
> Our lock'd embrasures, strangles our dear vows
> Even in the birth of our own labouring breath:
> We two, that with so many thousand sighs
> Did buy each other, must poorly sell ourselves
> With the rude brevity and discharge of one.

Troilus and Cressida IV, iv, 35–50

The words themselves actively render a metaphysical predicament, drawing us into a violent drama of love in which the frail human sentiment haplessly opposes itself to an indifferent universe of unpredictable chance and change.

Shakespeare presents his action as if the entire enterprise may turn upon each moment, whose consequence neither we nor the characters can anticipate as we live it through. Events are dramatized so that they seem to be enacting themselves before our eyes, and taking us into the minds of the participants. We are party to the precarious condition of the characters themselves, sharing their wary sense of possibilities and

---

[4]In an interview with Hugh Herbert, *The Guardian*, 2 April 1979.

searching of the consequences, their calculation of the responses of others and of their own chances. Shakespeare may rely as much for his effect as the Greek tragedians on the fact that we already know the outcome, as when Cressida vows truth to Troilus, or Antony prepares for Actium. Yet our awareness of the upshot doesn't override the hope of the moment, even when the reasons for what will occur are already ironically discernible within the present state. Our interest is more analytic than judicial, more humane than doctrinal, and in any case must be highly complex. We follow out the unfolding of a state of mind, or condition of circumstances, observe the dynamic interplay of decisions, wills, deeds, at the same time as we appraise a sheer quality of living.

Shakespeare gives dramatic substance to our sense of being caught up in time. He asks us to share the consciousness of people who are confronted moment by moment with changing circumstances which pose them choices. Far from being kept at a lofty remove from the cockpit of choice, so that we have no more to do than assent to the moralizing of a completed action, we are put in the position of participants who have some power to shape their world. The plays sift us, as we sift their characters.

The shift in dramatic tense is decisive. In dramatizing present actuality, miming the process of occurrence, Shakespeare asks us to do more than just weigh up an action in the past whose outcome has long been resolved. He moves us into the centre of decision, putting the possible courses of action before us as well as before the characters, and inviting us not only to enter into their predicament but to search our own lives if we can. Process itself becomes the stuff of drama. Resolution only matters as a final disclosure of the workings of the inner processes of mind and feeling, the interplay between impulses and characters, the sheer human quality of the life. The dramatist is no moralizer but a compassionate observer of the differences of men, curious anatomist of the ways in which people's several qualities show themselves and produce their consequences; and his very interest in the possibilities of human nature prompts him to try what people may make of themselves at the limits of their humanity.

Shakespeare renders love itself as a dynamic process, and an interplay of contending impulses. His lovers must painfully revise their expectation of a stable condition, or an ideal order to be attained:

> It is the cause, it is the cause, my soul,
> Let me not name it to you, you chaste stars:
> It is the cause, yet I'll not shed her blood,
> Nor scar that whiter skin of hers than snow,
> And smooth, as monumental alabaster;
> Yet she must die, else she'll betray more men.
> Put out the light, and then put out the light:
> If I quench thee, thou flaming minister,

I can again thy former light restore,
Should I repent me; but once put out thine,
Thou cunning pattern of excelling nature,
I know not where is that Promethean heat
That can thy light relume: when I have pluck'd the rose,
I cannot give it vital growth again,
It must needs wither; I'll smell it on the tree,
A balmy breath, that doth almost persuade
Justice herself to break her sword: once more:
Be thus, when thou art dead, and I will kill thee,
And love thee after: once more, and this the last,
So sweet was ne'er so fatal: I must weep,
But they are cruel tears; this sorrow's heavenly,
It strikes when it does love:

Othello V, ii, 1–22

Othello's speech as he moves in to kill Desdemona powerfully shows how Shakespeare's dramatic language implies action, choice, pitch of feeling. The movement of the syntax calls for a sustained intensity of resolve. Every word and phrase is a working force, prompting the actor to some powerful movement within himself, or towards other things. Othello's inward struggle is made apprehensible to us in a series of apostrophizing gestures which set up a kind of active dialogue between the several elements of his own nature, and between his mind and the universe around him:

it is the cause, my soul,

Let me not name it to you, you chaste stars:

yet I'll not shed her blood,
Nor scar that whiter skin of hers than snow,

Put out the light, and then put out the light:

I'll smell it on the tree,

Yet she must die,

once more . . . . once more, and this the last,

I must weep,

He appeals fiercely to his soul against himself, to the stars, to the universal condition of things, to his own desires. He thinks of his dagger or sword, and then arrests that lacerating impulse at once when it takes him on towards the sleeping Desdemona so that he glimpses the smooth whiteness of her skin, image of unsullied purity as well as of desirable beauty. He moves agitatedly around the chamber, trying to distract himself from the terrible necessity of decision by small practical actions, which only throw him back upon the one inescapable dilemma posed by the bed and its occupant — 'Put out the light, and then put out the light'. Then having got him to the bedside the words enact the fearful inward struggle between his aching sense and his self-appointed cause, communicating the agony of his attempt to see sleep as death as he bends above the warm, breathing, possessible body of his wife. We are party to a drama which involves not only the several elements of our nature but the larger nature they reach out to, putting Othello at the centre of a metaphysical debate. The irony is that he thinks he kills her to vindicate that impulse of the human spirit which can rise above sense and aspire to the pure spirituality of universal love itself. There's a more intimate and terrible irony in the way he sees in the sleeping woman stretched out in front of him her own alabaster funeral effigy, superimposing death upon life, the cold finality of the tomb upon the frail human flesh and blood. He holds before us as an imperative issue that fine yet absolute difference between being and not being which so preoccupied the Jacobean tragedians:

> Why does yon fellow falsify highways,
> And put his life between the judge's lips,
> To refine such a thing . . .?

The Revenger's Tragedy, III, v, 75–7

To take love for the process of a mutual relationship in time and in the world, and involve us so immediately in the competing claims of our own nature, is to value a devotion to another human being very differently from poets who represent love as a settled fealty of the lover which we can only look at from a distance and appraise. *Troilus and Cressida, Othello, Antony and Cleopatra*, involve us in love in action, taking us into the conduct of a compact which still has to find its accommodation with inhospitable circumstance, and with human nature itself. What these plays have to tell us of erotic love is implicit in the way each action is plotted. Shakespeare's rendering of love simply is the way the play works, not least the way the language works. Love takes on metaphysical moment because the plays are as much concerned with final values as with moral discriminations, and the way human nature sustains its most drastic impulses. They discover in erotic love a test of our capacity to make what we value endure in a universe of hazard and decay.

2

Time's Fools

that other curse of being short,

Donne, 'Farewell to Love'

reckoning Time, whose million'd accidents
Creep in 'twixt vows and change decrees of kings,

Shakespeare, Sonnet 115

Troilus and Cressida bursts in upon the house with a challenging peremptoriness:

In Troy there lies the scene.

Not only the aspect but the manner of this armed prologue is aggressively unsettling. His insistent historic present claims our prompt imaginative engagement. The language, at once highflown and muscular, bumps the mind on through outré terms and heraldic inversions only to pull us up short with a disdainfully curt dismissal:

From isles of Greece
The princes orgulous, their high blood chafed,
Have to the port of Athens sent their ships,
Fraught with the ministers and instruments
Of cruel war; sixty and nine, that wore
Their crownets regal, from th'Athenian bay
Put forth toward Phrygia, and their vow is made
To ransack Troy, within whose strong immures
The ravished Helen, Menelaus' queen,
With wanton Paris sleeps — and that's the quarrel.

If these are the means by which Shakespeare set out to quell a refractory Inns of Court audience at Christmas 1608[1] then he lets his distaste show

---

[1]As Neville Coghill argues in *Shakespeare's Professional Skills*, Cambridge, 1964, pp. 78–97, and in a letter to *TLS*, 30 March 1967 p. 274. The Prologue isn't given in the Quarto text of 1609; it first appears in the First Folio text of the play in 1623.

through in brusque contempt of the customary ingratiations. But whatever its occasion the prologue establishes a mode which will take us straight into the play.

Such relief as this unaccommodating verse affords comes quite abruptly, with the brief imitation of the disembarking at Tenedos:

> And the deep-drawing barks do there disgorge
> Their warlike fraughtage;

It is no more than a momentary respite. Labouring with the weight of these drawn-out terms the actor scarcely has time to get breath before the syntax launches him into an urgent assault upon his audience's composure:

> now on Dardan plains
> The fresh and yet unbruised Greeks do pitch
> Their brave pavilions: Priam's six-gated city,
> Dardan, and Timbria, Helias, Chetas, Troien,
> And Antenorides, with massy staples
> And corresponsive and fulfilling bolts,
> Sperr up the sons of Troy.
> Now expectation, tickling skittish spirits
> On one and other side, Trojan and Greek,
> Sets all on hazard —

Shakespeare has this theatrical rhetoric at command, prompting the actor to rouse the house on the instant with his own imaginative excitement as the battle noises rise about him. Yet now the lines abruptly check our involvement, recalling us to the circumstances of a performance and our own free power to judge such a display of art:

> and hither am I come
> A Prologue armed, but not in confidence
> Of author's pen or actor's voice, but suited
> In like condition as our argument,
> To tell you, fair beholders, that our play
> Leaps o'er the vaunt and firstlings of those broils,
> Beginning in the middle; starting thence away
> To what may be digested in a play.

Not that this prologue affects any such deference as that with which the first Chorus of *Henry V* solicits our indulgence — 'But pardon, gentles all, . . .'. On the contrary, we are confronted with a cavalier indifference to opinion, as if judgement must be a matter of whim:

> Like or find fault; do as your pleasures are:

Then as we settle ourselves to weigh such another version of an old tale his very last words wittily snatch us back again to lively involvement, switching our minds from the still undetermined prospects of the play to the arbitrary fortunes of battle as the long rising vowels clarion us up into the main action:

> 'tis but the chance of war.

What follows is a still more disconcerting turn-about however. For the Prologue's battle-alarm cues another explosive entry of a man in armour yet it doesn't bring the fray we anticipate. On the contrary, we catch this young warrior just in the act of desperately defying his role, renouncing and rejecting the manly sport of arms so that he may indulge his amorous daydreams in private:

> Call here my varlet; I'll unarm again:

The heady prospect of world in battle disconcertingly gives place to a confessional episode in a private boudoir, which offers us nothing more violent than the lamentings of an ardent young lover to his worldly-wise old confidant:

> O Pandarus! I tell thee, Pandarus —
> When I do tell thee there my hopes lie drowned,
> Reply not in how many fathoms deep
> They lie indrenched. I tell thee I am mad
> In Cressid's love.

We're not allowed to forget that this scene of privy self-indulgence here, mingling high passion and deflating earthiness, comes as a courtly paren-thesis to the exigent preoccupations of the world about it. Public voices insistently nag at the amorous truant, and burst in upon him at last with a summons to the day's casual traffic of blood.

Shakespeare realizes such cross-motives very powerfully, as when he has Brutus and Cassius debate Caesar's power in the deserted street while the crowd roars for Caesar near at hand. The offstage counterpointing gives the dialogue a jittery urgency, audibly putting it on the margin of big events from which the speakers are thus held back. Troilus's first scene immediately proposes a tension between public causes and private pieties, voicing a judgement which the play will continually hold before us upon such clamorous imperatives of state as falsify even a woman's beauty:

> Fools on both sides! Helen must needs be fair,
> When with your blood you daily paint her thus.

Yet all Troilus himself can oppose to the crassness of a war of honour is the bravery of a courtly lover, that exquisite brain-froth of dilemmas, trials, dreams and high-reaching conceits which Pandarus brings to earth as quickly as it is launched:

> Tell me, Apollo, for thy Daphne's love,
> What Cressid is, what Pandar, and what we?
> Her bed is India; there she lies, a pearl;
> Between our Ilium and where she resides
> Let it be called the wild and wandering flood;
> Ourself the merchant, and this sailing Pandar,
> Our doubtful hope, our convoy and our bark.

Moreover, these refined raptures aren't just left in balance with the realities of battle near at hand, but get summarily dismissed by the alarumed arrival of yet another armed man. For Aeneas' mere aspect, and his news of the morning's fortunes, are enough to turn Troilus back at once on his flat denunciation of a few moments earlier; as in Tasso's great inter-weaving of love and war, the sight of the battle-stained knights plucks Rinaldo from Armida's garden.[2] The two young princes rush off together to resume the habitual exercise of their caste.

From contemptuous dismissal of the war over Helen —

> I cannot fight upon this argument;
> It is too starved a subject for my sword

— we pass in a moment to an eager relish for the fight:

> *Troilus*:   But to the sport abroad: are you bound thither?
> *Aeneas*:   In all swift haste.
> *Troilus*:   Come, go we then together.

Such an ironic reversal of direction within some 20 lines frustrates our posing of alternatives. The old tension between eros and hero yields a new complexity. There'll be no secure hold for the mind in the way the ensuing action sets off courtly passion against heroic conflict, the war within ourselves against the war with others, not least because it also sets off all such high endeavours against the squalid chaos which is as native to our pursuit of passion and glory.

Troilus and Cressida shows us young untried lovers who expect everything from a returned passion and make, or express, an absolute commitment to love and to each other. Even their different dispositions in love are yet to prove. This is love in the teeth of circumstances such as all but crowd the lovers out of their own play, and pretty briskly wreck their bliss

[2]*La Gerusalemme Liberata* XVI, 27–35.

— war, grim necessity of state, policy, expedient temporizing, the assumptions of the casual game of sex. The lovers snatch their intimacies clandestinely from the public brawl of politics and blood, putting love in pawn to the big events beyond them, and to the frailty of human nature itself in an exploiting world. The still moment of their bliss, which they so pathetically seek to lift beyond alteration, stands vulnerable on all sides to the casual chances of a world in dynamic flux whose skirmishes and trumpets, council and stratagems, catch us up in its own preoccupation with change in time. We see that the apprehension of change turns even erotic life into politic dealing.

To cast the old story so is to oppose the values of the heart to the expedient shifts of a world hell-bent on its temporizing way to its relative ends. Yet the play leaves us in no doubt that the world has its necessary values to assert. Such politic devices may themselves be a means to uphold just order and stability against the chaos of conflicting wills to which love so powerfully contributes in the world as we have it.

Unsettling paradoxes, ironic juxtapositions, stark and bitter contrasts, bring out the vision of love in the world which this play enacts. The very first coming together of the unguarded young lovers whose history *Troilus and Cressida* purports to be occurs right in the middle of the play, with a ribald old pandar for mediator, between an urgent political debate and an episode of wanton dalliance. III, ii is a scene which marvellously concentrates the ripening of love from diffident misgiving to full fruition, and yet by the very power of that implied organic metaphor intimates inescapable change.

Troilus opens the scene at a pitch of passionate expectation such as no actuality could live up to, his conceited excesses already standing to be tacitly mocked by their remoteness from the down-to-earth ministerings of Pandarus:

Pandarus:	Have you seen my cousin?
Troilus:	No, Pandarus; I stalk about her door,
	Like a strange soul upon the Stygian banks
	Staying for waftage. O, be thou my Charon,
	And give me swift transportance to those fields
	Where I may wallow in the lily beds
	Proposed for the deserver! O gentle Pandar,
	From Cupid's shoulder pluck his painted wings,
	And fly with me to Cressid!
Pandarus:	Walk here i'th'orchard; I'll bring her straight.

Troilus anticipates in imagination an abandonment of self in the intense moment of passion, and strains towards that ecstasy of sense:

I am giddy; expectation whirls me round.
Th'imaginary relish is so sweet

That it enchants my sense. What will it be
When that the watery palate tastes indeed
Love's thrice repured nectar? — death, I fear me,
Swooning destruction, or some joy too fine,
Too subtle-potent, tuned too sharp in sweetness,
For the capacity of my ruder powers;
I fear it much, and I do fear besides
That I shall lose distinction in my joys,
As doth a battle, when they charge on heaps
The enemy flying.

Speaking here as if all his being is committed beyond compromise to this one end of a delicious oblivion, Troilus articulates the singleminded aspiration of an ardour not yet schooled by experience.

Pandarus' comic banter doesn't diminish the trembling intensity of this first encounter of undeclared lovers but daringly sets it off:

Troilus: You have bereft me of all words, lady.
Pandarus: Words pay no debts, give her deeds; but she'll bereave you o'th'deeds too, if she call your activity in question. What, billing again? . . . . Come in, come in; I'll go get a fire.
Cressida: Will you walk in, my lord?
Troilus: O Cressid, how often have I wished me thus!
Cressida: Wished, my lord? — The gods grant — O, my lord!
Troilus: What should they grant! What makes this pretty abruption? What too curious dreg espies my sweet lady in the fountain of our love? . . .
Pandarus: What, blushing still? Have you not done talking yet?

These brisk practicalities of the go-between punctuate love's tremulous exchanges with reminders of the everyday world; but Pandarus brings with him also a seamier sense of the world, that toying prurience of his courtly milieu which we've just seen tellingly displayed in the scene between Helen and Paris. His interjections at once make an ironic contrast with the ritual of courtship Troilus and Cressida are so touchingly caught up in, and a sceptical commentary on it. What they accidentally bring out is that for the lovers this is no mere perfunctory observance of the rules of the game, to an end well-recognized on both sides, but an impassioned debate which grows unpredictably out of their struggle with themselves and each other.

We see them wittily fencing with words by way of venturing forward in an unknown territory, pathetically offering and countering with the laws and rules of love as if to shore up their inexperience with the security of a common lore. They test themselves against their world in their very language:

Troilus:	. . . This is the monstruosity in love, lady — that the will is infinite and the execution confined; that the desire is boundless and the act a slave to limit.
Cressida:	They say all lovers swear more performance than they are able, and yet reserve an ability that they never perform; vowing more than the perfection of ten, and discharging less than the tenth part of one. They that have the voice of lions and the act of hares, are they not monsters?
Troilus:	Are there such? Such are not we. Praise us as we are tasted, allow us as we prove. Our head shall go bare till merit crown it: no perfection in reversion shall have a praise in present. We will not name desert before his birth; and, being born, his addition shall be humble. Few words to fair faith: Troilus shall be such to Cressid as what envy can say worst shall be a mock for his truth; and what truth can speak truest, not truer than Troilus.

Their timorous ripening towards consummation is marvellously suggested in a very few lines, so that we see for ourselves how the diffidences, reticences, shamed self-disclosures, gradually open into half-confession and then naked avowal:

Cressida:	Boldness comes to me now and brings me heart: Prince Troilus, I have loved you night and day For many weary months.

As a wooing of innocents this is altogether more human than the scene in *Hero and Leander*. These lovers are quite well aware of the fruition they seek, being supplied by their courtly world with a language of desire and sexual encounter, and confirmed by brilliant example. But they are less well assured how to approach their end decorously, without devaluing it or rendering themselves wholly vulnerable. They are frightened of their own natures, and of succumbing to their passions and one another as completely as they wish; frightened, also, of what they understand of the power of love, and of what love commits them to. Moreover, they are wary of love's frailty:

Cressida:	My lord, I do beseech you, pardon me: 'Twas not my purpose thus to beg a kiss. I am ashamed. O heavens! what have I done? For this time will I take my leave, my lord.
Troilus:	Your leave, sweet Cressid?
Pandarus:	Leave! An you take leave till tomorrow morning —
Cressida:	Pray you, content you.
Troilus:	What offends you, lady?
Cressida:	Sir, mine own company.
Troilus:	You cannot shun yourself.

Cressida:	Let me go and try.
	I have a kind of self resides with you,
	But an unkind self that itself will leave
	To be another's fool. I would be gone.
	Where is my wit? I know not what I speak.

Such self-struggles have a powerful release in the sudden elevation of their exchanges into mutual assurances, whose intensity Keats found apt to his love for Fanny Brawne,[3] and then into a litany of passionate vows which carries them beyond the frame of the fiction altogether:

Troilus:	O that I thought it could be in a woman —
	As, if it can, I will presume in you —
	To feed for aye her lamp and flame of love;
	To keep her constancy in plight and youth,
	Outliving beauty's outward, with a mind
	That doth renew swifter than blood decays!
	Or that persuasion could but thus convince me
	That my integrity and truth to you
	Might be affronted with the match and weight
	Of such a winnowed purity in love —
	How were I then uplifted! But, alas,
	I am as true as truth's simplicity,
	And simpler than the infancy of truth!
Cressida:	In that I'll war with you.
Troilus:	O virtuous fight,
	When right with right wars who shall be most right!

They lift themselves clear of historical circumstance, to challenge us directly with a timeless ecstasy of passion which even our better knowledge can scarcely mock:

	True swains in love shall in the world to come
	Approve their truths by Troilus. When their rhymes,
	Full of protest, of oath, and big compare,
	Want similes, truth tired with iteration —
	'As true as steel, as plantage to the moon,
	As sun to day, as turtle to her mate,
	As iron to adamant, as earth to th'centre' —
	Yet, after all comparisons of truth,
	As truth's authentic author to be cited,
	'As true as Troilus' shall crown up the verse
	And sanctify the numbers.
Cressida:	Prophet may you be!
	If I be false, or swerve a hair from truth,
	When time is old and hath forgot itself,

[3]Letter to Fanny Brawne, July 1820. In *Letters*, ed. M.B. Forman, 1935, p. 501.

When waterdrops have worn the stones of Troy,
And blind oblivion swallowed cities up,
And mighty states characterless are grated
To dusty nothing, yet let memory,
From false to false, among false maids in love,
Upbraid my falsehood! When they've said 'as false
As air, as water, wind or sandy earth,
As fox to lamb, or wolf to heifer's calf,
Pard to the hind, or stepdame to her son',
Yea let them say, to stick the heart of falsehood,
'As false as Cressid'.

The moment of exaltation doesn't stand forfeit to the irony of the vaunt, or to Pandarus's burlesque of their compact:

Pandarus: Go to, a bargain made. Seal it, seal it. I'll be the witness. Here I hold your hand; here my cousin's. If ever you prove false one to another, since I have taken such pains to bring you together, let all pitiful goers-between be called to the world's end after my name — call them all Pandars: let all constant men be Troiluses, all false women Cressids, and all brokers-between Pandars! Say 'amen'.

Troilus: Amen.

Cressida: Amen.

Pandarus: Amen. Whereupon I will show you a chamber with a bed; which bed, because it shall not speak of your pretty encounters, press it to death. Away!

This is compelling theatre, and a quite unnerving moment for the audience. These utterly committed human passions which have so caught us up suddenly shift into an eery perspective of time, presenting themselves as impulses which have been dust these 3,000 years; and the prospect complicates further if it strikes us that Shakespeare's characters are speaking to his audiences of 1603. The multiple irony of their youthful absoluteness echoes back at them from a gathering to which Troilus and Cressida and Pandarus are mere puppets in an old courtly rite. Yet it is an irony which doesn't spare us either, for the pathos of that brave defiance of time is not belied but made more disturbing by our awareness of its frailty. Then the mood shifts at once. Pandarus' sniggering innuendo dismisses the golden moment, bringing their passion down to the needs of practical performance — which have their place and truth, needless to say:

And Cupid grant all tongue-tied maidens here
Bed, chamber, pandar, to provide this gear!

The scene shows us lovers who, at the man's prompting, seek to idealize their love into an ordering certitude, ironically challenging time or bravely defying it; and it also shows us the way such an absolute gesture is promptly undercut by society and circumstances around them, the very language that is available to them, and the susceptibility of their own condition to the effects of time and change. It brings out the distance between the truth of the idyll, as it were, in its golden moment beyond time, and the actualities of life in the world, letting us stress the pathos or the irony as we will. A harder lesson follows, showing us how simply brute fortuity belies their commitment even while it is being made.

The immediate cut to the brief scene in the Greek camp, III, iii, quite harshly brings home to us the pathetic momentariness of all we've just seen:

> *Calchas:*   Now, princes, for the service I have done,
> Th'advantage of the time prompts me aloud
> To call for recompense . . . .
> You have a Trojan prisoner called Antenor,
> Yesterday took; Troy holds him very dear.
> Oft have you — often have you thanks therefore —
> Desired my Cressid in right great exchange,
> Whom Troy hath still denied. . . . Let him be sent, great princes,
> And he shall buy my daughter; and her presence
> Shall quite strike off all service I have done
> In most accepted pain.

The episode slips in here with an effect of ironic coincidence, suggesting that Calchas is demanding his daughter in exchange for Antenor even while she and Troilus are professing their eternity of love. We see that the affair of Troilus and Cressida is already doomed before it is even consummated, and that the very condition of their bliss is their ignorance of its brevity. The bleakness of Agamemnon's response to Calchas' request tells us in itself that the affairs of Troilus and Cressida are being settled without regard to their wills by the cold indifferent honouring of an agreement, a mere arrangement concluded elsewhere. A still further irony of the way the episode is placed is that it comes as little more than a casual parenthesis in the struggle of wills between the besieging captains, which is what really concerns the Greeks. The scene at once opens out into the leisurely dialectic of Ulysses' attempts upon Achilles, putting Troilus and Cressida beyond our consideration altogether for some little time.

The return to Troy in IV, i is powerfully dramatic, following out the consequence of Calchas's request as though within the hour of its being granted. A sudden street encounter in the darkness before dawn quickly resolves itself into the joint mission to conduct Cressida from Troy to the Greeks — torches meet and mingle, glimpsed faces are recognized, tense challenge and response give place to edged introductory civilities. The nervous despatch of these small-hour scenes reminds us that this embassy of the Greeks to a city under siege, with dawn coming on, is a business to be hastily concluded. Not that the effect of the meeting is single or simple. The barrack-room jokes at Paris's expense, the careful considerateness, the ambiguous courtesies, put a human face upon iron necessity. We recognize the familiar case of men who must summarily follow out the bitter disposition of the time in despite of their own natural sympathies.

Their rough summons rudely breaks in upon the tender solicitudes of the fulfilled lovers at their before-dawn parting. Shakespeare disposes his scenes so that we plot behind the intimate little tussle of love the progress of the mission which will end all such privities for them, cutting brilliantly from the search-party to the lovers to let us take the point that Aeneas is on his way to seek out Troilus and Cressida even as they emerge from Cressida's bed into the raw morning air. We expect that at any moment his knocking will break out, and admit the world upon their closeness.

The change the knocking brings on is shown in a vivid scurry of broken scenes, the action fragmenting as Shakespeare cuts rapidly between the several parties, the lovers, Aeneas, the posse kicking its heels outside, Pandarus and Cressida. The urgent tide of circumstance simply sweeps love aside. Troilus and Aeneas rattle through the customary moves in the game of manly discretion; there are tears and affirmations, voices insistently calling, pathetic reiterations of 'Be true!', the parting gifts of the glove and the sleeve; and then they are in the open way, with Diomed already laying claim to Cressida, and Troilus powerless to do more than fence with him in nice terms of honour.

Urgent brevity is the essence of this plotting, and we feel it the more in contrast with the expansiveness of the political scenes which surround the episode. Troilus' bliss lasts an hour or two in dramatic time, no more than a few minutes in the playing; and then Cressida is already on her way to the Greeks, the kissing game of IV, v and the betrayal of V, ii. We see that this cruelly brisk exchange of the bowers of Troy for the Grecian tents gives special point to Cressida's seeming metamorphosis in so short a space. 'So quick bright things come to confusion', or just change their style at the hard compulsion of circumstance.

The entire movement of this episode works to enlarge the instance of the momentariness of love into an emblem of our existence in the world. The lovers have their content only because they are unaware that its term is already set. But the vision of this play needs debate as well as images, casual detail as well as big set pieces. The relativeness of all the enterprises with which these people so totally identify themselves comes out sharply in a brisk little exchange between Paris and Diomed, who just happen to be left waiting together outside Cressida's house as Aeneas goes in to rouse the lovers. It is characteristic of Shakespeare to make such a telling vignette of a casual occasion when men merely pass the time of night. The *question d'amore* Paris pleasantly proffers for courtly debate between the two of them, whether Menelaus better deserves Helen than he himself, is quite savagely crushed by the realist Greek, as by a soldier putting down a courtier:

Paris: And tell me, noble Diomed, faith, tell me true,
            Even in the soul of sound good-fellowship,
            Who, in your thoughts, merits fair Helen most,
            Myself or Menelaus?

Diomedes: Both alike:
            He merits well to have her that doth seek her,
            Not making any scruple of her soilure,
            With such a hell of pain and world of charge;
            And you as well to keep her that defend her,
            Not palating the taste of her dishonour,
            With such a costly loss of wealth and friends.
            He, like a puling cuckold, would drink up
            The lees and dregs of a flat tamed piece;
            You, like a lecher, out of whorish loins
            Are pleased to breed out your inheritors.
            Both merits poised, each weighs nor less nor more;
            But he as he, the heavier for a whore.

Paris: You are too bitter to your countrywoman.

Diomedes: She's bitter to her country. Hear me, Paris:
            For every false drop in her bawdy veins
            A Grecian's life hath sunk; for every scruple
            Of her contaminated carrion weight
            A Trojan hath been slain; since she could speak,
            She hath not given so many good words breath
            As for her Greeks and Trojans suffered death.

Diomed harshly puts a view of the Trojan campaign which always stands in the play against the chivalric idea of it, reducing the war from noble sport to a squalid and costly squabble in a dishonoured cause. There's the realism of eight years in the field in his tacit recognition that he fights on now as a leading Greek champion simply because the situation gives him no choice. He cuts through talk of the honour of arms, and even of the rights and wrongs of the struggle, to the grim fact which counts, the number of the dead on either side for the sake of a frail beauty, whom we ourselves have just seen lightly toying with Paris as it happens. And at once Paris courteously undercuts him in turn with the taunt of sour grapes. Diomed runs Helen down so vindictively only because he himself would have her if he could:

Paris: Fair Diomed, you do as chapmen do,
         Dispraise the thing that you desire to buy;

There's enough force in that, as in Diomed's hack at the roots of heroic chivalry, to deny us the assurance of an absolute judgement. We are left with the sense that men espouse their fine causes according to circumstance, and even the state of their sexual appetites.

One marvellous scene in Act V suffices to settle the affair of Troilus and Cressida, nicely offsetting III, ii and the ensuing flurry. But it matters that we reach love's wrack through the truce of IV, v and the long pause in the action which that expansive set-piece imposes. No less pointedly than the feast on the galley in *Antony and Cleopatra*, IV, v of *Troilus and Cressida* shows us the drawing together of deadly opponents who now mingle in chivalrous emulation, courteous fellow-feeling, even love, well recognizing the small consequence of the cause that divides them:

> *Nestor*:   . . . I knew thy grandsire,
> And once fought with him. He was a soldier good;
> But, by great Mars the captain of us all,
> Never like thee. O, let an old man embrace thee;
> And, worthy warrior, welcome to our tents.
> *Aeneas*: 'Tis the old Nestor.
> *Hector*: Let me embrace thee, good old chronicle,
> That hast so long walked hand in hand with time;
> Most reverend Nestor, I am glad to clasp thee.
> *Nestor*: I would my arms could match thee in contention,
> As they contend with thee in courtesy.
> *Hector*: I would they could.

They consciously share a rare moment of celebration which they have snatched from time and circumstance, a humane intermission in the inescapable process of mutual ruin:

> *Agamemnon*:   . . . understand more clear,
> What's past and what's to come is strewed with husks
> And formless ruin of oblivion;
> But in this extant moment, faith and troth,
> Strained purely from all hollow bias-drawing,
> Bids thee, with most divine integrity,
> From heart of very heart, great Hector, welcome.

The tensions of habitual rivalries give the encounter flavour, heightening their awareness of what they owe to each other simply as men. Then Greeks and Trojans go together to banquet in Agamemnon's tent and carouse with Achilles, as if to a feast of love, before the ensuing day's butcheries and betrayals. It is from the tail of this hospitable procession that Diomed suddenly steals away; and Ulysses at once detaches Troilus for that torch-led scamper across the darkening plain to Calchas' tent, where a private betrayal of love will be enacted.

Troilus and Cressida V, ii is masterly theatre, not least in its power to engage the mind through the imagination. The bare elements of the stage setting are intensely realized for our eyes and ears in the lines themselves, the night-overtaken field and distant noises of revelry, the approaching flare of Diomed's torch, the dim glow of Calchas' tent. Then Diomed emerges, his appearance before the tent being followed at once by the covert entries of Ulysses and Troilus to one side of the stage, and Thersites opposite and further down, where he can privately mediate the love-duel to his audience. Ulysses' muttered injunction marks their shadowy arrival for us — 'Stand where the torch may not discover us'; and the abrupt urgency of that voice from the shadows pitches the scene. The place is dangerous, the enterprise illicit, the coming revelation not in their power to control.

Faces half-glimpsed to one side of the stage, and a mere misshape bulking above us at the other side, frame the low lit central tableau. Once the scene is set its voices sound against each other like instruments, at different levels of tone and pitch. The mood modulates subtly; and the several speakers follow their own ways, alternating one with another in an ironic counterpoint of short antiphonal phrases:

Troilus:	Cressid comes forth to him.
Diomedes:	How now, my charge!
Cressida:	Now, my sweet guardian! Hark, a word with you.
Troilus:	Yea, so familiar!
Ulysses:	She will sing any man at first sight.
Thersites:	And any man may sing her, if he can take her clef; she's noted.
Diomedes:	Will you remember?
Cressida:	Remember? Yes.
Diomedes:	Nay, but do then;
	And let your mind be coupled with your words.
Troilus:	What should she remember?
Ulysses:	List.

The scene is intellectually exacting in that like a fugue it asks us to attend to several arguments going forward at once, interweaving the tense little game which is being played out so adroitly upstage with the muffled struggle nearer at hand between passion and cold reason, and the stream of cynical wit snarled straight into our faces at the other side:

Cressida:	Guardian! Why, Greek!
Diomedes:	Foh, foh! adieu; you palter.
Cressida:	In faith, I do not; come hither once again.
Ulysses:	You shake, my lord, at something; will you go?
	You will break out.
Troilus:	She strokes his cheek!
Ulysses:	Come, come.

Troilus:	Nay, stay; by Jove, I will not speak a word;
	There is between my will and all offences
	A guard of patience. Stay a little while.
Thersites:	How the devil luxury, with his fat rump and potato-finger,
	tickles these together! Fry, lechery, fry!
Diomedes:	But will you then?
Cressida:	In faith, I will, la; never trust me else.

Diomed and Cressida here continue a game in progress whose end they both know very well, even if they don't will it equally. Diomed's wooing style makes a nice contrast with Troilus's impassioned innocence in III, ii; we recognize a man who has played this game many times before and understands every move in it. He knows what he is after, and how to get it; and once Cressida consents to play at all there's no doubt that he will get it.

We must take their debate as enacting a betrayal, though it doesn't invite anyone to represent it as a surrender to sense, much less an implied copulation. It comes to us quite unerotically as a little contest between Cressida and Diomed, a drama whose powerful climax, which settles all, is no more than the gift of a love-token:

Diomedes:	Give me some token for the surety of it.
Cressida:	I'll fetch you one.
Ulysses:	You have sworn patience.
Troilus:	Fear me not, sweet lord;
	I will not be myself, nor have cognition
	Of what I feel. I am all patience.
Thersites:	Now the pledge; now, now, now!
Cressida:	Here, Diomed, keep this sleeve.
Troilus:	O beauty! where is thy faith?
Ulysses:	My lord —
Troilus:	I will be patient; outwardly I will.
Cressida:	You look upon that sleeve; behold it well.
	He loved me — O false wench! Give't me again.

That the turning point comes here, and Cressida will soon abandon herself wholly to Diomed, is marvellously intimated in the scuffle for the sleeve and in Cressida's regretful recollections of Troilus:

Diomedes:	Whose was't?
Cressida:	It is no matter, now I have't again.
	I will not meet with you tomorrow night.
	I prithee, Diomed, visit me no more.
Thersites:	Now she sharpens; well said, whetstone!
Diomedes:	I shall have it.
Cressida:	What, this?
Diomedes:	Ay, that

Cressida:	O, all you gods! O pretty, pretty pledge!
	Thy master now lies thinking in his bed
	Of thee and me, and sighs, and takes my glove,
	And gives memorial dainty kisses to it,
	As I kiss thee. Nay, do not snatch it from me;
	He that takes that doth take my heart withal.
Diomedes:	I had your heart before; this follows it.
Troilus:	I did swear patience.
Cressida:	You shall not have it, Diomed; faith you shall not;
	I'll give you something else.
Diomedes:	I will have this. Whose was it?
Cressida:	It is no matter.
Diomedes:	Come, tell me whose it was.
Cressida:	'Twas one's that loved me better than you will.
	But now you have it, take it.
Diomedes:	Whose was it?

On Cressida's part this is a struggle with herself which Diomed skilfully manipulates:

Cressida:	Well, well, 'tis done, 'tis past — and yet it is not;
	I will not keep my word.
Diomedes:	Why then, farewell;
	Thou never shalt mock Diomed again.
Cressida:	You shall not go; one cannot speak a word,
	But it straight starts you.
Diomedes:	I do not like this fooling.
Troilus:	Nor I, by Pluto; but that that likes not you
	Pleases me best.
Diomedes:	What, shall I come? the hour?
Cressida:	Ay come. O Jove! do come; I shall be plagued.
Diomedes:	Farewell till then.
Cressida:	Good night; I prithee, come.

What makes the scene so disturbing is that it presents her as reluctant victim, not only of Diomed's skills but of her situation, and no doubt of her own erotic nature too. Old affection and loyalty still linger, and struggle impotently with her need to come to terms with things as they now are. Shakespeare brings out the poignant irony of her own recognition of the way the world goes when he has her invoke Troilus, even address him directly to excuse herself, not knowing that he overhears all she says:

> Troilus, farewell! One eye yet looks on thee,
> But with my heart the other eye doth see.
> Ah, poor our sex! this fault in us I find,
> The error of our eye directs our mind;
> What error leads must err — O, then conclude
> Minds swayed by eyes are full of turpitude.

Thersites:	A proof of strength she could not publish more,
	Unless she said 'My mind is now turned whore'.

It could only impoverish the sense of these lines to play them as though Cressida is not deeply torn and troubled here, as truly moved for Troilus as for herself yet quite incapable of drawing back.

V, ii most resembles an operatic ensemble in its bold theatrical counter-pointing of unlike voices and motives which yet always hold together in one conception, working out a pattern which has its own continually unexpected modulations, and a satisfying wholeness. Beginning in whispering urgency it mounts to its agitated climax, then subsides in the quiet rumination of an experience wholly played out. We feel the completing of the gesture in the response of the onlookers when the lovers have gone, and in Troilus' self-perplexed outburst afterwards:

Ulysses:	All's done, my lord.
Troilus:	It is.
Ulysses:	Why stay we then?
Troilus:	To make a recordation to my soul
	Of every syllable that here was spoke.
	But if I tell how these two did co-act,
	Shall I not lie in publishing a truth?
	Sith yet there is a credence in my heart,
	An esperance so obstinately strong,
	That doth invert th'attest of eyes and ears;
	As if those organs had deceptious functions,
	Created only to calumniate.
	Was Cressid here?
Ulysses:	I cannot conjure, Trojan.
Troilus:	She was not, sure.
Ulysses:	Most sure she was.
Troilus:	Why, my negation hath no taste of madness.
Ulysses:	Nor mine, my lord; Cressid was here but now. . . .
Thersites:	Will 'a swagger himself out on's own eyes?
Troilus:	This she? No; this is Diomed's Cressida.
	If beauty have a soul, this is not she;
	If souls guide vows, if vows be sanctimonies,
	If sanctimony be the gods' delight,
	If there be rule in unity itself,
	This is not she. O madness of discourse,
	That cause sets up with and against itself! . . .
	Instance, O instance! strong as Pluto's gates:
	Cressid is mine, tied with the bonds of heaven.
	Instance, O instance! strong as heaven itself:
	The bonds of heaven are slipped, dissolved and loosed,
	And with another knot, five-finger-tied,
	The fractions of her faith, orts of her love,
	The fragments, scraps, the bits and greasy relics
	Of her o'ereaten faith are given to Diomed.

We're bound to put this alongside Troilus' idealizing expectations in III, ii which produce a like loss of bearings — like, but how unlike! In these later lines the young uncompromising absolutist confronts the evidence of his senses, sees for himself the relativeness of people's commitments in the world, feels the shock of hard necessity which is the primer of worldly wisdom. Hector's murder in treachery — or in politic realism if we judge the deed by its outcome — enlarges the lesson the world thrusts upon Troilus. It scarcely matters whether the play ends with his brave but impotent defiance of circumstance, or with Pandarus's self-pitying whimper in a corner as disaster closes in. In fact either scene makes such a telling close that Shakespeare may well have wanted both endings in the repertory.[4]

No one who engages imaginatively with *Troilus and Cressida* V, ii will doubt that its counterposing of unlike attitudes makes very particular sense. Shakespeare not only subjects the untried love of Troilus and Cressida to the iron imperatives of the world but surrounds the lovers with the world's voices and solicitations, brusque practicality, sceptical worldly wisdom, belittling cynicism; and by playing off all these attitudes and judgements against each other he keeps us sympathetically uninvolved, as the one party to the proceedings who can take a detached view of the whole range of human contradictions thus unfolded before us. The sheer alternation of plausible attitudes inhibits our attempt to identify ourselves with one or other party or cause but keeps us standing back to see the matter whole, and to understand rather than choose sides.

How then are we to take an enactment which affords us no easy lessons or judgements, provides no single focus for our sympathy, allows no categorical moral discriminations of motive and character? The episode has its effect partly by the way it plays off the attitudes against each other, never allowing us to settle for the voice we've just heard but immediately jolting us into fresh recognition with a quite different account of the matter, continually shifting the point of view to show another side of human nature. Shakespeare stages the betrayal of Troilus as a witty counterpoint, which repeatedly thwarts our will to complacent sympathy by opposing us with a contrary, yet no less plausible attitude, compelling us to recognize the limitations of each partial cause. The scene seems pointedly designed to deny us any settled moral bearings, when the attitudes to human nature its characters disclose have truth in themselves and yet so ironically contradict one another.

Shakespeare often invites a divided response to a scene, and provokes unlike or quite contrary impulses in his audience. The witty villains win their laughs, and even some sympathy for their exposure of human

---

[4]See Coghill *op. cit.* Both the Quarto and the Folio texts of the play have Pandarus's epilogue, but there is evidence in the Folio text that Shakespeare first thought to end the play at V, x, 34 with Troilus's public vow of revenge for Hector's death.

frailty, while we condemn their destructive double-dealing and pity their victims. It's a peculiarly Shakespearean effect to offset tragedy or pathos with a mock which yet doesn't diminish or invalidate it, as when Prince Hal's dignified tribute over Hotspur's body gets an ironic application to Falstaff, who grotesquely shams death just behind him:

> this earth that bears thee dead
> Bears not alive so stout a gentleman.

1 Henry IV, V, iv, 92–3

Wit is engaging, in villains as buffoons, when it ingeniously turns things round to show us the actuality behind the pose, or opens another way of looking at something we had taken for granted. Thersites presents the extreme case of a squalid wit which doesn't even offer itself candidly to our approval as the means of self-advancement, but expresses a reductive cynicism about all human endeavours and aspiration. Yet he sustains his rapport with the house, scores all the time, gets his laughs, even finds the final word for the entire imbroglio — 'Lechery, lechery! Still wars and lechery! Nothing else holds fashion. A burning devil take them!' Our laughter partly approves the reduction allowing it for some part of the truth about the Trojan war and much high human endeavour, as if a right view of our doings requires this corrective of a raw realism which the reformulations of a more genteel age scarcely hit — 'Wenching, wenching, still wars and wenching. . . .'[5]

Yet it is vital that these commenting voices don't overbalance the scene:

Cressida:	Sweet honey Greek, tempt me no more to folly.
Thersites:	Roguery! . . .
Cressida:	What would you have me do?
Thersites:	A juggling trick — to be secretly open.

We laugh because Thersites continually offers to strip away the nice trappings of courtship, derisively reminding us of the common end of the game beyond its ritual moves, and exposing the animal impulse behind the honeyed words, nice demurs and delicate hesitations. Ulysses is coldly contemptuous of the game, as Thersites wittily derides it. They offer us ways of looking at Cressida, and sexual encounter, which don't invalidate for us a very different understanding of women and love, or even of Cressida and what is going on in this scene. A full response to the scene may well allow her the understanding she implicitly pleads for, and

---

[5]The line is amended so in J.P. Kemble's prompt copy of the play in the Folger Shakespeare Library, Washington DC. Kemble prepared the text for performance at some time in the 1780s or 1790s, though he seems never to have staged this version of it.

a measure of sympathy as well, if only because she and her love for Troilus seem such pathetic casualties of circumstance, all too apt to figure the frailty of our firmest human commitments when time and occasion change. What compassion we admit for Troilus himself can scarcely exclude all fellow-feeling for his reluctant betrayer..

Such a dramatic counterposing of dissimilar attitudes has truth to the extent that we find ourselves responding to each voice in turn with assent, or surprised recognition. We can't take a simple view of Cressida, Thersites' view or any other, without impoverishing the vision of a scene whose very point is that it holds together in tense equipoise the most diverse responses to the same events. C.L. Barber's elegant formula gets us some way further forward with Shakespeare's habitual contrarieties: 'By incarnating ritual as plot and character, the dramatist finds an embodiment for the heart's drastic gestures while recognizing how the world keeps comically and tragically giving them the lie.'[6] But *Troilus and Cressida* V, ii offers us more than a debate between the heart and the world. The several attitudes to love we encounter in the scene express unlike expectations of our human nature and concerns, each of which is valid to the extent that we can verify in ourselves such an account of what we are and might be. Shakespeare brings together in a rich theatrical metaphor some perpetual human differences, and representative attitudes to ourselves as unlike as the promptings of head, heart, hands and lower organs.

We must take account of the extent to which the entire play offers to test in action the economy of our own nature:

> Then everything includes itself in power,
> Power into will, will into appetite;
> And appetite, an universal wolf,
> So doubly seconded with will and power,
> Must make perforce an universal prey,
> And last eat up himself. Great Agamemnon,
> This chaos, when degree is suffocate,
> Follows the choking.

> The great Achilles, whom opinion crowns
> The sinew and the forehand of our host,
> Having his ear full of his airy fame,
> Grows dainty of is worth,. . . .
> And, like a strutting player whose conceit
> Lies in his hamstring. . . .

> I take today a wife, and my election
> Is led on in the conduct of my will;
> My will enkindled by mine eyes and ears —

[6]*Shakespeare's Festive Comedy* (1959), 1963, p. 22.

> Two traded pilots 'twixt the dangerous shores
> Of will and judgement — how may I avoid,
> Although my will distaste what it elected,
> The wife I chose?

The images of right and aberrant order which these insistent metonymies continually hold in tension before us are the more urgently offered because characters in all parts of the action simply assume an organic model, the relation of parts to whole in a healthy or a diseased body:

> They tax our policy and call it cowardice,
> Count wisdom as no member of the war,
> Forestall prescience, and esteem no act
> But that of hand; the still and mental parts
> That do contrive how many hands shall strike
> When fitness calls them on, and know by measure
> Of their observant toil the enemy's weight —
> Why, this hath not a finger's dignity:
> They call this bed-work, mappery, closet-war;
> So that the ram that batters down the wall,
> For the great swing and rudeness of his poise,
> They place before his hand that made the engine
> Or those that with the fineness of their souls
> By reason guide his execution.

> This lord, Achilles — Ajax, who wears his wit in his belly and his guts in his head — I'll tell you what I say of him.

People move continually, and critically, between the order of the human constitution and the ordering of affairs of state, inviting us to seek an identity of nature between our own well-being and moral harmony in an army, a kingdom, a body politic, a common wealth, the animal creation, the cosmos itself:

>   Agamemnon,
> Thou great commander, nerve and bone of Greece,
> Heart of our numbers, soul and only spirit,
> In whom the tempers and the minds of all
> Should be shut up, hear what Ulysses speaks.

>   imagined worth
> Holds in his blood such swollen and hot discourse
> That 'twixt his mental and his active parts
> Kingdomed Achilles in commotion rages
> And batters down himself.

> The reasons you allege do more conduce
> To the hot passion of distempered blood

Than to make up a free determination
'Twixt right and wrong: for pleasure and revenge
Have ears more deaf than adders to the voice
Of any true decision . . . . If this law
Of nature be corrupted through affection,
And that great minds, of partial indulgence
To their benumbed wills, resist the same,
There is a law in each well-ordered nation
To curb those raging appetites that are
Most disobedient and refractory.

The characters themselves keep before us in continual debate such questions concerning our constitution as Shakespeare offers for more radical inquiry in the fictions of his late comedies. What does the temper of a particular nature owe to birth, and what to nurture, circumstance, age, experience of the world? How far may we attribute a motivating trait of character, and even a settled attitude to the world, to the dominance in a man's make-up of this faculty or that organ? Should we see human society as a forced collocation of individual atoms, each looking out for itself? Or may we take these characters in the way that some of them see themselves and each other, as faculties in action, in harmony or disharmony with the body of which they are members? Are we gods, beasts or devils?

The conceit of organic order imposes no such cut and dried schematizing as we find elsewhere in Renaissance art:

The Army, compounded of diverse Princes, and of other Christian Soldiers, signifieth Man, compounded of Soul and Body; and of a Soul, not simply, but divided into many, and diverse Powers. Jerusalem, the strong City, placed in a rough and hilly Country, whereunto as to the last End, are directed all the Enterprises of the faithfull Army, doth here signify the civil Happiness, which may come to a Christian Man (as hereafter shall be declared) which is a Good very difficult to attain unto, and situated upon the Top of the Alpine and wearisome Hill of Virtue; and unto this are turned, as unto the last Mark, all the Actions of the politic Man. Godfrey, who by all the Assembly is chosen Chieftain, stands for Understanding, which considereth not only the Things necessary, but the mutable, and which may diversely happen, and those by the Will of God: and by the Princes he is chosen Captain of this Enterprise, because Understanding is from God, and by Nature made Lord over the other Virtues of the Soul and Body, and commands those, one with civil Power, the other with royal Command. Rinaldo, Tancred, and the other Princes are in lieu of the other Powers of the Soul; and the Body here becomes notified by the Soldiers less noble.

Tasso, *Allegoria del poema*, prefixed to the Bonna editions of *La Gerusalemme Liberata*, 1581. Transl. E. Fairfax (1600), 1749, p. 495.

Troilus and Cressida resists the attempt to express a system from it, whether of 'correspondences' or a great chain of being, because such ideas as its action engenders are imaginatively embodied in this complex dramatic fiction and have their meaning only there. The play offers such purchase to humane intelligence just because it continually tests in the clash of attitudes, and in outcome, what the characters say of themselves and each other. The metaphor of organic order itself is put before us with Shakespeare's customary openness to the diversity of experience, to be tried in human interaction.

Indeed, the play testifies in itself to the uniqueness of the human organism in a vital regard. All the talk of order assumes people's power to recognize and so affect the relation of parts to whole in their own constitution, making a moral principle of their ability to understand themselves. Like *Paradise Lost*, the play dramatizes the very process of coming to understand which is the condition of responsibility, as of prudence. In its way *Troilus and Cressida* V, ii offers its unschooled young lover as hard a recognition as the lesson Adam and Eve have to learn.

The play prompts a revision of Barber's formula, showing us how the world of our own being belies the heart's drastic gestures, checking them with the brain and mocking them with the lower organs. The diversity of licit responses to Cressida's betrayal of Troilus — the licitness of even contradictory responses — doesn't just reflect the variety of human attitudes in the world. Such differences are embedded in our nature. The play projects the diversity of impulses in ourselves, holding the different tendencies of our faculties in the tensions and contrarieties of our own constitution, which may become a self-destructive oppugnancy of elements. If V, ii offers us any lesson it's just that we can't afford to be categorical about human nature but must see it as it is, divided against itself. In Shakespeare's day this was evidently ceasing to be a truism. The need to embody a diversity of possible responses within the one gesture is clearly an impulse to wit, as to the distinctive metaphysic of love we find in seventeenth-century poets.

The relativeness of our judgements and values is implicit in the vision. Shakespeare's sudden shifts of viewpoint often offer us an ambiguous moral perspective, yet *Troilus and Cressida* must be his most radical attempt at a play whose intellectual life draws from no single moral centre by which every nuance of will may be proved. 'One of the reasons why *Troilus and Cressida* has been interpreted in so many different ways is that we are continually made to change our point of view.'[7] We can never say more than that our estimate of the worth of a motive or act depends upon the standard by which we judge it. Is Achilles' surprising of Hector to be rated by Hector's own code of chivalry and honour? Or should we approve it by its outcome, in that it gives Achilles the glory of vanquishing Hector, and marks the beginning of the end for Troy? The

---

[7]Kenneth Muir, 'Troilus and Cressida', *Shakespeare Survey* 8, 1955, pp. 28–39.

familiar issue between honour and *Realpolitik* seems posed with such
brutal starkness here just to show us that no final assurance of such matters is possible to us. It is a short step (which Shakespeare doesn't take) to
the presumption that no absolute order can hold good in human affairs at
all, if only because no certain knowledge is available to unaided human
understanding. *Troilus and Cressida* suggests that the times nurtured the
formal scepticism of a Donne, and that the prospect of an atomistic
universe in which will is law, such as Webster and Middleton portray,
was appalling men's minds quite early in the new century. The play also
discovers a double impulse which helped shape metaphysical poetry
down to Rochester, coupling an intense absorption in the moment with
the keenest apprehension of the way time nullifies human striving.

Kenneth Muir well remarked the way in which images of appetite and
revulsion link the themes of love, glory and time in this play.[8] The idea
that our attitudes and beliefs merely project the constitution of our own
nature, and even the momentary state of our appetites, is a prime article
of the naturalism Donne entertains in 'Farewell to Love' and the
Metempsychosis. The projections of sexual desire make a crucial case
because the urge can change so abruptly to its opposite, as both Donne
and Shakespeare forcibly bring out in their love poems. A sense of unpredictable instability in all human affairs is the likely consequence of the
assumption, however insensibly made, that in some way our sexual
appetites govern our lives. Shakespeare locates a motive which shapes
much seventeenth-century writing, and helped drive Rochester to the
brink of despair.

Shakespeare's management of love is as striking in *Troilus and Cressida*
as it is in *Romeo and Juliet* and *Othello*, and he places the climax of love
very tellingly. The effect of that sustained lyric encounter, which so
swiftly comes to its height once the lovers confess themselves, is to arrest
the flux of events as though their moment of ecstasy might really be
claimed from time and consciously eternalized; and then consummation
and the onset of ruin follow together. Their love meets no tragic fate;
rather, the mere alteration of circumstances brings on a casual temporizing to decay and the all-but-incidental leaking away of the bright
vision. In this play the promised eternity of love is denied before the love
is even consummated, as the audience must see.

Allowing the lovers only one short night of passion, Shakespeare gives
their plot itself a distinctive rhythm which he brings out more starkly
here than in the great tragedies of love. In this play the agent of change
comes from beyond the lovers — they are forced apart. Yet their love is
doomed thereafter as much by the inevitable alteration of things in time,
and the compromises the world compels, as by the iron wedge which fate
drives between them. Then the episodes are quite precisely plotted so

[8]*Op. cit.*

that we see the lovers in secure mutualness only for the moment before fruition, as innocents who don't suspect that dire change must follow. 'You men will never tarry' is the word soon enough, even while such niceties of motive still matter. The action has the force of dramatic metaphor, miming a process in which change and decay at once follow fulfilment.

The play powerfully holds before us the ironic condition of beings who pathetically yearn for absolutes and yet can't sustain them in the world, because the world and their own natures deny them. We see that the brute facts of their social existence are against these categorical young lovers, who swear to outlast time with their passion. They must compromise, temporize, settle for such expedient means as offer, if they are to go on living reasonably with others at all in an unaccommodating world. The mere change of circumstances and occasions undercuts their bravest vows, as it must, despite their wills. Above all, they are at the mercy of contrarious human nature itself, which never permits us to sustain an undivided response, or to be wholly confident that we ourselves won't belie our most absolute commitments of passion the moment they are sealed. The lover who is all willingness to come to terms with the world, and the lover who won't compromise even with the evidence of his own senses, are equally pathetic victims of circumstance.

Troilus and Cressida brings it home to us that it is we ourselves who go on giving the lie to the heart's drastic gestures even as we make them, tragically, comically, and always ironically then:

> Almost any tale of our doings is comic. We are bottomlessly comic to each other. . . . Yet it is also the case that life is horrible, without metaphysical sense, wrecked by change, pain and the close prospect of death. Out of this is born irony. . . .
>
> Iris Murdoch, *The Black Prince*

Heroic tragedy or reductive farce? *Troilus and Cressida* is Shakespeare's most explicit attempt at a dramatic metaphor for the contrarieties of our being, holding in ironic confrontation quite opposite human impulses and ways of looking at ourselves, while pointedly denying these pagan Greeks and Trojans any effective spiritual recourse beyond our own nature. The play takes us on to those great tragedies which so powerfully enact the vision of an existence at once momentous and absurd, and weigh a quality of being against the consequence of men's lives in time. The remarkable thing is that Shakespeare needed heroes as unlike each other as Troilus, and Othello and Antony to prove sexual love in a world of alteration.

3

The World's Great Snare

Love is a growing, or full constant light;
And his first minute, after noon, is night.

Donne, 'A Lecture upon the Shadow'

Shakespeare draws us into the affairs of Othello and Desdemona by subtle indirection, surrounding Cintio's simple drama of the Moorish officer who clandestinely marries the daughter of a prosperous senator with a strident charivari of Venetian life in the sixteenth century. He opens his play in the streets by having us overhear a passing altercation between a couple of nightwalking bloods, which ends in their bawling ribaldry up at the darkened windows of a family mansion so as to rouse the household, and bring down its menfolk armed into the public way. We see the sleeping streets come to startled life as torches appear, messengers scurry on their way, parties encounter and challenge each other in the dark. The local fracas swells into a larger disturbance. Gradually it emerges that the Venetian Senate sits in urgent session, even at so late an hour, under the threat of an impending Turkish attack from the sea. The stage fills with hurrying Senators and their retainers en route for the Council Chamber, where the Duke already presides over a council of war, which is reassessing the situation moment by moment as fresh intelligence comes in.

We find ourselves thus rudely embroiled in the affairs of a prosperous maritime state which feels itself to be at the centre of its world. Shakespeare catches the city in a moment of crisis such as the seaboard domains of Europe keenly feared while the Turks (not to say the Spaniards) were still making head. We enter into the alarm of an opulent mercantile community which is under dire threat of barbarous assault from the sea, and well realizes the urgency of the measures it takes to preserve itself. Men look anxiously to their families, property, place, and their own lives.

The values of family, possession, and place loom large in the Venice Shakespeare thus discovers to us. Even that casual squabble which begins the play turns upon an aspiring gallant's attempts upon a rich merchant's daughter, and a soldier's chagrin at seeing a rival get preferment to an office he had expected for himself. It discloses a familiar world of emulation and envy in which men watch their opportunity to do down a rival so as to advance themselves; or they serve their own turn by masking their real motives, while lamenting that honesty and loyal service no longer count for anything:

Iago:	But there's no remedy, 'tis the curse of service,
	Preferment goes by letter and affection,
	Not by the old gradation, where each second
	Stood heir to the first: now sir, be judge yourself,
	Whether I in any just term am affin'd
	To love the Moor.
Roderigo:	I would not follow him then.
Iago:	O, sir, content you.
	I follow him to serve my turn upon him:
	We cannot be all masters, nor all masters
	Cannot be truly follow'd. You shall mark
	Many a duteous and knee-crooking knave,
	That, doting on his own obsequious bondage,
	Wears out his time much like his master's ass,
	For nought but provender, and when he's old, cashier'd,
	Whip me such honest knaves: others there are,
	Who, trimm'd in forms, and visages of duty,
	Keep yet their hearts attending on themselves,
	And throwing but shows of service on their lords,
	Do well thrive by 'em, and when they have lin'd their coats,
	Do themselves homage, those fellows have some soul,
	And such a one do I profess myself, . . .

Malicious envy takes these two malcontents into the assault on Brabantio's peace, but a zestful savouring of their own gross wit carries them through it. The scene explodes into farce, whose coarse exuberance of language and invention knocks the stuffing out of pompous pride:

Roderigo:	What ho! Brabantio, Signior Brabantio, ho!
Iago:	Awake! what ho, Brabantio! thieves, thieves, thieves!
	Look to your house, your daughter, and your bags.
	Thieves, thieves!

BRABANTIO *at a window.*

Brabantio:	What is the reason of this terrible summons?
	What is the matter there?
Roderigo:	Signior, is all your family within?
Iago:	Are all doors lock'd?
Brabantio:	Why, wherefore ask you this?

Iago:	Zounds, sir, you are robb'd, for shame put on your gown,
	Your heart is burst, you have lost half your soul;
	Even now, very now, an old black ram
	Is tupping your white ewe; arise, arise,
	Awake the snorting citizens with the bell,
	Or else the devil will make a grandsire of you,
	Arise I say.
Brabantio:	What, have you lost your wits?

The barrack-room ribaldry quite hilariously reduces connubial rites to farmyard rutting:

Iago:	Zounds, sir, you are one of those that will not serve God, if the devil bid you. Because we come to do you service, you think we are ruffians, you'll have your daughter cover'd with a Barbary horse; you'll have your nephews neigh to you; you'll have coursers for cousins, and gennets for germans.
Brabantio:	What profane wretch art thou?
Iago:	I am one, sir, that come to tell you, your daughter, and the Moor, are now making the beast with two backs.
Brabantio:	Thou art a villain.
Iago:	You are a senator.
Brabantio:	This thou shalt answer, I know thee, Roderigo.
Roderigo:	Sir, I will answer anything, But I beseech you,
	If't be your pleasure, and most wise consent,
	(As partly I find it is) that your fair daughter,
	At this odd-even and dull watch o' the night,
	Transported with no worse nor better guard,
	But with a knave of common hire, a gondolier,
	To the gross clasps of a lascivious Moor: . . . .

The lights coming up all over the big house, the alarm and scurry of servants, Brabantio's reappearance in the street at the head of a household, all mark substance to be safeguarded. Brabantio, full of wary self-esteem, cuts a familiar figure at this point. He is the man of means whose marriageable only daughter has given him the slip. We can place him in that avid fair of vanities held up for us in the Renaissance satiric comedy, whose thriving citizens lock away their daughters or young wives from a jungle of predators only to find that women won't be treated as mere adjuncts of estate or blood, and ingeniously deceive them. All the characters might pass for social types in a Machiavellian intrigue; and they work at their roles with furious intensity. Like Jonson, Shakespeare renders in displays of dramatic energy the prevailing zest for gain, setting off the witty resource of the predators against the obsessive self-interest of the established citizens.

The display of double-dealing in action gives the scene savour in the theatre. Iago plays to his house here, flaunting himself before us as the exploiter of would-be exploiters. He adroitly jockeys people along, pushing his accomplice forward during the assault on Brabantio's house while he himself keeps back out of sight, slipping quietly away in an exquisitely timed exit the instant Brabantio leaves the window to come down, and then capping his performance when he re-emerges openly next moment at the head of the party he has just been doing down, and works upon Othello in quite a different character from the one he had presented to Roderigo. Iago operates at this point as another Scapino or Mosca in a city satire; and we may relish his artistry in the the game of self-advancement whatever we think of his means.

Shakespeare suggests just enough of the tension of that Council meeting in the small hours, when the fate of Venice itself may hang on a timely word, to let us see how self-importantly Brabantio interrupts the anxious conclave with his domestic complaint, and how humanely he is indulged. Outraged family feeling overrides his civic discretion. He elbows aside the traffic of intelligence and orders to get judgement against the Moor who has supposedly duped his daughter, and doesn't hesitate to question Othello's fitness to lead the counterattack upon the Turks. Even when it becomes plain that Othello himself is blameless, Brabantio determinedly finds him another role in a domestic farce:

> Look to her Moor if thou hast eyes to see
> She has deceived her father, and may thee.
> Prithee on to the business

It is from the midst of this inauspicious turmoil of the Venetian world that Othello and Desdemona publicly testify their love.

Even while Desdemona is still awaited in the Council Chamber, Othello's tale of how he wooed her comes as an idyll in the midst of tumult, a still centre of peace and mutual devotion won out of hardship, which she shared with him at least in sympathetic retrospect:

> She lov'd me for the dangers I had pass'd,
> And I lov'd her that she did pity them.

When Desdemona enters she at once finely confirms the mutual bond, with a firm dignity that sets her apart from the bluster she confronts. Called upon to defend their marriage in the middle of a council of war, the lovers make a mutual avowal which has no truck with self-advancement or equivocation. To propose such an apologia they both need a certain unworldliness, which Shakespeare carefully provides for. His lover here has reached middle years while remaining professionally unaccustomed to the guarded sophistication of cities; and the woman is a sheltered girl, as yet unexposed to the appetites that move the society which surrounds her. Shakespeare singles them out for their simple candour from the commerce of the Venetian world. Their uncalculating expectation of truth gives them a rare largeness of spirit; but it also disarms them in the world we've already encountered, whose working principle Iago voices:

> For when my outward action does demonstrate
> The native act, and figure of my heart
> In compliment extern, 'tis not long after
> But I will wear my heart upon my sleeve
> For doves to peck at.

Yet we can't take the Venice of *Othello* for another Claudius' Court or Viennese stew. Othello and Desdemona are civilly heard, and approved, against a leading senator who clearly has a case; Brabantio's own colleagues give love its just due in the trial with influence. We see that the city fathers themselves prize true quality of mind and temper, and allow it scope in civic life. Far from surrounding his lovers with the corrupt luxury for which Venice was notorious in his day, Shakespeare shows us a fairminded dukedom which remains throughout the arbiter of just values, and speedily repairs the local disorder wrought by Othello's unwariness.

Heroism here must be a matter of holding to a vision of love, and of human possibility, which our own nature partly undermines. If the avowals of Othello and Desdemona escape the expectations of the Brabantios of the world, they deny altogether the ill-willed worldliness of a Iago. The distance between the men of the world and the lovers appears in the stark contrasts of attitudes by which the play moves forward, marking extreme and uncompromising differences in the understanding of love and of human nature. Desdemona and Othello movingly make their profession in public at the climax of the first act:

> *Desdemona*: That I did love the Moor, to live with him,
> My downright violence, and scorn of fortunes,
> May trumpet to the world: my heart's subdued
> Even to the utmost pleasure of my lord:
> I saw Othello's visage in his mind,
> And to his honours, and his valiant parts
> Did I my soul and fortunes consecrate:
> So that, dear lords, if I be left behind,
> A moth of peace, and he go to the war,
> The rites for which I love him are bereft me,
> And I a heavy interim shall support,
> By his dear absence; let me go with him.
>
> *Othello*: Your voices, Lords: beseech you, let her will
> Have a free way; I therefore beg it not
> To please the palate of my appetite,
> Nor to comply with heat, the young affects

In my defunct, and proper satisfaction,
But to be free and bounteous of her mind;
And heaven defend your good souls that you think
I will your serious and great business scant,
For she is with me; . . . no, when light-wing'd toys,
And feather'd Cupid, foils with wanton dullness
My speculative and active instruments,
That my disports occupy and taint my business,
Let housewives make a skillet of my helm,
And all indign and base adversities
Make head against my reputation!

Not that Desdemona's sense of their love quite chimes with Othello's lofty idealism at this point, or in the revealing little exchange that follows:

Duke:	You must hence tonight.
Desdemona:	Tonight, my Lord?
Duke:	This night.
Othello:	With all my heart.

Less starkly than in *Troilus and Cressida* Shakespeare arranges the circumstances of his action so that the lovers have only a brief fulfilment, which they snatch out of alarms and uncertainties. For all her innocent modesty Desdemona seems to have the surer understanding of connubial love. Her words finely envisage a relationship much like that of unfallen Adam and Eve, in which mind and body may be wholly at one in mutual tenderness; and she properly feels the jar of the disturbance of their wedding rites. Othello exalts their marriage to a union of pure minds, and allows the proper satisfaction of their bodies only when it serves that higher end. He disdains the promptings of sense as frailties unworthy of a noble spirit. But then both lovers are as yet untried in love.

From these brave avowals amid the crisis of state we are brusquely returned to the buffoonery of Roderigo's Aguecheek-like bleatings as Iago ironically spurs him on. The change of attitude would be as harsh as the change of tone were it not that even Roderigo adds his involuntary testimony to Desdemona's worth:

Iago:	Virtue? a fig! 'tis in ourselves, that we are thus, or thus: our bodies are gardens, to the which our wills are gardeners, so that if we will plant nettles, or sow lettuce, set hyssop, and weed up thyme; supply it with one gender of herbs, or distract it with many; either to have it sterile with idleness, or manur'd with industry, why, the power, and corrigible authority of this, lies in our wills. If the balance of our lives had not one scale of reason, to poise another of sensuality, the blood and baseness of our natures would conduct us to most preposterous conclusions. But we have reason to cool our raging motions, our carnal

stings, our unbitted lusts; whereof I take this, that you call love, to be a sect, or scion.

Roderigo: It cannot be.

Iago: It is merely a lust of the blood, and a permission of the will. . . . It cannot be that Desdemona should long continue her love unto the Moor, . . . put money in thy purse, . . . nor he to her; it was a violent commencement, and thou shalt see an answerable sequestration: put but money in thy purse. . . . These Moors are changeable in their wills:. . . . fill thy purse with money. The food that to him now is as luscious as locusts, shall be to him shortly as acerb as the coloquintida. When she is sated with his body, she will find the error of her choice; she must have change, she must. . . .

Iago may be simply keeping Roderigo in play, but what he says of love has force and puts a question to us. Is love what Othello and Desdemona make of it? Or is it what Iago declares it to be? For Iago here love is no more than appetite unrestrained by will, an expression of our base nature; and to expect any better of it is just to project our cravings and aversions into hopeless self-deceit. Reason consists in understanding ourselves well enough to will our own exemption from such abject self-slavery, as from every other vulnerable attachment, in the furtherance of our own interests: ' 'Tis but applying wormseed to the tail'. We see how Iago carries through his code of politic calculation the instant Roderigo leaves him:

Thus do I ever make my fool my purse

If Iago's naturalism articulates itself in the voice of self-seeking worldliness, then the idealism of the lovers stands against that view of the world. In the quarrel between the manners and expectations of the Venetian streets, and the brave stand Othello and Desdemona take in despite of expedient compromise, our own nature is put in proof. We are to ask ourselves whether love may be an ideal union of minds or 'souls, whom no change can invade', which does not need sense or depend upon sensual appetite, or whether it is a mere function of sense which must be wholly subject to satiety and change while it lacks the politic regulation of the will. The very manner in which the play works on its audience suggests that we find it well within the capacity of our nature to approve both unlike terms, and that our divided response puts the same predicament to us as at once farcical and tragic. Iago's business with Othello can't be just to make him doubt Desdemona; it is to bring him to believe that people are creatures of appetite, while he still wholeheartedly wills a prospect of grace.

By the second act this counterposing of attitudes has become a continual dramatic excitement. Shakespeare sharpens the encounter by arranging the arrival at Cyprus so that the parties land at intervals, producing a lively clash of attitudes before even Desdemona and Othello come together again. Cassio finely acknowledges a spiritual sublimity in Desdemona, hailing her as a being in the highest state of blessedness:

> One that . . . in the essential vesture of creation
> Does bear all excellency. . . .
>
> . . . The divine Desdemona. . . .
>
> . . . Hail to thee lady! and the grace of heaven,
> Before, behind thee, and on every hand,
> Enwheel thee round!

So Dante might have celebrated Beatrice or the angel greeted Mary; and the transcendent salutation is followed at once by Iago's caricaturing mirror for women, held up to the very same lady as well as to his wife:

> Come on, come on , you are pictures out of doors;
> Bells in your parlours; wild-cats in your kitchens;
> Saints in your injuries; devils being offended;
> Players in your housewifery; and housewives in your beds.

His wit has force in a different order of being from Cassio's celebration, invoking the manners of the *novella* or of domestic farce. In fact the debate seems to have not two terms here but three, putting the same woman before us as a spiritual being, a domestic creature and an animal sensibility. The ensuing action will prove Desdemona's quality without discounting other possibilities of woman's nature.

Iago's reading of the courtesies between Cassio and Desdemona gives us a precise emblem of the forces now in play:

> *Iago*:   He takes her by the palm; ay, well said, whisper: as little a web as this will ensnare as great a fly as Cassio. Ay, smile upon her, do: I will catch you in your own courtesies:

Cassio ensnares himself here by his very openness to Desdemona's worth, refining for himself the web in which Iago will trap him. The irony is that any such innocent ceremony makes people vulnerable in the world a Iago inhabits:

> In this world's warfare, they whom rugged Fate,
> (God's commissary,) doth so throughly hate
> As in the Court's squadron to marshal their state
>
> If they stand armed with silly honesty,
> With wishing prayers, and neat integrity,
> Like Indian 'gainst Spanish hosts they be.

> Donne, *To Sir Henry Wotton*, 'Here's no more news, than virtue'

In Iago's terms anything that limits the scope of self-interest is to that extent a self-impediment.

Then Othello enters to be reunited with Desdemona and at once they reach the height of their mutual ecstasy, as venturers who suddenly gain a calm prospect out of storm:

> O my soul's joy,
> If after every tempest come such calmness,
> May the winds blow, till they have waken'd death,
> And let the labouring bark climb hills of seas,
> Olympus-high, and duck again as low
> As hell's from heaven. If it were now to die,
> 'Twere now to be most happy, for I fear
> My soul hath her content so absolute,
> That not another comfort, like to this
> Succeeds in unknown fate.

Desdemona: The heavens forbid
> But that our loves and comforts should increase,
> Even as our days do grow.

Othello: Amen to that, sweet powers!
> I cannot speak enough of this content,
> It stops me here, it is too much of joy:
> And this, and this, the greatest discord be
> That e'er our hearts shall make!

Iago: O, you are well tun'd now,
> But I'll set down the pegs that make this music,
> As honest as I am.

The passage is harrowingly full of ironies and ambiguities, and not only because Iago looks on enviously like a Satan in Eden, reminding us of what we know will come. The disturbance in the elements which seems the means to so sublime a peace may just as well be taken to portend a more inward disturbance. Even the terms of their rapture innocently raise an issue between them, Othello speaking of a consummate ideal which here attains its fixed perfection while Desdemona implores the homelier blessing of an increase in affection and contentment; as if love must change, but may by singular grace grow still better. Is love an ideal of perfection? or is it a condition of change? The question will be tried in action; and it is telling that here again Shakespeare gives his lovers the highest expression of their love immediately before love's bodily consummation, when their union is already threatened or doomed. This is their last moment of pure bliss.

Iago and Roderigo enter at once to give us quite another understanding of love. It seems all in the way of the world when Iago assures Roderigo that 'Desdemona is directly in love with' Cassio despite her protestations to her husband, and backs up the plausible lie with a whole naturalistic psychology of sensual appetite:

. . . Her eye must be fed, and what delight shall she have to look on the devil? When the blood is made dull with the act of sport, there should be again to inflame it, and give satiety a fresh appetite, loveliness in favour, sympathy in years, manners and beauties; all which the Moor is defective in: now, for want of these requir'd conveniences, her delicate tenderness will find itself abus'd, begin to heave the gorge, disrelish and abhor the Moor, very nature will instruct her to it, and compel her to some second choice.

The catalogue of Cassio's favours which must lead Desdemona to fancy him supports a wilful misconstruction of his courtesies to Desdemona, such as Iago directly promised us:

> a knave very voluble, no farther conscionable than in putting on the mere form of civil and humane seeming, for the better compassing of his salt and hidden affections: a subtle slippery knave, a finder out of occasions; that has an eye can stamp and counterfeit the true advantages never present themselves. Besides, the knave is handsome, young, and hath all those requisites in him that folly and green minds look after; a pestilent complete knave, and the woman has found him already.

Roderigo: I cannot believe that in her, she's full of most blest condition.
Iago: Blest fig's-end! the wine she drinks is made of grapes: if she had been blest, she would never have lov'd the Moor. Didst thou not see her paddle with the palm of his hand?
Roderigo: Yes, but that was but courtesy.
Iago: Lechery, by this hand: an index and prologue to the history of lust and foul thoughts:

Iago gives a sharp enough account of the way people commonly behave in the world he speaks of; indeed the force of his words is that they plainly come of acute observation, and so often prove true. Iago can be sure of a guffaw at 'Blest fig's end!' from any audience which takes the coarse allusion. He simply assimilates Desdemona and Cassio to the manners of marital farce. It scarcely matters whether he believes what he says. He is a willing victim of his own coarse faith that the world runs by appetites, feeding upon the fantasy that his wife lusts after Othello even as he factitiously invents such a motive for jealousy. He simply plays out his own expectation of his world.

The conflict of values moves inward. Cassio's downfall is a fearful emblem of the contradictions in a man's own nature. In the dialogue just before Iago brings about that swift lapse, he tries to draw Cassio out with his banal barrack-room ribaldries:

> . . . 'tis not yet ten o'clock: our general cast us thus early for the love of his Desdemona, who let us not therefore blame: he hath not yet

made wanton the night with her; and she is sport for Jove.

Cassio: She is a most exquisite lady.

Iago: And I'll warrant her full of game.

Cassio: Indeed she is a most fresh and delicate creature.

Iago: What an eye she has! Methinks it sounds a parley of provocation.

Cassio: An inviting eye, and yet methinks right modest.

Iago: And when she speaks, 'tis an alarm to love.

Cassio: It is indeed perfection.

Iago: Well, happiness to their sheets. . . .

This is a delicately managed bit of dramatic fencing, in which unlike responses to a woman's beauty set each other off quite precisely; and we must put it against what we see of Cassio almost at once. As always Iago tells us what he is about:

> If I can fasten but one cup upon him,
> With that which he hath drunk to-night already,
> He'll be as full of quarrel and offence
> As my young mistress' dog. . . .

Then only moments later Cassio really does change so and is no longer master of himself but the creature of the booze, and of Iago, transformed from humane courtesy into doggish unreason and wilful vanity. It is disturbing that he can be so promptly brought down to Iago's expectation of him, so easily mastered by his animal nature at the application of a mere cup of wine. Yet the capacity is in himself to change so hideously. In a sense Iago proves his case upon him, as he will shortly work to prove it upon Othello.

The real power of Iago over other people, as over us in the theatre, is that he speaks with our voice, or with one of our possible voices. We may recognize him for an aspect of ourselves, at once divertingly down-to-earth and destructively belittling. He confides in us to the point:

> And what's he then, that says I play the villain,
> When this advice is free I give, and honest,
> Probal to thinking, and indeed the course
> To win the Moor again? For 'tis most easy
> The inclining Desdemona to subdue,
> In any honest suit; she's fram'd as fruitful
> As the free elements: and then for her
> To win the Moor, were 't to renounce his baptism,
> All seals and symbols of redeemed sin,
> His soul is so infetter'd to her love,
> That she may make, unmake, do what she list,
> Even as her appetite shall play the god
> With his weak function.

To suppose that Desdemona's appetite plays the god with Othello's weak function is to accommodate the lovers to a common case, that of people in thrall to their own desire, which readily deceives them into idolizing its object and as quickly disillusions them once it is sated:

> Whilst yet to prove,
> I thought there was some deity in love
>   So did I reverence, and gave
> Worship;. . . .
>   Thus when
> Things not yet known are coveted by men,
>   Our desires give them fashion, and so
> As they wax lesser, fall, as they size, grow.
>
>   But, from late fair
> His highness sitting in a golden chair,
>   Is not less cared for after three days
> By children, than the thing which lovers so
> Blindly admire, and with such worship woo;
>   Being had, enjoying it decays:. . . .
>
>   Donne, 'Farewell to Love'

Othello's attachment to Desdemona doesn't stand apart from common nature. It scarcely takes a Iago to find the fillip of such a marriage in a nubile girl's hold over an ageing man, who even makes a god of her power to engross his slackened desire. We wait to see how far that plausible view of their relationship is borne out in their conduct of love.

Iago's expectation of human nature has force while it appeals to what we know of ourselves, and persuades us that he only shows people as they really are behind the forms of social behaviour, and their own self-deceits. He cuts himself off from us just at the point where he turns from sceptical man-of-the-world to malicious wrecker, taking the action beyond laughter altogether, if not quite beyond farce. As we re-encounter the play we are continually being asked what it means to be human, how far we are creatures of appetite, what there is in our behaviour which can't be reduced to the attempt to gratify some lust of other, and whether we are gods, animals, or devils. The action moves instantly between the extreme alternative possibilities of our nature, as in the big scene in IV, i in which Iago misrepresents to Othello the transactions between Cassio and Bianca over the handkerchief; so that we get comic jealousy on one side of the stage, and tragic torment on the other:

Iago: Before me! look where she comes.
Cassio: 'Tis such another fitchew; marry, a perfum'd one.
          What do you mean by this haunting of me?

Bianca:	Let the devil and his dam haunt you, what did you mean by that same handkerchief you gave me even now? I was a fine fool to take it; I must take out the whole work, a likely piece of work, that you should find it in your chamber, and not know who left it there! This is some minx's token, and I must take out the work; there, give it the hobby-horse, wheresoever you had it, I'll take out no work on't.
Cassio:	How now, my sweet Bianca, how now, how now?
Othello:	By heaven, that should be my handkerchief!
Bianca:	An you'll come to supper to-night, you may, an you will not, come when you are next prepar'd for.

[*Exit.*

Iago:	After her, after her.
Cassio:	Faith, I must, she'll rail i' the street else.
Iago:	Will you sup there?
Cassio:	Faith, I intend so.
Iago:	Well, I may chance to see you, for I would very fain speak with you.
Cassio:	Prithee come, will you?
Iago:	Go to, say no more. [*Exit Cassio.*
Othello:	[*Advancing*] How shall I murder him, Iago?
Iago:	Did you perceive, how he laughed at his vice?
Othello:	O Iago!
Iago:	And did you see the handkerchief?
Othello:	Was that mine?
Iago:	Yours, by this hand: and to see how he prizes the foolish woman your wife! she gave it him, and he hath given it his whore.
Othello:	I would have him nine years a-killing; a fine woman, a fair woman, a sweet woman!

Iago on the way of Venetian women of the world is not only plausible but likely to be justified, as far as he goes:

I know our country disposition well;
In Venice they do let God see the pranks
They dare not show their husbands; their best conscience
Is not to leave undone, but keep unknown

Whatever the irony of such arguments when he applies them to Desdemona, yet they are probable enough in nature:

Not to affect many proposed matches,
Of her own clime, complexion, and degree,
Whereto we see in all things nature tends;
Fie, we may smell in such a will most rank,
Foul disproportion; thoughts unnatural.

Othello's soliloquy which follows may be painfully wrong about his own case but it shows only too well the way he now sees the common lot of husbands, and of all who let their desires enthral them to a woman:

> She's gone, I am abus'd, and my relief
> Must be to loathe her: O curse of marriage,
> That we can call these delicate creatures ours,
> And not their appetites! I had rather be a toad,
> And live upon the vapour in a dungeon,
> Than keep a corner in a thing I love,
> For others' uses: yet 'tis the plague of great ones,
> Prerogativ'd are they less than the base,
> 'Tis destiny, unshunnable, like death:
> Even then this forked plague is fated to us,
> When we do quicken:;

Here we see Othello at the mercy of his aroused senses, caught in the erotic agitation he had earlier disdained and rushing from intense love to intense loathing. In effect, the degrading of his understanding of our nature brings him to prove in himself the power of sense in sexual love, even though the intolerable actuality of staled marriages still struggles in his mind with the earlier vision of Desdemona:

> If she be false, O, then heaven mocks itself,
> I'll not believe it.

In his own eyes Othello demeans himself to the contemptible cuckold of farce, who is content not to recognize his state:

> *Othello*:   I had been happy if the general camp,
> Pioners, and all, had tasted her sweet body,
> So I had nothing known: O now for ever
> Farewell the tranquil mind, farewell content:
> Farewell the plumed troop, and the big wars,
> That makes ambition virtue: O farewell,

Yet at once there's this powerful shift from farce to tragic grandeur within the same line of verse:

> So I had nothing known: O now for ever. . . . .

Iago fosters Othello's jealousy by working upon his sensual imagination, as in the fiction of Cassio's dream, which racks Othello the more because it plays upon his newly aroused senses. The 'Lie with her, lie on her' speech in IV, i 35–43, marvellously realizes a jealous man's imaginings of the intimacies which most inflame him. Othello's 'I am your own forever' at the end of this scene marks among other things his agonized conversion to Iago's expectation of the world. By the middle of the play Othello seems possessed with the sense that love may be as arbitrary in its satisfactions as is appetite. His touching little tale of the magical embroidery makes his wife's handkerchief the figure of a power by which a woman might hold a man wholly to her love while she keeps it, but would at once turn the love to loathing and revulsion should she lose it. If this is chastity he speaks of, it operates very like the power to sustain desire.

Othello swings between opposite extremes of passion as suddenly as the action itself shifts between tragedy and farce. His agony is insupportable because he is torn between irreconcileable ideas of Desdemona, loving her and hating her at once:

Othello: I would have him nine years a-killing; a fine woman, a fair woman, a sweet woman!
Iago: Nay, you must forget.
Othello: And let her rot, and perish, and be damned to-night, for she shall not live; no, my heart is turn'd to stone; I strike it, and it hurts my hand: O, the world has not a sweeter creature, she might lie by an emperor's side, and command him tasks.

Shakespeare powerfully brings home to us what has happened to Othello by putting alongside this frenzy of the passion-torn *geloso* the picture of a leader of unshakeable dignity which Lodovico brings from Venice, reminding us what Othello had been only a few days before:

Lodovico: Is this the noble Moor, whom our full senate
Call all in all sufficient? This the noble nature,
Whom passion could not shake? whose solid virtue
The shot of accident, nor dart of chance,
Could neither graze, nor pierce?
Iago: He is much chang'd.

This ought to be a powerful moment in the theatre, though it rarely is. Shakespeare has reserved until now the known character of a great man, so that we can feel the shock of comparison, and see where thwarted sensual rage has brought the serenely self-sufficient general. The most shocking testimony to the transforming force of the passion must be that it is so far from Othello's native temper to be thus affected. We see how powerfully sexual jealousy works, just because this is a nature which no one could have expected to admit such a convulsion. We have no reason to discount Lodovico's picture of Othello, or to question his astonishment that one so notoriously immune to perturbation should succumb to sexual rage. People who know Othello well, and thought him beyond the reach of passion, have good reason to be dismayed by the alteration in him here; for if he can change so abruptly into a creature of wilful frenzy then a man may have no more confidence in his own nature in love than in drink. The arbitrariness of the transformation shows up the more because we ourselves are never allowed to take Iago's version of love for the play's truth. The evidence of its destructive inadequacy is always before us in Desdemona's innocence. She is what she is, and remains what she had seemed to Othello's mind, while he becomes the prey of his kindled senses. His sensual imagination is all too ready to bewilder him and underwrite Iago's prompting, even in face of the plain truth.

The very loftiness of Othello's innocent vision of love makes him more vulnerable to his own experienced imaginings. He had not reckoned with the involvement of his body in his love, which he now terrifyingly feels:

> O thou weed, who art so lovely fair and smellest so sweet
> That the sense aches at thee

It is his misfortune that by the time he does recognize the power of sense he is already disposed to take the woman for no more than a creature of appetite. He never loses the vision of a love beyond sensuality, even though he cannot reconcile it with the force of his passion now, and blames that rage wholly upon Desdemona's supposed disaffection; indeed he remains the absolutist whose faith has been tragically betrayed:

> Had it pleas'd heaven
> To try me with affliction, had he rain'd
> All kinds of sores and shames on my bare head,
> Steep'd me in poverty, to the very lips,
> Given to captivity me and my hopes,
> I should have found in some part of my soul
> A drop of patience; but, alas, to make me
> A fixed figure, for the time of scorn
> To point his slow unmoving fingers at . . . oh, oh.
> Yet could I bear that too, well, very well:
> But there, where I have garner'd up my heart,
> Where either I must live, or bear no life,
> The fountain, from the which my current runs,
> Or else dries up, to be discarded thence,
> Or keep it as a cistern, for foul toads
> To knot and gender in! Turn thy complexion there;
> Patience, thy young and rose-lipp'd cherubin,
> I here look grim as hell!

When Othello confronts Desdemona in IV, ii we see the worldliness he has learned from Iago completely mastering him. He addresses Emilia as a brothel-keeper, and contemptuously degrades himself to a client, as well as the stock cuckold of Italian comedy. Yet Shakespeare still won't allow us to take his self-lacerating grossness simply as aberration. At the very end of the willow scene, that episode which most pathetically seals our sense of Desdemona's unassailable innocence and purity, Emilia bursts out in humorous indignation against Desdemona's refusal to believe that there are women who would wrong their husband 'For the whole world':

> Why, the wrong is but a wrong i' the world; and having the world for your labour, 'tis a wrong in your own world, and you might quickly make it right.

She goes on to urge that since wives have sense as husbands do, and by the frailty of sense husbands change to others for sport and affection, then wives may do the same:

> And have we not affections?
> Desires for sport? And frailty, as men have?

Her reasoning seems unassailable; and it suddenly shifts our point of view in the way which is so characteristic of Shakespeare. No doubt it holds true for another world than Desdemona's, in which people must come to terms with the caprices of their sensual natures, if only because they see that sense is not in the control of will.

Othello's entry in V, ii explosively confirms a metaphysical drama:

> It is the cause, it is the cause, my soul,
> Let me not name it to you, you chaste stars:
> It is the cause, yet I'll not shed her blood,
> Nor scar that whiter skin of hers than snow,
> And smooth, as monumental alabaster;
> Yet she must die, else she'll betray more men.
> Put out the light, and then put out the light:

Yet the universal cause enlarges a dire inward conflict. The impulse to kill Desdemona struggles in Othello with the impulse to enjoy her. The very texture of the lines shows us that both impulses are expressions of the same sexual passion; and we feel the dilemma of sense in that anguished poring over Desdemona's body, as if he wills the icy purity of death upon the warm breathing woman who arouses his desire:

> when I have pluck'd the rose,
> I cannot give it vital growth again,
> It needs must wither; I'll smell it on the tree,
> A balmy breath, that dost almost persuade
> Justice herself to break her sword: once more:
> Be thus when thou art dead, and I will kill thee,
> And love thee after: once more, and this the last,
> So sweet was ne'er so fatal: I must weep,
> But they are cruel tears; . . . .

For all its physical energy the speech is an extraordinary inward realization of sexual jealousy, which we see here to be only the thwarted side of
possessive sexual love. Late-awakened sexuality intertwines the mind's
vision of pure beauty with the hunger of sense for physical union; intellect and feeling are inseparably interinvolved. But sexual love may
impose its own categoricalness, and 'his first minute, after noon, is
night'. Shakespeare takes care to show us Othello's state of mind before
their night of consummation as well as after, so that we may see how
easily jealousy and the sense of loss set in. The sheer precipitancy of
Othello's turn against Desdemona brings out the effect of that move
which has so suddenly metamorphosed an image of ideal innocence into a
creature of sense and pleasure. There's a Iago already at the back of
Othello's mind, because the passion puts him there. The sensual
absolutist connives at his own reduction to absurdity.

The discomforting irony is that Othello prosecutes his misconceived
cause with such heroic grandeur of spirit. He brings to the killing of
Desdemona not only intense feeling, but a sustained spiritual elevation
which invests the scene with the majesty of a solemn sacrifice.
Shakespeare lets the trappings conspire with him, evoking in the lines
themselves the draped dimly-lit chamber, the white bed with its ceremonial sheets and motionless figure, the tapers, the drawn blade. Yet the
scene is shaped in the language and comportment which confirm
Othello's own exalted vision of what he is about:

>   I must weep,
> But they are cruel tears; this sorrow's heavenly,
> It strikes when it does love: she wakes.
>
> *Desdemona*: Who's there? Othello?
> *Othello*:   Ay, Desdemona.
> *Desdemona*: Will you come to bed, my lord?
> *Othello*: Have you pray'd to-night, Desdemona?
> *Desdemona*:   Ay, my lord.
> *Othello*: If you bethink yourself of any crime,
>   Unreconcil'd as yet to heaven and grace,
>   Solicit for it straight.
> *Desdemona*: Alas, my lord, what may you mean by that?
> *Othello*: Well, do it, and be brief, I will walk by,
>   I would not kill thy unprepared spirit,
>   No, heaven forfend, I would not kill thy soul.
> *Desdemona*: Talk you of killing?
> *Othello*:   Ay, I do.
>
> *Desdemona*:   Then heaven
>   Have mercy on me!
> *Othello*:   Amen, with all my heart!

We need not be so superfluous as to ask how far this is self-deceit. What matters is that both participants suppose themselves to be acting in a domain of grace:

Othello:	Sweet soul, take heed, take heed of perjury,
	Thou art on thy death-bed.
Desdemona:	Ay, but not yet to die.
Othello:	Yes, presently:
	Therefore confess thee freely of thy sin,
	For to deny each article with oath
	Cannot remove, nor choke the strong conceit,
	That I do groan withal: thou art to die.
Desdemona:	Then Lord have mercy on me!
Othello:	I say, amen.
Desdemona:	And have you mercy too! I never did
	Offend you in my life, . . . never lov'd Cassio,
	But with such general warranty of heaven,
	As I might love: I never gave him token.
Othello:	By heaven, I saw my handkerchief in his hand:
	O perjur'd woman, thou dost stone thy heart,
	And makest me call what I intend to do
	A murder, which I thought a sacrifice;. . . .

The very terms of Othello's dialogue with Desdemona transform what might have been a wilful act of revenge into an extreme unction. The difference between *Othello* and a tragedy of blood is that Othello thinks he ministers to a just and pure universe, as well as his wife's soul, in sacrificing what he loves; and it is devastatingly ironic that he makes himself an instrument of hellish malice while believing himself to be furthering heaven's cause. The scene harrows us with its parody of a sacrament, even as it invites our admiration for the austere aspiration of the betrayed human spirit.

The murder of Desdemona, relieving the intolerable compulsion of sense, prepares a bitter self-realization. To recognize that the heart has been mocked in its most drastic gestures is to disable one's moral being. Emilia's abuse brings Othello down to what he soon perceives himself to be, and he rushes to reduce himself to such a figure of scorn as he had killed Desdemona to avert. He is an abject figure in his own eyes at this point, no tragic hero or avenging instrument of justice but the poor gull in a farce, a dolt 'As ignorant as dirt', or worse, a murderous fool and coxcomb. Yet his very invocation of everlasting torment confirms his spiritual resoluteness, offsetting the intense wish to expiate his error by mortifying himself, with the recognition that an eternity won't suffice to do it:

Whip me, you devils,
From the possession of this heavenly sight,
Blow me about in winds, roast me in sulphur,
Wash me in steep-down gulfs of liquid fire!

He acknowledges heaven even while he recognizes that he has enacted hell, and destroyed his own bliss — 'This last pain for the damned the Fathers found. . . .'

Othello believes his deed to be damnable because he has so mistaken heaven for the world; though he has done no more than was expected of a wronged husband in the world of his day, and few proud *signori* would have cavilled much over an error or so in defence of their honour. Speaking his own funeral oration he pronounces himself to be a man who was not prone to the impulses that destroy him,but has been more surely destroyed just because they are alien to his nature; and he justly sees himself as one ensnared and baffled by his own good qualities. He fell such easy prey to Iago partly out of simple innocence of his own nature, and of other natures too. This final self-recognition is his sufficient punishment, condemning him to the secular hell of a good man's consciousness that he has wreaked irredeemable harm and folly:

> then must you speak
> Of one that lov'd not wisely, but too well:
> Of one not easily jealous, but being wrought,
> Perplex'd in the extreme; of one whose hand,
> Like the base Indian, threw a pearl away,
> Richer than all his tribe;. . . .

More salutary than his bitterly won self-insight is this final revelation of Desdemona, the acknowledgement that something in her stood apart from the common course of nature in the world. Her innocence has proved to be of a different order from Othello's highminded unawareness of his own temper; and it wasn't so much forfeited with sexual experience, as transformed into a living testimony that it is within the capacity of our nature to find grace through the mutualities of flesh and blood.

Cassio has the final word on his friend, as Othello stabs himself and dies:

> This did I fear, but thought he had no weapon,
> For he was great of heart.

Othello is great of heart here in a cause such as Antony's, killing himself rather than endure his self-earned ignominy. Beyond the tragic consequences there's the tragedy of the man, which is implicit in the tribute paid him at his end by one who well knows what little provocation of sense will transform us, how easily a fine nature may be degraded by something within itself. Yet Othello and Desdemona surely aren't belittled by Iago's reductive practice upon them. Their honesty isn't cheapened because it disarms them in the world; nor does the wreck of their marriage impugn the high reach of their love. The very manner of their deaths vindicates them against the envious and calumniating circumstances which might seem to mock all our unguarded endeavours. Their love isn't alms for oblivion, however intimately it persuades us that an unschooled heart may be vulnerable to its own austerity, and that the awakening to the life of sense carries some danger.

4

Crowning the Present

'Tis greatest now, and to destruction
Nearest; there's no pause at perfection.

Donne, *Metempsychosis*

All other things, to their destruction draw,

Donne, 'The Anniversary'

The opening of *Antony and Cleopatra* is powerfully direct. An officer of
Antony's enters, expostulating with an emissary from Rome and
embroiling us at once in the old quarrel between manly valour and amorous indulgence. Then the whole court entourage sweeps in on the wave
of Cleopatra's jealous taunting of Antony. Messengers from Rome are
announced, provoking her to still keener gibes and him to still vaster professions of love; they resolve for sport rather than Caesar's despatches of
state; and they're gone, leaving the two bystanders just a moment of head-
shaking wonderment, and unconfident hope for a better-minded Antony
next day.

This is a masterly start in its forceful subtlety of exposition, the rich-
ness of motives displayed and complexity of the issues proposed, its
enactment of a sudden eruption of vivid energy into the quiet continuum
of being. We're abruptly caught up in the casual broils of people many
centuries back, who carry their unquiet world around with them in their
conscious exercise of vast imperial power; and the play establishes itself
for us in an image of intense vitality such as sustains or may ruin a state.

The scene is dynamically conceived, as a clash of powerful impulses
which the language directly enacts. We encounter the lovers not at a
moment of climax or passion but caught up in their continuing crisis of
conflicting imperatives which demand a choice. In just 62 lines we are
drawn into an entire turbulent world of powerfully charged tensions and
conflicts, domestic as well as political, in which personal causes inter-
work with events going forward over several continents. The very first

speech of the play, uttered by a character who exists just to open the argument to us thus abruptly, puts Antony before us as the profligate of his virility who can now scarcely sustain his former magnificence; and ensuing events will try this estimation.

Philo's brief speech establishes the manner of a dramatic language which realizes in its syntax the modulating energies of its subjects, and continually offers us judgements to be tested in action. We are made to feel as well as see the dissipation of a potent vitality in a loose expense of spirit, the lavishing of power where it evokes no response, or exhausts itself unprofitably:

> those his goodly eyes,
> That o'er the files and musters of the war
> Have glow'd like plated Mars, now bend, now turn
> The office and devotion of their view
> Upon a tawny front: his captain's heart,
> Which in the scuffles of great fights hath burst
> The buckles on his breast, reneges all temper,
> And is become the bellows and the fan
> To cool a gipsy's lust.

His 'behold and see' at once invites us to approve upon the Antony we see for ourselves his soldierly reprobation of such a disregard of measure.

The very first entry of the lovers counters the voice of Roman prudence with their extreme commitment to each other, quite radically opposing prowess in love to might in war. Antony is characterized for us here precisely through the working energy of his language, and a habit of authority which displays itself in his peremptory address, and masterful bearing:

Cleopatra:	If it be love indeed, tell me how much.
Antony:	There's beggary in the love that can be reckon'd.
Cleopatra:	I'll set a bourn how far to be belov'd.
Antony:	Then must thou needs find out new heaven, new earth.
	Enter an Attendant.
Attendent:	News, my good lord, from Rome.
Antony:	Grates me, the sum.

He speaks gnomically in powerful imperatives, whose very disposition sets in play forces which are barely contained and purposeful, or self-entangled and struggling:

> *Antony*:   Fie, wrangling queen!
> Whom every thing becomes, to chide, to laugh,
> To weep: how every passion fully strives,
> To make itself, in thee, fair and admired!
> No messenger but thine, and all alone,

> To-night we'll wander through the streets, and note
> The qualities of people. Come, my queen,
> Last night you did desire it. Speak not to us.

We can't doubt the energy of spirit in Antony's first speeches, or the imperious manhood they convey. Yet it is Antony's manhood that Cleopatra at once impugns in the opposite cause from Philo's, setting one expression of his powers in destructive conflict with another as if his obligation to anything but her must threaten his independence, and even his virility. We feel the pain of their self-laceration in this superb realizing of sexual possessiveness, and the inherent danger of the uncompromising demands they make upon each other in the face of a world which sustains itself by compromise.

The characters launch themselves into the unknown, at each stage shaping their drama hazardously by acts of choice; indeed we share their awareness of the possibilities which are open to their election. The play continually puts Antony's predicament before us, asking us how he should decide now and so define himself. Antony shows himself well aware that his circumstances put a defining choice upon him:

> Let Rome in Tiber melt, and the wide arch
> Of the rang'd empire fall! Here is my space,
> Kingdoms are clay: our dungy earth alike
> Feeds beast as man; the nobleness of life
> Is to do thus: when such a mutual pair,
> And such a twain can do't, in which I bind,
> On pain of punishment, the world to weet
> We stand up peerless.

He justifies his determination for love, and proclaims his own nature which chooses so, by appealing to what is noble in our lives; as if some moral imperative of our being prompts us to prize nobility of spirit, and the impulses which best distinguish us as men. No doubt there's something self-defiant in his vehement assertion of the paradox that love is nobler than feats of arms, for patently he still has to convince himself that he need choose between Cleopatra and Rome at all. Yet a commitment which affirms itself in such unqualified prodigality of spirit leaves us putting some questions to ourselves. Is it idle of these lovers to claim that their embrace sums up 'the nobleness of life'? What does it really mean to live nobly, and why should a man strive to do it? Which ends best befit us as human beings? For that matter, what is it to be human, and what is our human nature capable of? One exhilaration of this manner of direct enactment is that it keeps such defining possibilities of our nature in play in our minds as we experience it, quite unlike that prescriptive mode of drama which puts the articulation of moral emblems at the centre of concern. In its very syntax Shakespeare's language enacts the tensions and cross-pulls of impulses which also pose oppositions of value.

Cleopatra meets Antony's defiant avowal with a challenge of her own, in a gesture which superbly mingles scorn with affirmation:

> Nay, pray you, seek no colour for your going,
> But bid farewell, and go: when you sued staying,
> Then was the time for words: no going then;
> Eternity was in our lips, and eyes,
> Bliss in our brows' bent; none our parts so poor,
> But was a race of heaven. They are so still,
> Or thou, the greatest soldier of the world,
> Art turn'd the greatest liar.

For all the disdain she affects, hers is another mode of that vaunting hyperbole by which the lovers monumentalize themselves in their assurance of an eternity of fame. Yet her speech moves quite unlike Antony's. Its abrupt shifts of mood, within a subtle cross-pattern of syntax and stresses, at once imitates impassioned thinking and sets off one state against another, the momentary against the unconditional absolute. The language works at a high degree of syntactical complexity, rendering an inner life whose warring imperatives frustrate each other. Is it to be an achievement in the public world? Or does anything else matter than the empire such lovers triumphantly comprehend in themselves when they vow an eternity of love? These issues pass into the argument of the play, to be advanced by the ensuing action.

We see Antony and Cleopatra caught up in the jostle of emergent events, and the decisions of the moment. However they may seek to define their love in opposition to the conduct of empire, they nonetheless inhabit the world of contingency and relative valuations whose insecurity they apprehend in themselves. The very language of their first scenes projects into gesture and policy the inflections of their passion, in a way which Shakespeare makes peculiar to them:

> *Antony:*   Quarrel no more, but be prepar'd to know
> The purposes I bear; which are, or cease,
> As you shall give the advice. By the fire
> That quickens Nilus' slime, I go from hence
> Thy soldier, servant, making peace or way,
> As thou affects . . .
> *Cleopatra:*   Courteous lord, one word:
> Sir, you and I must part, but that's not it:
> Sir, you and I have lov'd, but there's not it;
> That you know well, something it is I would —
> O, my oblivion is a very Antony,
> And I am all forgotten.

We see that they habitually define their love by their sway, and their mastery of the game of power. In his own mind at least Antony's prowess as a lover is of a piece with his stature as a soldier and emperor; his sexuality and his greatness of spirit are both modes of his manly virility. The antithetical choices his circumstances seem to pose aren't available to him in practice; and his uncompromising first commitment to love is ironically countered at once, not only by events but by his own will:

	Enter another Messenger.
Antony:	From Sicyon how the news? Speak there!
First Messenger:	The man from Sicyon, — is there such an one?
Second Messenger:	He stays upon your will.
Antony:	Let him appear.
	These strong Egyptian fetters I must break,
	Or lose myself in dotage.

Moreover, the world these lovers apprehend in each other isn't set apart from the world beyond them. On the contrary, they are conscious of inhabiting the centre of their own universe; and the curious double focus of an action in which close domestic interest continually alternates with global politics never lets us lose sight of the whole nature which holds together such diverse elements. The Plutarchian amplitude of the action only follows out the vision of a full engagement of our humanity, allowing the playwright to hold in dramatic tension seemingly unlike orders of concern.

The moment Antony gets away from Cleopatra we find him urgently soliciting the messages from Rome after all; and he opens a prospect of a huge game of power politics, played across the chessboard of the entire known world:

Messenger:	Fulvia thy wife first came into the field.
Antony:	Against my brother Lucius?
Messenger:	Ay:
	But soon that war had end, and the time's state
	Made friends of them, jointing their force 'gainst Caesar,
	Whose better issue in the war, from Italy,
	Upon the first encounter, drave them.
Antony:	Well, what worst? . . .
Messenger:	Labienus —
	This is stiff news — hath with his Parthian force
	Extended Asia: from Euphrates
	His conquering banner shook, from Syria
	To Lydia, and to Ionia;
	Whilst —
Antony:	Antony, thou wouldst say, —
Messenger:	O, my lord!
Antony:	Speak to me home, mince not the general tongue:
	Name Cleopatra as she is call'd in Rome;

> Rail thou in Fulvia's phrase, and taunt my faults
> With such full license, as both truth and malice
> Have power to utter.

For all the participants, Antony's affair with Cleopatra is a main factor in the game. What comes out at once by this sharp juxtaposition of statecraft and love is that the politic game of sex has a good deal in common with the politics of rule, at least as Cleopatra manages it:

Cleopatra:	Where is he?
Charmian:	I did not see him since.
Cleopatra:	See where he is, who's with him, what he does:
	I did not send you. If you find him sad,
	Say I am dancing; if in mirth, report
	That I am sudden sick. Quick, and return.
Charmian:	Madam, methinks if you did love him dearly,
	You do not hold the method, to enforce
	The like from him.
Cleopatra:	What should I do, I do not?
Charmian:	In each thing give him way, cross him in nothing.
Cleopatra:	Thou teachest like a fool: the way to lose him.
Charmian:	Tempt him not so too far. I wish, forbear;
	In time we hate that which we often fear.

Enter Antony.

	But here comes Antony.
Cleopatra:	I am sick, and sullen.
Antony:	I am sorry to give breathing to my purpose, —
Cleopatra:	Help me away, dear Charmian, I shall fall.
	It cannot be thus long, the sides of nature
	Will not sustain it.
Antony:	Now, my dearest queen, —
Cleopatra:	Pray you stand farther from me.
Antony:	What's the matter?
Cleopatra:	I know by that same eye there's some good news.
	What, says the married woman you may go?
	Would she had never given you leave to come!
	Let her not say 'tis I that keep you here.
	I have no power upon you; hers you are.
Antony:	The gods best know —
Cleopatra:	O, never was there queen
	So mightily betray'd! yet at the first
	I saw the treasons planted.
Antony:	Cleopatra, —
Cleopatra:	Why should I think you can be mine and true
	(Though you in swearing shake the throned gods)
	Who have been false to Fulvia? Riotous madness,
	To be entangled with those mouth-made vows,
	Which break themselves in swearing!
Antony:	Most sweet queen, —

Holding on to such a man of the great world seems to be something which calls for study like a campaign, and must be worked at and contrived by whatever shifts and subterfuges might play upon his will and desires. The wavering contest of political wills and wits which dominates Act II is pointedly paralleled in the scene in Alexandria, which Shakespeare slips into the midst of the political manoeuvrings.

Messenger:	Will't please you hear me?
Cleopatra:	I have a mind to strike thee ere thou speak'st:
	Yet if thou say Antony lives, is well,
	Or friends with Caesar, or not captive to him,
	I'll set thee in a shower of gold, and hail
	Rich pearls upon thee.
Messenger:	Madam, he's well.
Cleopatra:	Well said.
Messenger:	And friends with Caesar.
Cleopatra:	Th'art an honest man.
Messenger:	Caesar, and he, are greater friends than ever.
Cleopatra:	Make thee a fortune from me.
Messenger:	But yet, madam, —
Cleopatra:	I do not like 'But yet,' it does allay
	The good precedence, fie upon 'But yet,'
	'But yet' is as a gaoler to bring forth
	Some monstrous malefactor. Prithee, friend,
	Pour out the pack of matter to mine ear,
	The good and bad together: he's friends with Caesar,
	In state of health, thou say'st, and thou say'st, free.
Messenger:	Free, madam, no; I made no such report,
	He's bound unto Octavia.
Cleopatra:	For what good turn?
Messenger:	For the best turn i' the bed.
Cleopatra:	I am pale, Charmian.
Messenger:	Madam, he's married to Octavia.
Cleopatra:	The most infectious pestilence upon thee!
	[Strikes him down.
Messenger:	Good madam, patience.
Cleopatra:	What say you? Hence,
	[Strikes him.
	Horrible villain, or I'll spurn thine eyes
	Like balls before me; I'll unhair thy head,
	She hales him up and down.
	Thou shalt be whipp'd with wire, and stew'd in brine,
	Smarting in lingering pickle.

News of Antony's marriage to Octavia, which is the immediate outcome of political dealing some thousand miles away, moves Cleopatra to a fierce turmoil of passions; though her fury soon concentrates itself in just such a shrewd calculation of expedients and chances as lies only just beneath the guarded courtesies of the political bargaining itself:

Cleopatra:	. . . Come thou near.
Messenger:	Most gracious majesty!
Cleopatra:	Didst thou behold Octavia?
Messenger:	Ay, dread queen.
Cleopatra:	Where?
Messenger:	Madam, in Rome; I look'd her in the face, and saw her led Between her brother and Mark Antony.
Cleopatra:	Is she as tall as me?
Messenger:	She is not, madam.
Cleopatra:	Didst hear her speak? is she shrill-tongu'd or low?
Messenger:	Madam, I heard her speak; she is low-voic'd.
Cleopatra:	That's not so good: he cannot like her long.
Charmian:	Like her? O Isis! 'tis impossible.
Cleopatra:	I think so, Charmian: dull of tongue, and dwarfish! What majesty is in her gait? Remember, If e'er thou look'st on majesty.
Messenger:	She creeps: Her motion and her station are as one: She shows a body, rather than a life, A statue, than a breather.
Cleopatra:	Is this certain?
Messenger:	Or I have no observance.
Charmian:	Three in Egypt Cannot make better note.
Cleopatra:	He's very knowing, I do perceive 't, there's nothing in her yet. The fellow has good judgement.
Charmian:	Excellent.
Cleopatra:	Guess at her years, I prithee.
Messenger:	Madam, She was a widow —
Cleopatra:	Widow? Charmian, hark.
Messenger:	And I do think she's thirty.
Cleopatra:	Bear'st thou her face in mind? is't long or round?
Messenger:	Round, even to faultiness.
Cleopatra:	For the most part, too, they are foolish that are so. Her hair what colour?
Messenger:	Brown, madam: and her forehead As low as she would wish it.
Cleopatra:	There's gold for thee, Thou must not take my former sharpness ill, I will employ thee back again; I find thee Most fit for business. Go, make thee ready, Our letters are prepar'd.

The opposite pulls of their ambiguous commitment, to each other and
to empire, gives the play its tension; but Shakespeare brings out some

likeness between sexual life and the conduct of power. Both activities offer ironic proof that the more compassionate involvement in the affairs of the world is also the more vulnerable; and we see that in sexual life as in politics tacit compromises are to be made, expedients sought and offered, nice moral scruples subdued to the furtherance of one's own will. Such parallels are scarcely surprising in an action which projects both enterprises from the contrarious impulsions of our own nature. Erotic life reveals itself as the domestic mode of a condition of contingency and relativeness which politics and history display at large.

We move from the tussling lovers to the political manoeuvring in Act II with no sense of disjunction. Those great political scenes effectively show us the world of contingency in action, giving shape to its dynamic uncertainties in a way that reminds us how far Shakespeare's dramatic vision altogether is shaped by his sense of what it is to have our wills free. The characters in this play are free at least to decide between the several promptings of their nature, and to recognize their responsibility for the outcome. Even when his concern is only politics Shakespeare nonetheless keeps changing his focus, alternating the widest panorama of action with closely observed local detail. Events occurring over the known world are played off against each other in a series of brief vignettes, and momentary epiphanies. Here rebellious Pompey weighs up his military chances with his generals; there the Roman leaders risk their alliance in a contest of will and pride. Here a couple of old campaigners quietly mull over the prospects of an alliance founded in Antony's fidelity to Octavia; there Enobarbus elegiacally recalls, and immortalizes, Antony's first meeting with Cleopatra. Here the brothers-in-law embrace; there Antony consults his Egyptian soothsayer, and is told that he can never hope to succeed in contest with Caesar. Here Antony promises loyalty to Octavia; there Cleopatra receives news of Antony's marriage. Here Antony is despatching a general to Parthia; there Lepidus, Maecenas and Agrippa hurry on their way to the confrontation with Pompey. Here a night of noisy revelry is ending in boozy farewells; there solemn funeral music sounds as Ventidius parades the body of a vanquished Parthian prince.

In its variety, subtlety and scope this must be accounted a *tour de force* of imaginative organization; and it is also quite thrillingly alive. Our minds are kept at stretch by the sheer range of interest and concern, the brisk alternation of big set-pieces with brief glimpses of the issues and consequences. The plotting follows out the vision of a world of colliding wills in the way the scenes set one another off so as to intensify dramatic uncertainty, or imply inner parallels and contrasts. We see how a political resolution here has immediate domestic effects far away in another country, how the tense alternation of political fortunes and wills in the contest of empire tries men's domestic virtues. We are made party to the understanding that the conduct of power can't be isolated from sexual disposition, if only because both proclivities are subject to like rhythms and laws, which express human nature itself.

Powerful contrasts emerge. The furious whirl of vivid sense-impressions in which Pompey catches Antony's caprices in II, i, 19–27 — 'He dreams' — is set off by the golden stasis of Enobarbus's marvellous celebration in II, ii, 191–218 of the lovers' first meeting, whose effect is to arrest altogether the flux of political manoeuvre from which it emerges while the voice moves in ecstatic contemplation over a timeless past, and a glory beyond time. To take the speech out of its place here, as Capell and Garrick do in their version of the play (1758),[1] is to lose the force of Shakespeare's vision, which partly depends upon our awareness that Enobarbus implicitly demonstrates the power of art to make such a moment endure when he relives the scene in the very voice of ancient commentary, and the manner of a poet of Augustus's court. Time is momentarily annulled in the syntax itself, with its breathtaking switch to a continuous present, and lavish surge of the phrasing:

Maecenas:	Now Antony must leave her utterly.
Enobarbus:	Never; he will not:
	Age cannot wither her, nor custom stale
	Her infinite variety: other women cloy
	The appetites they feed, but she makes hungry,
	Where most she satisfies.

Enobarbus's hyperboles, coming just at this point, transform the play. They give an ideal character to the terms of sexual prodigality in which people constantly talk of Antony's obsession with Cleopatra; as Donne's 'The Canonization' transmutes into a unique condition of mutual love the common detraction of coitus:

We die and rise the same, and prove
Mysterious by this love.

Love scenes and political scenes prove ironically alike in the way the dramatic uncertainties of events in pawn to time stand against a condition which seems to rise beyond stratagem altogether. It's a character of Shakespeare's plotting that the shifts of policy are picquantly set off by such moments of simple celebration.

The two episodes of politic parleying, II, ii and II, vi, seem to be pointedly paralleled. In both scenes the uncertain tussle of wills and wits sets up a prolonged tension out of which the climactic decision emerges quite suddenly, to be followed by a quick winding down, and then a slack period in which bystanders comment on the events and their likely

---

[1]They transfer the speech to I, i, with all the rest of the scene, giving it instead of the dialogue between Philo and Demetrius which follows the exit of the lovers.

consequences. Yet the second negotiation doesn't follow the course of the first; on the contrary, the two scenes stand against each other by reason of their crucially different effects; and the difference implies a point of its own. That like confrontations should have wholly unlike consequences isn't fortuitous but a measure of the different qualities and wills of those who shape them.

The long-delayed encounter between Antony and Caesar is masterfully rendered. Shakespeare keeps us in just the participants' extreme uncertainty as to its outcome; and it is all the more tense because something is to be decided on which so much depends, not only for the action of the play but in the world and in history altogether. Yet everything hangs in the most precarious balance between these two contestants here, and the exchanges are kept at high pitch because every small gesture thus takes on such moment.

The scene is brilliantly observed and developed in the way it follows out the moves of the game, from the affected indifference of the principals' entries, chatting with friends, through the tensely formal over-courtesies — 'Sit, sir!' —, to the delicate probing and fencing of the bargaining itself. Shakespeare brings out the personal involvement of the two statesmen in the public issue between them, letting us see how ready they are to find offence in each other's words and supposed motives, and how stiffly obdurate are their wills, hardened as much by self-esteem as by their cause. In this merciless game of manoeuvring for pride of place to be reasonable is to be ineffectual; and what clearly emerges is that the contest of such peremptory dispositions can have no settlement in the terms they entertain. It is suspended rather than resolved by Agrippa's suggestion that Antony should marry Octavia, the project which brings about that extraordinary climax of their sudden confederation against Pompey. Things might easily have gone quite a different way from that; and the very uncertainty of the outcome reminds us how shrewdly Shakespeare keeps us level with the thinking of his characters. The bargain which brings about that abrupt turn against the common enemy is too evidently a short-term expedient rather than a real solution, and will itself prove a source of future trouble; but then at least one of the parties to it is already calculating his chances either way.

These political scenes show us the world of contingency at work, powerfully giving shape to the drama created by the interplay of free independent wills. Sheer uncertainty from moment to moment pitches the mood. We find ourselves caught up in the exigencies of competing claims, made privy to the inner conflict of motives as well as the outward clash of wills, invited to appraise the likely effects of the exercises of cunning, the politic shifts, the shows of self-conscious pride, the spasms of moral scruple. Above all, we share the calculation of chance and choice which gives these people responsibility for their fortunes. Such scenes live vividly for us because they open a condition of perpetual possibility, not so much drawing out resolved moral dispositions as figuring a state of dynamic change.

Far from resolving characters into moral stereotypes this world of possibility proves people by their effectiveness in it, and not least by the degree of their success in imposing their will upon themselves and others. Lepidus' fairminded attempts at mediation cruelly show us how far out of his depth he is in the conduct of a power which he formally shares with Antony and Caesar. We see him blundering anxiously between great men who find their own reputations at stake, as well as the peace of the world. The scene on Pompey's galley makes a still deadlier judgement upon him, drawing out his amiable qualities into feeble ineffectualness and public imbecility. The comments of the servants, always a telling sign in Shakespeare, make explicit the amused contempt we all feel for a well-disposed fool in high office:

> *First Servant*:   To be called into a huge sphere, and not to be seen to move in't, are the holes where eyes should be, which pitifully disaster the cheeks.

People are tried in action in surprising fashions. Those who succeed make their way because they understand their world and how to use it, if it's only that they have a keen eye to circumstance, and know just when their own endeavours best feed the will and pride of their great masters. The odd yet vivid little episode of Ventidius' success in Parthia shows us a captain who refuses to follow up a decisive military advantage because it would attract to him the glory which should be Antony's. How to serve one's prince so as to serve oneself? We make what we may of such prudent deference to authority, which in itself limits the power it serves as it happens.

Pompey's temper is put to trial in a particularly bold comparison of attitudes and fortunes. The second parleying scene, II, vi, makes such a telling contrast with the first partly because Pompey is a more reasonable man than his rivals, who shows himself ready to consider the offered conditions on their merits without insisting on his own proud will. He is fatally ready as it proves; for if that episode doesn't tell us enough about Pompey's chances in this jungle then there's the decisive irony of a little epiphany in the midst of the banquet on the galley, II, vii. But then that marvellous scene is ironic through and through in the way it permeates a politic gala of state with the spirit of a feast of love.

The reconcilement of deadly political rivals is a tense and wary affair at first, following so soon upon some knife-edge negotiation:

> *Lepidus*:   Well met here.
> *Pompey*:   I hope so, Lepidus, thus we are agreed:
> I crave our composition may be written
> And seal'd between us.

Caesar:	That's the next thing to do.
Pompey:	We'll feast each other, ere we part, and let's Draw lots who shall begin.
Antony:	That will I, Pompey.
Pompey:	No, Antony, take the lot: but, first or last, Your fine Egyptian cookery shall have The fame. I have heard that Julius Caesar Grew fat with feasting there.
Antony:	You have heard much.
Pompey:	I have fair meanings, sir.
Antony:	And fair words to them.
Pompey:	Then so much have I heard, And I have heard Apollodorus carried —
Enobarbus:	No more of that: he did so.

But then they board the galley, the wine begins to flow, and tension is soon released in festive revelry. Drunken buffoonery takes over; indeed the way men hold their drink becomes a measure of their quality as men. Lepidus holds his so badly that his colleagues openly rib him:

Lepidus:	What manner o' thing is your crocodile?
Antony:	It is shap'd, sir, like itself, and it is as broad as it hath breadth: it is just so high as it is, and moves with its own organs. It lives by that which nourisheth it, and the elements once out of it, it transmigrates.
Lepidus:	What colour is it of?
Antony:	Of its own colour too.
Lepidus:	'Tis a strange serpent.
Antony:	'Tis so, and the tears of it are wet.
Caesar:	Will this description satisfy him?
Antony:	With the health that Pompey gives him, else he is a very epicure . . . These quick-sands, Lepidus, Keep off them for you sink.

There's music; old adversaries dance the Egyptian bacchanals together; and then in the beautiful obliviousness of booze they find a kind of humane innocence, in which men momentarily esteem each other just as fellow beings. Like IV, v of *Troilus and Cressida* this is a moment as it were snatched from the workaday use, an interlude of mere humanity before the world's affairs press in again and men begin once more to tear each other apart. Yet even as he whips up the revelry Shakespeare slips in a quick parenthesis. A piratical sea-captain of Pompey's, one Menas, sidles up behind Pompey and tries to draw him aside. Pompey is keeping the wine flowing and won't even listen at first, but Menas persists, and he finally gets Pompey to walk apart with him in some irritation — 'I think th'art mad!' While Pompey continues to urge on the guests around the table Menas whispers behindhand to him — 'Wilt thou be lord of all the world?' Pompey doesn't take it in for a time, thinking this is more drunken foolery. But then he suddenly grasps that Menas is cold sober, and in deadly earnest:

Pompey: Show me which way.
Menas: These three world-sharers, these competitors,
Are in thy vessel. Let me cut the cable;
And when we are put off, fall to their throats.
All there is thine.
Pompey: Ah, this thou shouldst have done,
And not have spoke on't. In me 'tis villainy:
In thee't had been good service. Thou must know
'Tis not my profit that does lead mine honour:
Mine honour, it. Repent that e'er thy tongue
Hath so betray'd thine act. Being done unknown,
I should have found it afterwards well done,
But must condemn it now. Desist, and drink.
Menas: For this,
I'll never follow thy pall'd fortunes more.
Who seeks, and will not take when once 'tis offer'd,
Shall never find it more.
Pompey: This health to Lepidus!

The brief exchange poses a nice little trial of political principle; and as Menas sees, this is a moment of defining choice for Pompey. Like Giovanpaolo Baglioni in Machiavelli's *Discorsi* (1.27) Pompey chooses honour, or the name of honour; and he dooms himself to the inevitable consequences of putting his fair fame before the cold political reality. That's the end of him in fact. We are left with some nice questions, not only about the morality of such political mastery as the calculating Caesar aims at, but about the qualities that bring men success, and the issues that set them to destroy each other. It's almost incidental that we see how an entire civil order hangs by a cable here.

The play continually invites our attention to the way that people's natures affect their fortunes, and are tried by circumstance. Events don't allow us the assurance of unqualified moral judgement. Our view of Enobarbus shifts with his shifting condition, because he always earns our sympathetic understanding as he passes from shrewd commentator to expedient deserter, and then to heartbroken penitent; and his progress invites a continual revision of our moral preconceptions in itself. Octavia is a good woman who would be an admirable wife to someone, yet her very virtues make her no match for an Antony; and the little we hear of Fulvia sets her up for us as a great spirit driven to extremes by her own demanding vitality, which has no other release once Antony has deserted her for Cleopatra. Cleopatra herself seems so unpredictably various to us because we are continually revising our expectation as circumstances call out fresh qualities in her; and no simple moral category will contain a creature in whom such pettiness and low cunning coexist with god-like aspiration and magnificence.

Yet our judgement is continually solicited. From the first words of the play the participants appraise one another, implicitly inviting us to approve their discernment as well as their accuracy; indeed the accompaniment of commentary is so persistent and pointed as to govern the way the play works upon us. We get to the political scenes in Act II with the sense that they try in action a whole gallery of witness we've already been offered, Philo on Antony in I, i, Antony on Pompey in I, iii, Caesar and Lepidus on Antony in I, iv, Caesar on Pompey in I, iv, Pompey on his several opponents in II, i. Nor are we weighing only what the great political adversaries make of each other. The voices of friends, servants, even disinterested bystanders, surround the principals with their practical observations at every stage, and amount to a kind of choric iteration of settled experience in the ways of the world.

As in Plutarch's *Parallel Lives* themselves the protagonists show their mettle in the choices they make, and are held up for our comparative appraisal. We size them up not only by what people say of them but by what we directly see, by the consequences of their actions and choices, by the ineluctable fact that certain things come about and others don't; and the verdict of history upon them is just another irony in the pattern. What seems clear is that our estimations will vary according to the point of view we take, and that none of these perspectives can exclude the others. Final and absolute judgement isn't within the scope of the world we see in this play, for such finality is no more available to us than it is possible to the participants in this ancient theatre of policy. The nature of the world itself ordains that good qualities here may be bad there, that the very qualities which make men unamiable and unadmirable as men may produce great good for humanity at large, while admirable human qualities may bring about chaos and disaster. Our estimation of events in time must be inherently relative when the events themselves admit no absolute measure.

How are we to weigh the difference in the qualities and fortunes of an Antony and an Octavius? Relatively, perforce, for the play won't be reduced to a moral formula. Shakespeare doesn't even allow us the comfortable prescription that Caeser is a man of destiny, while the lovers live intensely in their moment. His Antony and Cleopatra are wholly creatures of the world of power, embodiments of temporal magnificence who share its vulnerableness to time and alteration. Nor does their love in itself set them beyond the mutations of the world, so that they might share Donne's vaunt — 'Only our love hath no decay'. On the contrary, it is peculiarly vulnerable just because their magnificence and their power also define them as lovers.

The pattern of the play follows the vicissitudes of the lovers' travail, even the rhythm of their erotic life, in a way that sharply contrasts such mutable fortunes with the progress of a Caesar. Shakespeare picks up Plutarch's narrative just at a stage of Antony's career which impels us to try his uncertain success against his former prowess. The play opens with an Antony whose powers are coming in question with the people around him, so that they watch for the sign of a falling off, and think they find it in his dotage on Cleopatra. They put it to us that the tide of his manhood stands at the turn, if it isn't already on the ebb. The prodigiously protracted climax in Acts III and IV, which catches the extraordinary wavering of Antony's hopes, keeps us at a telling distance from Antony's own reading of events, concentrating our interest on his need to come to terms with the prospect that he can never again be as good as he was. An Antony will not be less than himself. Yet we onlookers are well prepared for his failure, not only by the soothsayer's prediction that he must always lose in contest with Octavius, and by Enobarbus's desertion, but by the intimate connection Shakespeare depicts in the language of the play between his virility and his power. Plutarch reports that Antony was in his fifties when these events took place. We measure his momentary triumphs against his inescapable decline. His resolves and elations, twists and turns of self-will, rages, despairs, revulsions, are all carefully anatomized for us; and we see that it is a double defeat in his own eyes when faltering military judgement is taken for failing manhood:

Antony:	The queen shall then have courtesy, so she Will yield us up.
Ambassador:	He says so.
Antony:	Let her know't. To the boy Caesar send this grizzled head, And he will fill thy wishes to the brim, With principalities.
Cleopatra:	That head, my lord?
Antony:	To him again, tell him he wears the rose Of youth upon him; from which, the world should note Something particular: his coin, ships, legions, May be a coward's, whose ministers would prevail Under the service of a child, as soon As i' the command of Caesar: I dare him therefore To lay his gay comparisons apart And answer me declin'd, sword against sword, Ourselves alone.

Behind all Antony's conduct in the play is a sense of the insecurity of his hold upon Cleopatra, and of his own powers as a lover. His very fear of the younger man starts there:

Antony:	Triple-turn'd whore, 'tis thou Hast sold me to this novice, and my heart

> Makes only wars on thee. Bid them all fly:
> For when I am reveng'd upon my charm,
> I have done all. Bid them all fly, be gone.

We feel Antony's debility after Actium through the slacker patterning and weakened verbs of his speeches:

> I have fled myself, and have instructed cowards
> To run, and show their shoulders. Friends, be gone,
> I have myself resolv'd upon a course,
> Which has no need of you. Be gone,
> My treasure's in the harbour. Take it: O,
> I follow'd that I blush to look upon:
> My very hairs do mutiny; for the white
> Reprove the brown for rashness, and they them
> For fear, and doting. Friends, be gone, you shall
> Have letters from me to some friends, that will
> Sweep your way for you. Pray you, look not sad,
> Nor make replies of loathness; take the hint
> Which my despair proclaims. Let that be left
> Which leaves itself: to the sea-side straightway;
> I will possess you of that ship and treasure.
> Leave me, I pray, a little: pray you now,
> Nay, do so: for indeed I have lost command,
> Therefore I pray you: I'll see you by and by.

Recurrent anxieties emerge like bugbears from the depth of his mind, embodying themselves in extreme images. He is preoccupied with his status as Antony, with the loyalty of those he relies on, with the likelihood of sexual betrayal, with the designs of the young man who has defeated him. Nothing reveals his misgiving so much as his veteranly contempt for the novice, and vaunts of superior skill. Samson-like, he himself now seeks excuse for lost strength in his uxorious blindness — 'My sword, made weak by my affection'; and he swings between self-pity and sentimental bravado, rushing from lament over lost manhood to the conceit which is such empty consolation here, that Cleopatra's tear is worth the whole world.

When we feel the old power still it is turned back on itself in self-lacerating savagery, coming through less in active verbs than in images of self-disgusted violence:

> You were half blasted ere I knew you: ha?
> Have I my pillow left unpress'd in Rome,
> Forborne the getting of a lawful race,
> And by a gem of women, to be abus'd
> By one that looks on feeders?

Cleopatra:	Good my lord, —
Antony:	You have been a boggler ever,
	But when we in our viciousness grow hard —
	O misery on't! — the wise gods seel our eyes,
	In our own filth drop our clear judgements, make us
	Adore our errors, laugh at's while we strut
	To our confusion.
Cleopatra:	O, is't come to this?
Antony:	I found you as a morsel, cold upon
	Dead Caesar's trencher: nay, you were a fragment
	Of Gnaeus Pompey's, besides what hotter hours,
	Unregister'd in vulgar fame, you have
	Luxuriously pick'd out. For I am sure,
	Though you can guess what temperance should be,
	You know not what it is.
Cleopatra:	Wherefore is this?

His humiliated sexual pride, like Othello's, finds nothing gross enough to relieve it but what it normally revolts from, savagely savouring its own animal degradation. Cleopatra's politic dalliance with Thidias provokes a blatant extremity of jealous rage, which is the more painfully revealing because the occasion seems so slight — 'O that I were/Upon the hill of Basan, to outroar/The horned herd, for I have savage cause,'. Antony's habit of speaking of himself in global images takes on bizarre cosmic scope as he extends his ruin outward to eternity, in a vision of final destruction:

> He makes me angry,
> And at this time most easy 'tis to do't:
> When my good stars, that were my former guides,
> Have empty left their orbs, and shot their fires
> Into the abysm of hell.

It seems a character of their passion that Cleopatra seeks to conciliate him by outdoing him in ferocious hyperbole:

> Ah, dear, if I be so,
> From my cold heart let heaven engender hail,
> And poison it in the source, and the first stone
> Drop in my neck: as it determines, so
> Dissolve my life; the next Caesarion smite
> Till by degrees the memory of my womb,
> Together with my brave Egyptians all,
> By the discandying of this pelleted storm,
> Lie graveless, till the flies and gnats of Nile
> Have buried them for prey!

The contrast between this state of mind and Antony's wildness comes home to us in the coherence of her thinking. Her reply starts as a violent personal conceit, spreads outward to involve more and more supposed people in an entire historical process, and finishes up in general doom, positing an earthly hell more tangible than any to which Antony's stars now lure him. Here we find visionary force purposefully directed to a denoument which is stunning in its conclusiveness, and proceeds not as disordered raving but in strict control of the conditional mode: 'If I be so, . . . let heaven. . . .' For all her moods and passions she is never the fool of her former greatness, as Antony is.

Antony's rejuvenated mood shows its strength only in the ferocity of a forced bravado:

> I will be treble-sinew'd, hearted, breath'd,
> And fight maliciously: for when mine hours
> Were nice and lucky, men did ransom lives
> Of me for jests: but now, I'll set my teeth,
> And send to darkness all that stop me.

He reminds us of a Lear or a hard-pressed Macbeth in the way he whips up his resolve; and he seeks relief of frustrated courage in extreme gestures, now by forcing his captains to drink till their wounds spout wine, now in the all-or-nothing fling of a personal challenge to Caesar. Enobarbus' deflating comment as soon as Antony is gone hits just our sense of the self-destructive savagery of his vaunts:

> Now he'll outstare the lightning; to be furious
> Is to be frighted out of fear, and in that mood
> The dove will peck the estridge; and I see still,
> A diminution in our captain's brain
> Restores his heart; when valour preys on reason,
> It eats the sword it fights with: I will seek
> Some way to leave him.

The image of a valour which preys on its own instrument makes Enobarbus' desertion more than a pathetic signal of Antony's decline. It suggests that Antony's very judgement is irreparably corrupted by powers which now turn back upon themselves.

It is still far from a random energy that we see in IV, iv:

>   'Tis well blown, lads.
> This morning, like the spirit of a youth
> That means to be of note, begins betimes.
> So, so; come, give me that: this way; well said.
> Fare thee well, dame, whate'er becomes of me:
> This is a soldier's kiss: rebukeable,
> And worthy shameful check it were, to stand
> On more mechanic compliment; I'll leave thee

Now like a man of steel. You that will fight,
Follow me close, I'll bring you to't. Adieu.

Whatever it may lack of the contained force of earlier speeches this leave-taking has its own brusque strength. Yet so conscious an enactment of the steel-encased man comes here as sadly ironic; and it is the pathetic irony of all their hopes that Shakespeare brings out at this stage. He moves from its place in Plutarch the brief episode of Antony's triumph in a preliminary skirmish, so that it immediately follows instead of preceding the elegiac farewells, and the episode of Hercules's withdrawal. The marvellous hyperbole of the lovers' greeting when Antony returns from battle thus comes on us as a trumpet of false hope, a dying flourish if not a posthumous echo of glory:

> O thou day o' the world,
> Chain mine arm'd neck, leap thou, attire and all,
> Through proof of harness to my heart, and there
> Ride on the pants triumphing!
>
> *Cleopatra*:   Lord of lords,
> O infinite virtue, com'st thou smiling from
> The world's great snare uncaught?

Antony's reply takes virility at a lower rate, with its vaunting talk of getting 'goal for goal of youth'. Almost to the end he apprehensively grounds his predicament in his rivalry with the younger man. His conscious whipping up of the zest for heroic deeds quite ironically spends itself in a bravura flourish of trumpets and drums.

The raging of IV, xii, following so hard upon their splendid vaunt, miserably reminds us that such absoluteness can't be the last word while they still so recklessly entangle themselves in the world's snare. Antony's language here expresses a still keener sense of self-frustration, and of self-tormenting vitality, as if his powers already converge upon that transfixion with his own sword which finally drains his life. His mad rage of suspicion that she has sold him to a novice renews a dire self-war — 'my heart/Makes only wars on thee' and 'when I am reveng'd upon my charm' — which delivers him to the Macbeth-like despair of 'bid them all fly', and resolves him for self-destruction even before Cleopatra's feigned death. His mind wearily draws together in one laboured image Cleopatra's treachery, the desertions of friends, and the blossoming of Caesar with the favours which might revive an Antony:

> O sun, thy uprise shall I see no more,
> Fortune and Antony part here, even here
> Do we shake hands. All come to this? The hearts
> That spaniel'd me at heels, to whom I gave

> Their wishes, do discandy, melt their sweets
> On blossoming Caesar: and this pine is bark'd,
> That overtopp'd them all.

The speech is obscure in the Folio, and further confused by Hanmer's emendation of Folio 'pannelled' to 'spaniel'd'; but its very incoherence expresses Antony's struggle to find the cause of his waning fortunes in some agency beyond himself, as though his vital sap dries up just because the showers that sustained him now fall on the younger man. The implied image of the dissolving cloud will recur to his mind within a couple of scenes as a figure of his own condition. When he turns to abuse Cleopatra he compacts what she has cost him in the very word which had seemed to sum up most memorably all his gain by her: 'Beguil'd me, to the very heart of loss'. By this point the play is a texture of such correspondences, which set each other off as if they disclose the unadmitted crosscurrents in the mind. Motifs recur with ironic complexity, and the very emblems of manliness prove fatally ambiguous:

> O, thy vile lady!
> She has robb'd me of my sword.

Rinaldo in Armida's garden bears a mirror at his side instead of a sword, which shows him images of his enervate enslavement (*La Gerusalemme Liberata* xvi, 20–3). Antony's sword is to be turned against its master in deluded honour, not altogether effectively, and taken to Caesar imbrued with Antony's life blood. Shakespeare aspires to a complexity of metaphor which is quite beyond Tasso's scope.

Antony's marvellous response to the false report of Cleopatra's death alternates imperatives with less peremptory moods, as if massive eruptions of power continually lose themselves in bitter realization, or fall away into impotence:

> Unarm Eros, the long day's task is done,
> And we must sleep. [*To Mardian*] That thou depart'st hence safe
> Does pay thy labour richly; go.   [*Exit Mardian.*
>   Off, pluck off,
> The seven-fold shield of Ajax cannot keep
> The battery from my heart. O, cleave, my sides!
> Heart, once be stronger than thy continent,
> Crack thy frail case! Apace, Eros, apace!
> No more a soldier: bruised pieces, go,
> You have been nobly borne. From me a while.
> I will o'ertake thee, Cleopatra, and
> Weep for my pardon. So it must be, for now
> All length is torture: since the torch is out,
> Lie down and stray no farther. Now all labour
> Mars what it does: yea, very force entangles
> Itself with strength: seal then, and all is done.

We see him struggling to revive the ebbed magnificence, or project it into a life beyond the present ruin. The brief ejaculatory imperatives impel extreme gestures, between which the mind can only beat in on itself, pathetically dwelling on the past or on the hope of future idyll. His wrestle with himself takes him from spasms of impassioned action to a despairing bewilderment, and then at last to revived hope:

Eros! — I come, my queen: — Eros! — Stay for me,
Where souls do couch on flowers, we'll hand in hand,
And with our sprightly port make the ghosts gaze;
Dido, and her Aeneas, shall want troops,
And all the haunt be ours.

His call to Eros at this point signals a new resolution, which is more than the courage of despair:

Come, Eros, Eros!

Shakespeare disposes the events as if to show how mere contingency may belittle even the greatest human lives. Antony is made the fool of a dreadful irony of circumstance, such as mocks and betrays his direst extremity. Our awareness of Cleopatra's miscalculated device lets us take his attempt at suicide for an unnecessary gesture of proud will, which is botched in itself, and merely enacts his final subjection to crass casualty. We see a splendid man brought low, reduced by pure mischance to a drained and helpless heap of animal flesh. The alteration is put before our eyes, even drawn out for our contemplation — 'The miserable change now at my end. . .'. We are invited to compare this state with his former magnificence, and to see our human condition thus defined by its subjection to chance, change and death. The more human the more vulnerable, might be the lesson of an Antony's downfall.

The ironies of Antony's Roman gesture keep us at a distance from his own assumption that such a death is a noble self-conquest. We see well enough what his nobility owes to sheer pride, and how far his revival of spirit *in extremis* is inspired by the prospect of a new and unsurpassable glory in death. Nothing could more cogently bring it home to us that these people are creatures of a heroic and not a Christian universe than Antony's consciously fostered uniqueness, his attempt to make self-slaughter a final demonstration of our mastery over fate.

The lovers themselves are always mindful of their heroic status. Their very exchanges remain public utterance. Even in the extremity of Antony's end they speak to each other, and of themselves, in the third person and by title — 'Antony' . . . 'Egypt'. This is the voice of universal celebration rather than of private grief or intimate leavetaking. Pity is scarcely in place. Antony's death leaves us only with the awed sense that something incomparably great is willingly departing the earth. It's not so much the waste we regret (for what could that amount to now!) as the inevitable withdrawal of something rich and irreplaceable, whatever new order it may make way for:

> The miserable change now at my end
> Lament nor sorrow at: but please your thoughts
> In feeding them with those my former fortunes
> Wherein I liv'd: the greatest prince o' the world,
> The noblest; and do now not basely die,
> Not cowardly put off my helmet to
> My countryman: A Roman, by a Roman
> Valiantly vanquish'd.

These two present themselves as the last representatives of a dying ethic, embodiments of a vulnerable magnificence which will now be replaced by competent policy; and their downfall signals a general contraction of life, a loss of the ancient greatness of heart. Their celebration of themselves is also a looking back, like Fulke Greville's memorial of Sidney, to proclaim that vanishing glory for the last time.

Yet what we remark above all in these exalted antiphonal vaunts as Antony's life ebbs is the sheer high-heartedness of human beings in the face of extinction, who have no spiritual recourse yet will to transcend their own mortality, if only so that death may be denied the conquest it would inflict upon them. They make the world the loser by their withdrawal from it:

> Noblest of men, woo't die?
> Hast thou no care of me, shall I abide
> In this dull world, which in thy absence is
> No better than a sty? O, see, my woman:
> The crown o' the earth doth melt. My lord?
> O, wither'd is the garland of the war,
> The soldier's pole is fall'n: young boys and girls
> Are level now with men: the odds is gone,
> And there is nothing left remarkable
> Beneath the visiting moon.

So vivid an enactment ('O, see, my women . . .') makes us hang upon Antony's passing, and mark for ourselves how brightness falls from the air with the lapse of such a being into mere clay. Our involvement gives special poignancy to Cleopatra's assumption of both their fames when she professes to honour death by encountering it so, and takes issue with the gods just for imposing such a privation upon the world:

> It were for me
> To throw my sceptre at the injurious gods,

To tell them that this world did equal theirs,
Till they had stol'n our jewel. All's but naught:
Patience is sottish, and impatience does
Become a dog that's mad: then is it sin
To rush into the secret house of death,
Ere death dare come to us?. . . . Look,
Our lamp is spent, it's out. Good sirs, take heart
We'll bury him: and then, what's brave, what's noble,
Let's do it after the high Roman fashion,
And make death proud to take us. Come away,
This case of that huge spirit now is cold. . . .

In Cleopatra's high conceit the lovers requite in a final triumph all the vicissitudes of their lives, meeting death with a whole will, and yet celebrating the scope of their worldly being:

Cleopatra:	I dreamt there was an Emperor Antony.
	O such another sleep, that I might see
	But such another man!
Dolabella:	If it might please ye, —
Cleopatra:	His face was as the heavens, and therein stuck
	A sun and moon, which kept their course, and lighted
	The little O, the earth.
Dolabella:	Most sovereign creature, —
Cleopatra:	His legs bestrid the ocean, his rear'd arm
	Crested the world: his voice was propertied
	As all the tuned spheres, and that to friends:
	But when he meant to quail, and shake the orb,
	He was as rattling thunder. For his bounty,
	There was no winter in't: an autumn 'twas
	That grew the more by reaping: his delights
	Were dolphin-like, they show'd his back above
	The element they lived in: in his livery
	Walk'd crowns and crownets: realms and islands were
	As plates dropp'd from his pocket.
Dolabella:	Cleopatra!
Cleopatra:	Think you there was, or might be such a man
	As this I dreamt of?

Cleopatra's lavish hyperbolizing of Antony for Dolabella, with its huge stride of the vaunt from one element to another, transforms into perfected image the global terms which had defined him, as if he really were the world of his own empire, and his empire had been no more than a projection of his full humanity. We follow out the vision of a godlike nature, which needs no spiritual rebirth because it apprehends that capacity of grandeur already within itself — 'I think I am becoming a god' (Seutonius, *Vespasian* xxiii).

However we take it Dolabella's startling response, 'Gentle madam, no',

brings us straight back to earth. Is this a courteous intimation of the way
Antony's greatness must inevitably be belittled when it becomes the
sport of envious and calumniating time? The demur will evoke its echo in
the audience, if only because it reminds us of the frailty of a fame which
lives in the minds of a few generous understanders. Still more cogently, it
keeps us in mind that even such a celebration of human magnanimity
can't stand unqualified, marking the ambiguity of all our ideas of ourselves and our own doings. Like Philo's 'Behold and see', Dolabella's
reply throws the question to us. What are we to make of an Antony? No
simple category of praise or blame will hold such a full humanity as this.

The two great scenes of apotheosis are quite drastically separated, so
that between the peaks of elegaic exaltation we get a close view of the
plight of vanquished power in the world. It shocks to see one who has
already confronted death so triumphantly wriggling and dodging in her
attempt to evade the consequence of their defeat by outsmarting Caesar
after all. Cleopatra has this in common with Vittoria Corombora, that she
tries to exploit her sexuality right up to the moment when she recognizes
that she has no way to preserve her will and dignity but by dying.
Seleucus's intervention makes its point. Cleopatra's attempt at a petty
deceit in the accounting of her assets seems mean shift enough after the
grandeur of her tribute to Antony, and in prospect of her own immola-
tion. That attachment to double-dealing marks the paradox of the divided
human spirit. It is the concentration of the will upon a death they
deliberately elect in preference to decline and dishonour that frees these
lovers from their commitment to the precarious world of contingents,
which has so betrayed them.

Then Antony and Cleopatra are the fools of time and history in a larger
sense. Shakespeare sets off his version of their lives and deaths against a
very different way of looking at these events, which takes Caesar's victory
for the triumph of a great vision over some petty faction-mongers, who
disturbed the world for a time with their private amours:

> The Roman Empire was helped to its perfection by miraculous intercession;
> therefore it was willed by God, and consequently it existed and exists by right.
>
> (Dante, *De Monarchia* 2.4)

> perchè tu veggi con quanta ragione
>   si move contr'al sacrosanto segno
>   e chi 'l s'appropria e chi a lui s'oppone. . . .
> Piangene ancor la trista Cleopatra,
>   che, fuggendola innanzi, dal colubro
>   la morte prese subitana e atra.
> Con costui corse infino al lito rubro;
>   con costui puose il mondo in tanta pace,
>   che fu serrato a Iano il suo delubro.
>
> (*Par.* vi, 31–3, 76–81)

[so that you may see with how little reason they move to oppose the sacred standard, both those who appropriate it and those who oppose it. . . . The woeful Cleopatra still weeps because of it, who, fleeing before it, took from the snake sudden and fearful death. With him [Augustus Caesar] it ran as far as the shore of the Red Sea; with him it set the world at such peace that the temple of Janus was locked.]

'The time of universal peace is now at hand'. Shakespeare sounds the Virgilian note ironically enough when he reminds us how the Augustan peace has hung in balance with the proclivities of lovers who aren't gods in their sensual lives, but all too human.

These deaths can scarcely be called a relinquishing of the world. On the contrary, the lovers carry their imperial bearing into death with them. Cleopatra responds to Iras's bleak truth —

Finish, good lady, the bright day is done,
And we are for the dark

— with a fine defiance of the unknown, which matches the spirit of an Antony who runs into his death as to a bridegroom's bed:

Show me, my women, like a queen: go fetch
My best attires. I am again for Cydnus,
To meet Mark Antony.

This is no sentimental repining ('Nessun maggior dolor . . .'), or vain ambition to be petrified in the posture of her greatness,[2] but a proud re-enactment of her glory as a prelude to the final hyperbole:

Give me my robe, put on my crown, I have
Immortal longings in me. Now no more
The juice of Egypt's grape shall moist this lip.
Yare, yare, good Iras; quick: methinks I hear
Antony call. I see him rouse himself
To praise my noble act. I hear him mock
The luck of Caesar, which the gods give men
To excuse their after wrath. Husband, I come:
Now to that name, my courage prove my title!
I am fire, and air; my other elements
I give to baser life. So, have you done?
Come then, and take the last warmth of my lips.

[2]Duke Vincenzo 1 of Mantua (1562–1612) willed that his body should be displayed sitting on a marble throne with his sword drawn, and then buried in the same attitude. The instruction was disregarded. (Wills of 18 July 1608 and 3 February 1612. See R. Signorini, 'Gonzaga Tombs and Catafalques' in *Splendours of the Gonzaga*, ed. D. Chambers and J. Martineau, 1981, p. 7).

> Farewell, kind Charmian, Iras, long farewell.
> Have I the aspic in my lips? Dost fall?
> If thou and nature can so gently part,
> The stroke of death is as a lover's pinch,
> Which hurts, and is desir'd.

The imperious authority of the syntax sustains the timeless blazon. Shakespeare's Cleopatra goes beyond her original in Plutarch, who simply lies out on her bed to die. She encounters death as an emperor receives an equal, displaying in nice ceremonial protocol this last chivalric amplitude of spirit. We must admire, however we may disapprove, the stoic grandeur of the will to transcend common fortune while she holds the means in her own hand:

> O, couldst thou speak,
> That I might hear thee call great Caesar ass,
> Unpolicied!

She wills a death which may negate mere policy and fulfil the exuberant sexuality of their lives, receiving it as a sensual ecstasy whose instrument is a lover's bite, a phallus, a baby at her breast, as well as a sword. Her passing itself becomes no more than a triumphal progress to rejoin a lusty lover:

> If she first meet the curled Antony,
> He'll make demand of her, and spend that kiss
> Which is my heaven to have.

The physical horror of the bite of an angry snake is intensely enough realized in the lines to bring home to our senses the difference between this death and a clean self-stabbing:

> Come, thou mortal wretch,
> With thy sharp teeth this knot intrinsicate
> Of life at once untie: poor venomous fool,
> Be angry, and despatch.

Our shudder of repulsion brings home to our senses this bizarre likening of the snake's fatuous malice with her enemy's, and her welcoming of what we instinctively fear. We are provoked to feel the triumph of the will which so transforms horror into a glorious consummation, and makes an amorous swoon of the ebbing of consciousness itself:

> As sweet as balm, as soft as air, as gentle.
> O Antony! . . .

We follow her through her slow dissolution as we follow the stages of Brachiano's death; only here the effect is pointedly unlike Webster's. It isn't the onset of a fearful degeneration we mark — 'There's death in's face already' — but the imperceptibility of the fatal change; as though the difference between life and death is of small account in the end, and the sheer force of her own conceit might really carry her through to a trans-figured being beyond organic decay. When the world breaks in on them at length we feel the shock of its bustling impertinence, then the awe of the physical confrontation of dead queen and living emperor, between whom such a gulf has opened in a moment. Octavius's bureaucratic manner all but parodies itself when we encounter it here, so hard upon Cleopatra's dying splendours, which belittle his clipped functional questions and manner of command. Yet Caesar himself is momentarily moved to wonder, catching up in a last equivocal transformation the serpentine motif which runs through the play:

> but she looks like sleep,
> As she would catch another Antony
> In her strong toil of grace.

The statesman reasserts himself soon enough in a shrewd discrimination of honours which makes a funeral eulogy serve his own fame:

> Take up her bed,
> And bear her women from the monument;
> She shall be buried by her Antony.
> No grave upon the earth shall clip in it
> A pair so famous: high events as these
> Strike those that make them: and their story is
> No less in pity than his glory which
> Brought them to be lamented. Our army shall
> In solemn show attend this funeral,
> And then to Rome. Come, Dolabella, see
> High order, in this great solemnity.

These last momentous scenes fulfil the movement of the play in the way they oppose the onward sweep of historical incident with an enduring image of stillness, which the passing show can't touch. There is that in the play which the very syntax sets apart from the modes of time and his-tory, and which isn't finally mocked by the ironies of circumstance. Shakespeare gives his lovers the casual power to perfect such moments, simply as a condition of their being. The splendour of self-conceit in their language continually lifts them beyond the petty limitations of their material condition, and the frailty of sense, not so much transcending time as giving as absolute value to the quality of their secular lives:

> Eternity was in our lips, and eyes,
> Bliss in our brows' bent; none our parts so poor,
> But was a race of heaven.

The irony of their lavishness of spirit is always before us in its effects, and in its roots in personal pride. They win their monumental sublimity out of the turbulence and squalor, even because of the petty accidents of the moment. Lacking the Christian hope of transcending their condition they transform their own state, deifying themselves as sovereign conquerors of all that might diminish our lives, and willing their immortality in their attitudes as they lived. They are right to anticipate a still greater empery after death, not as the legacy of power or their passion, but by the immemorial magnificence which art, at least, may give them.

The play attests the power of the human spirit to rise out of the wrack of circumstance and defy time by its own inherent splendour. It figures a triumph of untransformed human nature over the contingencies of our existence, as if to proclaim the possible grandeur of being human, and to hold against Augustus Caesar's realized vision of a great work in time a quality of present being, and a self-exaltation such as wills to perpetuate its conceit of its own sublimity:

> The intellect of man is forced to choose
> Perfection of the life, or of the work,

Shakespeare offers us a larger prospect than Yeats. The image Antony and Cleopatra achieve is no mere compensation for their careers, a perfected work of art which the mind somehow sublimes out of the heart's foul rag-and-bone shop, but a glory in their lives such as warrants their eternity of fame. The testimony to the power of the image is the play itself, in whose language it is so tellingly recreated.

In thus vividly reanimating causes which worked themselves out 1600 years before it was written, the play leaves a question with us. What endures and has value, of all our striving? In Shakespeare's day, and after, the Augustan concord scarcely needed justifying. The verdict of history must be that it was well an Augustus rather than an Antony survived to perfect a civil order:

> I instance the way things stood among mortal beings when the son of God took on the form of man for man's salvation, whether he awaited such a state or disposed it according to his will. For if we call to mind all the conditions and times of men from the lapse of our first parents, which began all our strayings, we shall find that only under the divine ruler Augustus was there a perfect monarchy, when the world was peacefully at one. And the human race was happy then in the tranquility of universal peace, as all the historians testify, as well as the illustrious poets, and even the scribe of the meekness of Christ; and lastly Paul called this most happy state 'the fulness of time'. . . .

> (Dante, *De Monarchia* 1.16)

Yet Shakespeare's Caesar himself finds as much to celebrate in the lives of the dead lovers as in his own triumph. The play resists easy alternatives as it resists simple choices, neither putting statecraft before love nor proving the world well lost. Its characters judge each other on grounds which we are invited to understand, rather than to uphold or condemn. The Roman view of a great soldier's infatuation with a scheming seductress stands against Alexandrian contempt for mere politic bureaucracy. We are offered not so much a scales or a moral blueprint as an optic glass, which sympathetically seeks out what happened and why, the differences in the qualities of people, the different fortunes these qualities beget, how people comport themselves *in extremis*. Shakespeare's concern with the way people behave is undoubtedly moral; yet all we may say of his view of human nature in *Antony and Cleopatra* is that he believed it capable of this.

Nonetheless the play doesn't deny us a stable point of view. However people may differ in their estimates of conduct, they don't undercut each other's motives and values. It's a familiar irony of the situation that the adversaries have so much in common. Least of all might it satisfy a full experience of the play to seek out flaws of character, which makes the lovers bring on their own downfall. If it means anything to lift one's spirit beyond mere chance then they enjoy a triumph as real as Caesar's, and Cleopatra's stoic paradox has truth:

My desolation does begin to make
A better life: 'tis paltry to be Caesar:
Not being Fortune, he's but Fortune's knave,
A minister of her will: and it is great
To do that thing that ends all other deeds
Which shackles accidents, and bolts up change;
Which sleeps, and never palates more the dung,
The beggar's nurse, and Caesar's.

Shakespeare invites us to understand and admire before we judge. Who are we to judge an Antony anyway! We are asked to see what it is to be human, what being human may mean. The play provides no ready lessons for conduct if only because it keeps us so keenly aware of the limits of such successes and failures as we see, the doubtfulness of the very idea of a triumph or a downfall when outward events matter so much less than the spirit in which a being wills to encounter them. Northrop Frye is surely right when he argues that Shakespeare's manner of continually setting off one kind of effect against another defeats our attempts to pin him to a single meaning, and throws us back on the way a scene works.[3]

Yet is doesn't follow, as Frye assumes it must, that Shakespeare practises a structural art whose effects are purely artistic in that they have no

[3]*A Natural Perspective*, 1965, *passim*, but especially pp. 46–53.

coherent moral tendency; so that he is best understood by the critic for whom the literary form is an end in itself (p. 33). True the majesty of Cleopatra's death can't be isolated from the clown's low comedy (which might even seem quite pertinently macabre), or the sheer grotesqueness of the means, or Caesar's brusque disposal of her corpse as of a last impediment to universal peace. Yet we sell such high art fatally short if we suppose that the pattern of these counterbalancing effects makes a sufficient end. The clown and Caesar offset Cleopatra's dying splendour without diminishing it; they merely complicate the vision of our being by pointing the ironies of our condition in the world. Each attitude has its own truth, which doesn't nullify other quite different kinds of truth. Human nature has this capacity of grandeur; but the largeness of spirit yokes with clownishness and with cool calculation, and is given scope to display itself at a price. This play proposes that it may not coexist with the qualities which bring universal peace. Shakespeare's moral vision is embodied in these complex effects and structures, which enact our nature in its diverse, not to say contradictory possibilities. The ironic contrapositions so define us to ourselves that the farce and the tragedy, the animal and the godlike, are never wholly separate; and the tragic and the comic modes themselves seem to be just different ways of looking at our state:

> man, proud man,
> Dress'd in a little brief authority,
> Most ignorant of what he's most assur'd —
> His glassy essence — like an angry ape
> Plays such fantastic tricks before high heaven
> As makes the angels weep; who, with our spleens,
> Would all themselves laugh mortal.

> *Measure for Measure*, II, ii 118–2.

Shakespeare's art is moral to the extent that it feeds the consciousness from which morality draws. It enlarges our sense of the possibilities of life, while sharpening our awareness of the conditions on which they may be realized. In Shakespeare's tragedies of love it's the sensed apprehension of their own mortality which quickens the lovers to their vision of what is sublime and inextinguishable in our nature.

5

The Course of Altering Things

i

> that she, and that thou,
> Which did begin to love, are neither now;
> You are both fluid, changed since yesterday;

Donne, *The Second Anniversary*, 391–3

Donne is no less preoccupied than Dante with the metaphysical worth of love, but the two poets write so unlike one another that they must be speaking of quite different orders of experience. Yet Dante's lyrics have many of the qualities we attribute to Donne's. They open arrestingly, show great strength of line, use a vivid colloquial diction, make a metaphysical drama of our being:

> Angelo clama in divino intelletto
>   e dice: 'Sire, nel mondo si vede
>   maraviglia ne l'atto che procede
>   d'un anima che'nfin qua su risplende'.

[An angel cries out in the divine intelligence and says 'Lord, in the world is seen a marvel, in the act that proceeds from a soul which shines even up to this height'. Heaven, which has no defect save the lack of her, asks her of its Lord, and every saint implores this favour. Only Pity takes our part, for God speaks, and refers to my Lady: 'My loved ones, now suffer in peace, that your hope may be fixed for as long as pleases me there where there is one who waits to lose her, and who will say in the inferno, "O you accursed, I have seen the hope of the blessed" '.]

La Vita Nuova xix, 7–8

Few later hyperbolists of love would match the scope of this metaphysical conceit, asserted as simple fact, which takes in heaven, earth and hell, and brings God himself, as well as the angels and the rest of creation, to attest the marvel of a human creature.

If we put some familiar lines of Donne against Dante's love poems we find ourselves in a different world:

I wonder by my troth, what thou, and I
  Did, till we loved? were we not weaned till then, . . .?
                              'The Good Morrow'

Dante's exaltation, which the great arch of his cadence so superbly sustains, is gone and the scene has shifted to domestic life. A sudden thought
breaks in upon the intimacies of lovers, and utters itself as if spon-
taneously in the lively turns of speech of the day. The brusque attack
buttonholes us with its promise of confidence, and intimates even before
the second stanza proclaims it, that they are wholly absorbed in one
another. Pitched thus, as if to let us overhear one of the voices in a com-
munion of lovers, the poem seems to speak to us immediately and
authentically. It catches the impulse of the moment in all its avid inflections, modulating the excitement of sexual discovery with tenderness,
self-mockery, wonderment, pleasure, pride. We can't doubt that Dante
Alighieri knew such moments but his love poetry is about experiences of
a different kind, which make no call upon domestic affections.

It is Donne's awareness of the frailty of our nature that gives the
guarded hyperboles of 'The Good Morrow' their brave poignancy:

    If our two loves be one, or, thou and I
  Love so alike, that none do slacken, none can die.

The love Dante owes to Beatrice is not subject to the way of the world:

Mai non t'appresentó natura o arte
  piacer, quanto le belle membra in ch'io
  rinchiusa fui, e sono in terra sparte;

[Neither nature nor art ever presented you with a greater pleasure than my fair
members, which are now scattered in the earth. And if this consummate pleasure failed you by my death what mortal thing ought you to have been drawn
to desire thereafter! Certainly at the first arrow of false things you should have
risen up after me who was such no longer.]

                            Purgatorio xxxi, 49–57

Dante's poem allows the lover no turning back upon his great commitment. The love he enacts in his lines is beyond gainsaying because his
earthly experience of it carries him on without break to the bliss of
heaven; the impulse to love Beatrice takes a wholly transcendental direction, and makes him a metaphysical poet. Dante's progress from the *Vita
Nuova* to the *Paradiso* marvellously comprehends the entire creation in a
scale of being up which he advances by settled degrees of a love that
includes moral understanding, as if to fulfil a providential pattern of self-
transcendence. He is brought to see that his love of Beatrice is one with
the love which turns the created universe itself:

La mente innamorata, che donnea
  con la mia donna sempre, di ridure
  ad essa li occhi piú che mai ardea:

[My enamoured mind, which communed perpetually with my lady, burned
more than ever to turn my eyes back to her . . . But she, who saw my longing,
began to speak, smiling so happily that God seemed to joy in her
countenance. . . . 'this heaven has no other place than the divine mind, in
which is kindled the love that turns it and the *virtú* which it rains down. Light
and love comprehend it in one circle, as it comprehends all other things. . . .']

Paradiso xxvii, 88–90, 103–5, 109–13

After Dante, men lost the hope of an unbroken continuum of existence in
fallen creation. When Donne discovers powers beyond nature in the
innocence and beauty of a young woman, they show him that the world is
irredeemably corrupt:

     thou hast but one way, not to admit
The world's infection, to be none of it. . . .
For the world's beauty is decayed, or gone,

The First Anniversary, 245–6, 249

The devotion apotheosized in the *Paradiso*, just because it is so
pointedly removed from our ordinary experience, lets us see how far common human love is defined by its frailty. Donne's professions of love are
sharpened by his ever-present sense of the precariousness of human
commitments, and of the impulsions in a man's own nature which resist
sexual dependence. Love poets well recognized that the very nature of the
passion produces sudden reversals of feeling and fortune. Changing vows
into curses, or denouncing the love which had engrossed one's being, is
so much part of a petrarchan understanding of love that it became a recognized move in the game. Courtly lovers reasserted their independence
after years of unrewarded service by bravely turning on their lady and the
enslaving passion itself, as Wyatt does:

Ffarewell Love and all thy lawes for ever:
  Thy bayted hookes shall tangill me no more;. . .
  For hetherto though I have lost all my tyme
  Me lusteth no lenger rotten boughes to clymbe.

Harsher alternatives presented themselves to people who found no way
between the life of the senses and contempt of the world. How might a
lover reconcile his amorous urges with his yearning to be one with God?
In love poetry which aspires to map moral life an attempt to renounce
love figures an intolerable dilemma. It shows how a man may be caught

between the opposite incitements of his own nature, and compelled to ask himself what his passion for a woman has to do with eternal reality. St Augustine admits no compromise:

> It was sweet to me to love and to be loved, but still more sweet to enjoy the body of my beloved. Thus I polluted the spring of friendship with the filth of concupiscence, and clouded its purity with the lust of hell. . . .
>
> In this vast forest full of snares and perils see how many of them I have cut off and driven out of my heart, as you have enabled me to do, God of my salvation;. . . .
>
> *Confessions* III, i and X, xxxv

In Petrarch's *Secretum Meum,* which debates the worth of devotion to a woman, it is St Augustine who condemns the poet's long preoccupation with his ideal of earthly womanhood and compels him to recognize the absolute incongruity of a secular passion with heavenly love:

> From the time you fell victim to love nothing but disconsolate groans issued from your breast; the tears and sighs which the voluptuousness of love stirred up in you kept you from sleep, so that you passed whole nights repeating her name. . . . You loved the laurel, with which poets are crowned as well as emperors, the more ardently because her name was Laura, and you wrote hardly a line of poetry that didn't mention it. . . . Such is the effect of love, miseries unbelievable and indescribable to one who hasn't experienced it. But the greatest misery of love is the forgetfulness it produces both of ourselves and of God. Indeed, while the love-vanquished heart bows under the weight of so many ills, entangled in the mud, how may it raise itself to God, the one pure fount of well-being?[1]

Petrarch's long tussle with himself and St Augustine, which he drama-tizes so powerfully, puts his lifelong devotion to an idea of womanhood in direct conflict with his spiritual well-being. Throughout the *Canzoniere* he strives to find a way in which his ardour for Laura may transcend sense, and not simply divert him from his true moral end. His emphatic verdict is that an obsession with a mortal object is mortal error. Love of a woman, however the lover may strive to idealize it, cannot in the end be reconciled with love of God; on the contrary, all sexual passion is a damning distraction from right love. The *Canzoniere* itself, which Renaissance poets would take for a manual of love, is framed by a severe judgement on the 31 years of devotion it celebrates:

---

[1] *Secretum Francisci Petrarche de Florencia Poete laureati De Contemptu Mundi. . . .,* Strasburg,? 1470, 32ᵛ-33ᵛ. The work was written about 1342 when Petrarch was thirty-eight. There is an English translation of it by W. H. Draper, *Petrarch's Secret: or the Soul's Conflict with Passion,* 1911.

del vario stile in ch'io piango e ragiono
fra le vane speranze e'l van dolore,
ove sia chi per prova intenda amore,
spero trovar pietà, non che perdóno.

[by the varied style in which I weep and argue among vain hopes and vain suffering I hope to find the pity, not to say pardon, of anyone who knows love by
experience. . . . And the only fruit of my vanity is shame, repentance, and the
clear recognition that whatever pleases the world is a brief dream.]

Canzoniere 1, 'Voi ch'ascoltate'

Omai son stanco, e mia vita reprendo
di tanto error che di vertute il seme
ha quasi spento; e le mie parti estreme,
alto Dio, a te devotamente rendo,
    pentito e tristo de' miei sí spesi anni,

[Now I am tired, and reproach my life with so much error that the seed of
virtue is almost spent in it, and I devoutly give back my remaining years to
you, high God, repentant and sad at my ill-spent years. . . . Lord, who have
closed me in this prison, draw me out of it safe from eternal torments, for I
know my error and I don't excuse it.]

Canzoniere 364, 'Tennemi Amor anni vent'uno ardendo'

The dilemma Petrarch proves is inherent in a chivalric understanding
of love. Love may be a refining devotion which elevates, ennobles, keeps
the lover chaste; but if it has any sensible reality it remains a fixation upon
an earthly object, and inevitably falls subject to the prompting of desire,
the incitement of the senses and passions. Such a love always contains in
itself the seeds of its own ruin, existing by self-contradiction and self-
frustration:

So while thy beautie draws the heart to love,
    As fast thy Vertue bends that love to good:
'But ah,' Desire still cries, 'give me some food.'

Sidney, *Astrophil and Stella* 71

Court poets seized on the paradox as a way of celebrating their Duchess's
miraculous combination of irresistible beauty and invincible chastity:

Deh dimme amor se gliè fuor di natura,
Da un cor di ghiaccio uscir fiamma chincende?

[Alas, tell me Love if it is something beyond nature that flames which set one
on fire should issue from a heart of ice?]

Serafino d'Aquila, *Strambotto*

More high-minded poets dramatize their dilemma as a dire self-war in which the lower faculties pull against the higher, flesh thwarts spirit, the sensible apprehension impedes intelligence:

> L' alma vaga di luce e di bellezza
> ardite spiega al ciel l'ale amorose,
> ma sí le fa l'umanità gravose
> che le dechina a quel ch'in terra apprezza;
>
> e de' piaceri a la dolce esca avvezza
> ove in candido volto Amor la pose
> tra bianche perle e mattutine rose
> par che non trovi altra maggior dolcezza;

[The soul, eager for light and beauty, boldly spreads its amorous wings heavenwards; but humanity makes them so heavy that they fall back to that which is valued on earth. And among such pleasures it accustoms itself to the sweet lure which Love has placed in a fair face among white pearls and morning roses, so that one might think it could find no greater sweetness. . . .]

Tasso, *Rime per Lucrezia Bendidio* lxvii

Spenser's inability to sustain his uncertain vision of intellectual love and beauty leads him in the end to condemn even the attempt to find truth through a passion for a woman:

> Many lewd lays (ah! woe is me the more!)
> In praise of that mad fit which fools call love,
> I have in th' heat of youth made heretofore

An Hymne of Heavenly Love

From a dilemma which seemed absolute just because it was locked in the contradictory terms of our own nature, a flat renunciation of love offered an extreme means of escape:

> Leave me o Love, which reachest but to dust
> And thou my mind aspire to higher things:

Sidney, *Certain Sonnets* 32

Such drastic ways of representing love imply a conception of our moral nature which is as striking in its exclusion as in its assumptions. Neither the theorists of love nor the Renaissance lyric poets found a licit place for sexual exchanges, or a mutual passion. The woman is taken for a celestial apparition, who lifts our understanding beyond the world of sense; or she is a paragon of chastity and beauty, whom we can't love in our intellect alone, as we ought, but must desire in ways that frustrate each other and distract the mind from God.

Either attitude supposes an absolute incompatibility between the sensible and intellectual elements of our nature, as between the orders of being in which we act and experience. Sense apprehends the chaotic and unstable world of matter, committing itself to momentariness and flux; whereas mind looks beyond the discrete particularities of the material world to the form that gives material things their coherence, reaching out thus to the order of absolute and immutable truth which is God's own essence. Our distinctive power of reason enables us to choose for ourselves between the life of sense and the life of mind. But in practice the choice can't be categorical, for we apprehend through sense, and the mind must rely upon sense so that it may grasp the world outside itself at all: *nihil in intellectu quod non prius in sensu*.

What may span the gap between sense and mind? Neoplatonists supposed that the senses themselves are qualitatively ordered, in accordance with the nature of their objects. Touch is the lowest sense because it knows only material objects which commit it to momentary and indiscriminate impressions; whereas sight, the highest sense, apprehends symmetry and order, acknowledging the triumph of form over matter which even physical beauty represents. Sexual love commits itself to the world of matter when the end it proposes is bodily coupling, so as to gratify the most material sense; and it is unappeasable or self-defeating then, for it craves impermanence and its own decay. But a love which is so refined by pure beauty that it heroically concentrates sense in a gaze of wonderment already looks to the world of form, and may soon transcend the senses altogether in its ascent from time to the timeless, from seeming to being, from false to real.

Petrarch was more oppressed by love and his own nature than were his transcendentalizing predecessors. He celebrates Laura's chaste beauty for an evidence from heaven, which lets him glimpse the universal form of beauty, and heavenly beauty itself:

> I'vidi in terra angelici costumi,
> e celesti bellezze al mondo sole;
> tal, che di rimembrar mi giova e dole,
> ché quant'io miro par sogni, ombre, e fumi.

Canzoniere 156

[I saw on earth the graces of angels, and heavenly beauties made familiar in the world; such that the memory of it both delights and pains me, and whatever I see now seems no more than dreams, shadows, and smoke.]

> In qual parte del ciel, in qual idea
> era l'essempio, onde Natura tolse
> quel bel viso leggiadro, in ch'ella volse
> mostra qua giù quanto lassu potea?. . . .
> Per divina bellezza indarno mira

chi gli occhi de costei gia mai non vide
come soavemente ella gli gira;

Canzoniere 159

[In what part of heaven, in what idea was to be found the pattern whence
nature took that fair delightful face, in which she wished to show down here
below what she was capable of there above?. . . .
   He looks for divine beauty in vain who never saw Laura's eyes, which move
with such grace.]

Yet he finds that it is just these heavenly qualities in her which kindle his
senses to desire:

Ma voi, occhi beati, ond'io soffersi
   quel colpo, ove non valse elmo ne scudo,. . . .

Canzoniere 95

[But you blessed eyes, which gave me such a blow to suffer as made useless hel-
met or shield;. . . .]

He is caught in the hopeless self-frustration of desiring her for that very
virtue which she would forfeit altogether if she yielded to him. Trapped
between the contradictory imperatives of his own nature, and of sensible
beauty itself, he is unable to love incarnate virtue save through his senses,
or detach the ideal he apprehends from the body which he craves to possess. Even Laura's death offers him no such way of transcendence as
Beatrice's death opened to Dante; and his only alternative to ruin in the
end, as St Augustine had warned him, is to renounce earthly beauty for
heavenly beauty. He turns from Laura to the Virgin:

Mortal bellezza, atti, e parole m'hanno
tutta ingombrata l'alma.
Vergine sacra et alma,
non tardar, ch'i'son forse a l'ultimo anno.

Vergine bella, 85–8

[My soul is wholly encumbered with mortal beauty, acts, and words. Virgin,
sacred and holy, don't delay, for I may be at the last hour.]

Succeeding poets seem to have found Petrarch's rendering of love more
congenial to them than the idealism of Cavalcanti, or the transcendentalism of Dante.

ii

Before, a joy propos'd; behind, a dream.

Shakespeare, Sonnet 129

Donne's rendering of love brings love poetry agreeably down to earth
from its rarefied Tuscan retreats:

> Whoever loves, if he do not propose
> The right true end of love, he's one that goes
> To sea for nothing but to make him sick . . .
> Rich Nature hath in woman wisely made
> Two purses, and their mouths aversely laid;
> They then, which to the lower tribute owe,
> That way which that exchequer looks, must go.
> He which doth not, his error is as great,
> As who by clyster gave the stomach meat.

Elegy 18: *Love's Progress*

> Licence my roving hands, and let them go
> Before, behind, between, above, below. . . .
> Then where my hand is set, my seal shall be.

Elegy 19: *To his Mistress Going to Bed*

> Thine age asks ease, and since thy duties be
> To warm the world, that's done in warming us.
> Shine here to us, and thou art everywhere;
> This bed thy centre is, these walls, thy sphere.

'The Sun Rising'

> Neither desires to be spared, nor to spare,
>   They quickly pay their debt, and then
> Take no acquittances, but pay again;
> They pay, they give, they lend, and so let fall
> No such occasion to be liberal.

An Epithalamion . . . on the Lady Elizabeth and Count Palatine . . .

Such poems as 'The Curse', 'The Indifferent', 'Love's Usury', 'The
Apparition', 'Love's diet', 'The Will', 'A Valediction: of my Name in the
Window', strike a pose which is more familiar in satiric comedy than in
love poetry. They open a young man's world in which women may be
carelessly tried, enjoyed and discarded, and a lover risks no greater
humiliation than the loss of his manly independence in an abject slavery
to his own desires. Faithful love is unnatural and inhibiting, an indignity
of middle age; and fidelity itself confirms a heresy, which had better be
purged if a man is to enjoy his due prerogative of change. The lover finds

ample scope for his wit in preserving his freedom to hawk at whom he pleases, and devising seductions which yield double or triple pleasure by their ingenious effrontery:

> Let me think any rival's letter mine,
>   And at next nine
> Keep midnight's promise; mistake by the way
> The maid, and tell the Lady of that delay;
> Only let me love none, no, not the sport;

'Loves Usury'

'The sport' is the hunt for sexual excitement, and even that pursuit will restrict a man's liberty if it is too much loved. At best love amounts to a bargain which is imposed by the exigencies of the chase, and may be evaded by legal quibbling like any other contract. A lover must take for granted his mistress's inconstancy and itch for change, however plausibly she justifies herself with highflown principles and pleas, which he might even choose to indulge if it suits his purpose: 'For by tomorrow I may think so too.' Women are frail creatures in a world of exploiters; they love 'diverse experience' by nature, and urge such scruples as chastity and honour just to gain a tactical advantage, which they won't hesitate to take for money, or pleasure, or in mere perverseness:

> Is it your beauty's mark, or of your youth,
>   Or your perfection, not to study truth?
> Or think you heaven is deaf, or hath no eyes?
>   Or those it hath, smile at your perjuries?
> Are vows so cheap with women, or the matter
>   Whereof they are made, that they are writ in water,
> And blown away with wind? Or doth their breath
>   (Both hot and cold) at once make life and death?
> Who could have thought so many accents sweet
>   Formed into words, so many sighs should meet
> As from our hearts, so many oaths, and tears
>   Sprinkled among (all sweeter by our fears
> And the divine impression of stolen kisses,
>   That sealed the rest) should now prove empty blisses?
> Did you draw bonds to forfeit? sign to break?
>   Or must we read you quite from what you speak,
> And find the truth out the wrong way? or must
>   He first desire you false, would wish you just?

Elegy 15: The Expostulation

> When thy inconsiderate hand
> Flings ope this casement, with my trembling name,
>   To look on one, whose wit or land,
>   New battery to thy heart may frame,

Then think this name alive, and that thou thus
        In it offend'st my Genius.

                And when thy melted maid,
    Corrupted by thy lover's gold, and page,
        His letter at thy pillow hath laid,
        Disputed it, and tamed thy rage,
    And thou begin'st to thaw towards him, for this,
        May my name step in, and hide his.

                        'A Valediction: of my Name in the Window'

When by thy scorn, O murderess, I am dead,
    And that thou think'st thee free
    From all solicitation from me,
    Then shall my ghost come to thy bed,
    And thee, feigned vestal, in worse arms shall see;. . . .

                                'The Apparition'

Donne's scepticism is as much an appraisal of the kind of world we inhabit as a judgement of women. There may once have been a condition in
which wives weren't 'cursed', wouldn't betray a husband by yielding
easily to his foes, didn't deceive him about the fatherhood of his children;
but we expect such depravity now, and regularly find it:

    Foxes and goats, all beasts change when they please,
    Shall women, more hot, wily, wild than these,
    Be bound to one man, and did Nature then
    Idly make them apter to endure than men?

                                Elegy 3: *Change*

    Fond woman, which wouldst have thy husband die,
    And yet complain'st of his great jealousy;
    If swoll'n with poison, he lay in his last bed,
    His body with a sere-bark covered,
    Drawing his breath, as thick and short, as can
    The nimblest crocheting musician,
    Ready with loathsome vomiting to spew
    His soul out of one hell, into a new,
    Made deaf with his poor kindred's howling cries,
    Begging with few feigned tears, great legacies,
    Thou wouldst not weep, but jolly, and frolic be,
    As a slave, which tomorrow should be free;

                                Elegy 1: *Jealousy*

Perhaps in some primal state of being women might be faithful as well as
beautiful, but in our world you will never find a woman who is both; or if
by some feat of exploration you should make such a discovery, then the

prodigy won't stay so for more than the few moments it takes you to announce it to the world:

> If thou find'st one, let me know,
>   Such a pilgrimage were sweet,
> Yet do not, I would not go,
>   Though at next door we might meet,
> Though she were true, when you met her,
> And last, till you write your letter,
>   Yet she
>   Will be
> False, ere I come, to two, or three.

Song: 'Go, and catch a falling star'

The attitudes which these poems present may lack heart, but they are far from crude or mindless. Nor do they seem insignificant when they are realized with such vitality and gusto, in witty extravagances and hyperboles which express such a keen relish for experience. Donne's lovers have style as well as zest, managing the civic jungle they inhabit with a jaunty elegance which is often outrageously funny. They challenge us to recognize ourselves and our world in the vivid little episodes they rehearse.

The ebullient self-sufficiency of 'The Indifferent' is far removed from courtly subservience to cruel caprice. 'The Flea' and 'The Damp' seem provocatively anti-courtly. Both poems are persuasions to bodily pleasure, in an Ovidean mode which proposes that women are to be outflanked by rhetorical virtuosity; but still more damaging to the high pretensions of lovers are the central devices announced in the titles. Donne makes a colloquy of lovers out of a Berni-esque *jeu d'esprit*,[2] wittily magnifying a trivial object so as to intimate that the end he seeks is not even faithful service but the sacrament of marriage:

> Oh stay, three lives in one flea spare,
> Where we almost, nay more than married are.
> This flea is you and I, and this
> Our marriage bed, and marriage temple is;
> Though parents grudge, and you, we'are met,
> And cloistered in these living walls of jet.

'The Damp' is still more brusquely unchivalric. It rehearses such properties of courtly love as disdain, honour, loyalty, concealment, simply to exorcise them brusquely. This lover doesn't profess concealment and

[2]The Florentine poet Francesco Berni (d. 1535) won himself European notoriety for his witty poems in praise of the plague, fleas, gluttons, being in debt, urinals, and the like. The fashion derived from Virgil's poem on a gnat and Ovid's poem on a flea.

constancy, or even love; and the lady will bring about his 'death' not by persisting in her disdain and honour but by abating them. The end his courtship proposes is their naked prosecution of love's war in bed, on equal terms:

> Here let me war; in these arms let me lie;
> Here let me parley, batter, bleed, and die.
> Thine arms imprison me, and mine arms thee,
> Thy heart thy ransom is, take mine for me.

Elegy 20: Love's War

Some of the *Songs and Sonnets* invite closer comparison with the orthodox attitudes of love. They present a lover as abject as any petrarchan. He suffers pain by her refusal of his love, then more pain when his lament is set to music and sung; he is brokenhearted, dying, dead of her hardheartedness or scorn; he complains that his faithful love, which seeks only marriage with her, is cheapened by her lightness. Or he cries out against the capricious tyranny of the god of love himself, who has killed him by making him love where he may expect no return and only insults the lady with his pleading, or whose usurpations have perverted the primal state in which love for love was the natural condition:

> Sure, they which made him god, meant not so much,
>   Nor he, in his young godhead practised it.
> But when an even flame two hearts did touch,
>   His office was indulgently to fit
> Actives to passives. Correspondency
> Only his subject was; it cannot be
>   Love, till I love her, that loves me.

'Love's Deity'

The properties of European petrarchism make up the *mise en scène* of Donne's drama of love. Yet his writing has a quite different tendency from the love poetry of Tasso, or Marino, or Gongora, not only because of the way he uses the devices he reworks but because he is always pulling even conventional materials round to point another way, and giving them rich new life. 'The Apparition' quite flaunts its routine plot of a lover who is dying of his mistress's disdain, and turns upon her to threaten a vengeful haunting. Yet the old familiar elements come to life in an ironic drama of sexual appetite which is ironically realized in the tense hissing deliberateness of tone and movement, the livid sharpness of the nightmare scene, the incessant play of comic wit:

> Then shall my ghost come to thy bed,
> And thee, feigned vestal, in worse arms shall see;

> Then thy sick taper will begin to wink,
> And he, whose thou art then, being tired before,
> Will, if thou stir, or pinch to wake him, think
>   Thou call'st for more,
> And in false sleep will from thee shrink,
> And then poor aspen wretch, neglected thou
> Bathed in a cold quicksilver sweat wilt lie
>   A verier ghose than I;

The laconic tail-line all but throws away the vivid little conceit that it is the covering of 'quicksilver sweat' which makes her more of a ghost than the ghost itself. In such poems the wit itself becomes a disposition of the lover, expressing no mere lust for ingenuity but a zest in the artistry of the performance, an ironic detachment from his own avowals, a commitment to the world of affairs beyond the engrossments of love:

> Now as those active kings
> Whose foreign conquest treasure brings,
> Receive more, and spend more, and soonest break:

'The Dissolution'

The shrewd political analogy claims equal interest with the paradox of love it points, or even outweighs so slight a truth. The emblematic play in 'A Jet Ring sent', with its cool appraisal of the value of the token and unruffled teasing out the worst of its possible messages, better persuades us of the lover's caginess than open disbelief might do, even while it quietly urges that the true trial of love isn't the exchange of toys, but marriage. The elaborate devices of such manifestos as 'The Legacy' and 'The Will' are exploited with a sardonic zest that keeps the lover at a mocking distance from his own misfortunes, which he discloses to us most divertingly:

> Before I sigh my last gasp, let me breathe,
> Great Love, some legacies; here I bequeath
> Mine eyes to Argus, if mine eyes can see,
> If they be blind, then Love, I give them thee;
> My tongue to fame; to ambassadors mine ears;
>   To women or the sea, my tears.
> Thou, Love, hast taught me heretofore
> By making me serve her who had twenty more,
> That I should give to none, but such, as had too much before. . . .

> Therefore I'll give no more; but I'll undo
> The world by dying; because love dies too.
> Then all your beauties will be no more worth
> Than gold in mines, where none doth draw it forth;
> And all your graces no more use shall have

> Than a sundial in a grave.
> Thou Love taught'st me, by making me
> Love her, who doth neglect both me and thee,
> To invent, and practise this one way, to annihilate all three.

'The Will'

Donne personates a lover who moves between guarded tenderness and sceptical detachment, never making an innocent commitment. Whole poems act out such a mocking wariness. 'Witchcraft by a Picture' sceptically reviews the lady's show of such customary tokens of sincere passion as tears, looks, sighs, and insists that they should be proved in her conduct before the lover may accept them. In 'The Token' itself the conventional device announced in the title, and meticulously tried out, is then simply discarded; as if the lover may work his way to a measure of assurance only by rejecting the common coin of wooers. He turns a sceptical eye on all such fanciful shifts, implying that they are altogether too childish to serve real love. The request he does make in the teeth of custom is deceptively humble, but gives the conceit of the love posie fresh force:

> But swear thou thinkst I love thee, and no more.

Love tokens are easy coin, and Troilus's favour may finish up in Diomed's coat; but lovers gain as much security as they may have when they are persuaded of each other's love. Truth to the way people think and feel comes before empty forms, modest but tried experience ousts mere show.

What most distinguishes Donne from idealizing love poets is his attitude to his own experience, and himself. 'Love's Deity' does much more than just refuse courtly servitude when it argues that an unreturned love is no love, and turns in the last lines to deny another article of the courtly code:

> Falsehood is worse than hate; and that must be,
>   If she whom I love, should love me.

Nothing could deflate more delicately the conceit of a divinity in love than the bland irony of that casually earnest approach, and seeming acquiescence in a stock character of the god of love. The sudden expostulations amusingly mock themselves:

> Rebel and atheist too, why murmur I,

Irony is no less finely poised in 'Twicknam Garden', where the self-dramatizing echo of 'Zefiro torna',[3] and the rueful solemnity of the final denunciation, are made to mock their own exaggeratedness, yet without ever denying that the lover's feelings are real and justified. The gravely ceremonious manner, and deflating realism of the emblems, make the poem a huge comic hyperbole which pays its subject the compliment of assuming that she is too intelligent to be impressed by fulsome praises:

> But O, self traitor, I do bring
> The spider love, which transubstantiates all,. . . .
>
> O perverse sex, where none is true but she,
> Who's therefore true, because her truth kills me.

The tone assures us that this is an admirer who is not likely to take either his subject or his own ardours over-solemnly. He makes love poems which burlesque their own professions without belittling them. 'The Triple Fool' is an ironic commentary on his love, and on his own poetic rendering of it, which wryly acknowledges the manifold folly of making love public in poems at all:

> To love and grief tribute of verse belongs,
> But not of such as pleases when 'tis read,
>   Both are increased by such songs:
> For both their triumphs so are published,
> And I, which was two fools, do so grow three;
> Who are a little wise, the best fools be.

'The Blossom' dramatizes this double attitude to his own predicaments as a colloquy between the lover and his heart, an encounter which cool judgement easily wins. Witty detachment couldn't go much further than the humouring self-indulgence the poet extends to a passion which is blind even to its own prospects; and his control is still more telling than his self-awareness:

> Well then, stay here; but know,
>   When thou hast stayed and done thy most;
> A naked thinking heart, that makes no show,
> Is to a woman, but a kind of ghost;
> How shall she know my heart; or having none,
>   Know thee for one?
> Practice may make her know some other part,
> But take my word, she doth not know a heart.

---

[3]Petrarch's sonnet which opens with these words tells how the return of spring has surrounded the lover with a reanimation that mocks him.

Meet me at London, then,
    Twenty days hence, and thou shalt see
Me fresher, and more fat, by being with men,
Than if I had stayed still with her and thee.
For God's sake, if you can, be you so too:
    I would give you
There, to another friend, whom we shall find
As glad to have my body, as my mind.

The Astrophil of Sidney's sequence, like so many other petrarchan lovers, and Petrarch himself, recognizes his grim plight but has no power to amend it while his heart rules his judgement. 'The Blossom' allows the heart its good reasons for hanging upon the lady's favour, but finds it unmanly to be so subservient to love.

The calm reasonableness with which 'The Funeral' chronicles the poet's fatal dependence on his mistress takes any severity out of the final turning of the tables on her, which is more of a last brave gesture of affection than a revenge:

Whate'er she meant by it, bury it with me,
    For since I am
Love's martyr, it might breed idolatry,
If into others' hands these relics came;
    As 'twas humility
To afford to it all that a soul can do,
    So, 'tis some bravery,
That since you would save none of me, I bury some of you.

Recrimination scarcely squares with this lover's fellow-feeling for the woman he addresses. Dante's exaltation and Petrarch's reverence are modes of another order of concern for a woman. The quite unexalted address of Donne's love lyrics carries its own assurance:

When I died last, and, dear, I die
    As often as from thee I go,
    Though it be an hour ago,
And lovers' hours be full eternity,

                          'The Legacy'

The conceits may be petrarchan but the lover isn't genuflecting before a demi-goddess or a paragon; on the contrary, he shows a touchingly tender respect for a companion. Donne's poems of parting, far from rehearsing an old routine of valediction, search real human predicaments as their fame implies:

> I . . . will conclude mine, with commending to his view, a Copy of Verses given by Mr *Donne* to his wife at the time that he then parted from her. And I beg leave to tell, that I have heard some Criticks, learned, both in Languages and Poetry, say, that none of the Greek or Latine Poets did ever equal them.[4]

They bring the lamenting lovers before us with vivid authenticity. A casual aside, or sudden realization, or snatched reassurance in the moment of parting, is made to evoke an attachment which the overhearer has to make out for himself, as in life:

> Sweetest love, I do not go,
>   For weariness of thee,

The lover's tender consolations present themselves most gracefully as a spontaneous impulse of his mind, in which asides and reflections qualify ardour as they do in any impassioned thinking. The opening words of 'The Expiration' catch a moment of extreme perplexity between opposite imperatives:

> So, so, break off this last lamenting kiss,
>   Which sucks two souls, and vapours both away,

We have come upon the lover in the act of pulling himself back from a passionate kiss, and of unwillingly denying her desperate attempts to prolong their last embrace. The vivid little scene is fixed in the first eight words, and prompts a stream of imperatives and justifications which convey his attempts to convince himself that their parting is necessary, or to make the best of it

> Turn thou ghost that way, and let me turn this,
>   And let ourselves benight our happiest day,
> We asked none leave to love; nor will we owe
>   Any, so cheap a death, as saying, Go;
> Go; and if that word have not quite killed thee,
>   Ease me with death, by bidding me go too.

Donne's writing graphically brings out by the slightest means both her unwillingness to let him go, and his struggles with himself. The simple repetition of 'Go' makes a little drama in itself. He has just asked her to 'Turn thou ghost that way', supposing that their separation will reduce

---

[4]Izaac Walton on 'A Valediction: forbidding Mourning', in the 1675 version of the *Life and Death of Dr Donne*.

them to mere bloodless shades of themselves, but that they may at least be spared the pain of a formal farewell or a forced leavetaking if she goes quickly. The second 'Go' undoes this hope at once. He must say the word after all, for she hasn't turned away; and he now has to make her leave him, and force himself from her as well. Donne's art humanizes wit:

> My rags of heart can like, wish, and adore,
> But after one such love, can love no more.

> 'The Broken Heart'

An old hyperbolic conceit of the impact of love, brilliantly exploited, is made to define a personal intuition, which also happens to be common truth.

Such writing invites the proof of familiar experience. In 'The Will' the common human bond is all that matters, a view Donne takes so much for granted that he could have had little sympathy with a transcendental love poetry such as Michelangelo's. The truth so carefully tested in 'The Token' is an acute perception of people's reasons for responding to one another as they do in matters of affection:

> Send me nor this, nor that, to increase my store,
> But swear thou think'st I love thee, and no more.

Even when the lover is for once made a slave of love, as in 'Love's Exchange', he affects no impassioned extravagances. Donne's ingenious figure of a siege-vanquished town puts the classic case of the rebel against love who eventually succumbs the more abjectly; but it also yields a singularly deft compliment by which Love's conquering demeanour becomes the lady's irresistible face. As he so often does, Donne represents the conventional show of sighs, tears, evasions and the like as the flimsy stock-in-trade of the professional lover; whereas the real lover is the hapless man who loves once, feels the shame of his humiliation, and asks for death rather than present torture. We are a long way from the courtly fiction of the lover who groans in secret under the strokes of a tyrant passion:

> Let me not know that others know
> That she knows my pain,

A love poetry which is subtly faithful to natural experience commends itself to readers who value a grasp of sexual motives in the world more than moral elevation, or an aspiration to truths beyond nature. Donne writes as a venturer who has tried the extent of amorous life, and is well in possession of his findings. The predicaments of earlier love poets scarcely come home to us so intimately, however magnificent the poetry they engender, and may even gain an adventitious interest by their remoteness from our own:

> I' vo piangendo i miei passati tempi,
> i quai posi in amar cosa mortale
> Senza levarmi a volo, havend'io l'ale,
> Per dar forse di me non bassi esempi.

Canzoniere 365

Petrarch's final renouncing of love marks a turn from the world, and dismissal of sensual life, which his successors could outgo only in lofty unworldliness:

> Then farewell world, thy uttermost I see,
> Eternall Love maintaine thy life in me.

Sidney, *Certain Sonnets* 31

> But all those follies now I do reprove,
> And turned have the tenor of my string,
> The heavenly prayses of true Love to sing.

Spenser, *An Hymne of Heavenly Love*

When Donne calls love in question he too puts his career as a lover in self-challenging perspective, and spurns the tyranny of sense; but his reasons aren't moral:

Love's Alchemy

> Some that have deeper digged love's mine than I,
> Say, where his centric happiness doth lie:
>   I have loved, and got, and told,
> But should I love, get, tell, till I were old,
> I should not find that hidden mystery;
>   Oh, 'tis imposture all:
> And as no chemic yet the elixir got,
>   But glorifies his pregnant pot,
>   If by the way to him befall
> Some odoriferous thing, or medicinal,
>   So, lovers dream a rich and long delight,
>   But get a winter-seeming summer's night.
>
> Our ease, our thrift, our honour, and our day,
> Shall we, for this vain bubble's shadow pay?
>   Ends love in this, that my man,
> Can be as happy as I can; if he can

Endure the short scorn of a bridegroom's play?
    That loving wretch that swears,
'Tis not the bodies marry, but the minds,
      Which he in her angelic finds,
      Would swear as justly, that he hears,
In that day's rude hoarse minstrelsy, the spheres.
Hope not for mind in women; at their best
    Sweetness and wit, they are but mummy, possessed.

Love is a bubble, whose pleasure is the shadow of a bubble; it has no true consummation or essential happiness, but imposes upon us with pitifully empty promises. Love doesn't refine but levels us, bringing initiate and clown alike to a humiliating congress whose heat lasts only a moment. The loving conjunction of minds is a myth; he is a fool who says that it isn't bodies that marry but minds, if only because women don't have minds. Even those women who by some special grace and life most suggest mind are mere dead flesh once you have had them; and at the best time in their lives, when they have at last gained some sweetness and wit, they are no more than living corpses, activated demonically. Like the alchemist, love promises you the elixir of life and the philosopher's stone and gives you mummy, the dross of all that ardour which at best 'Will cure the itch',[5] or leave some tang of sweetness behind it. The squalid consequence mocks the high presumption, and the truth is as you find it; or we might conclude that our experience is equivocal, and yields us no final certainty.

The poem which Donne's second editor aptly entitled 'Farewell to Love' assumes finality, and amounts to an intricate commentary on the lover's servitude to sense which is worth our teasing out. Commentators have counted it among the least accommodating of Donne's poems, and it remains to be seen how far the difficulty follows the subtlety of Donne's understanding of sexual life. The piece presents an aspect of elaborate ceremony:

    Farewell to Love
      Whilst yet to prove,
   I thought there was some Deitie in love,
    So did I reverence, and gave
Worship, as Atheists at their dying houre
Call, what they cannot name, an unknowne power,   5
    As ignorantly did I crave:
        Thus when
Things not yet knowne are coveted by men,

[5]Ben Jonson, *The Alchemist* 4.3.

Our desires give them fashion, and so
As they waxe lesser, fall, as they sise, grow.   10

    But, from late faire
His highnesse sitting in a golden Chaire,
   Is not lesse cared for after three dayes
By children, then the thing which lovers so
Blindly admire, and with such worship wooe;   15
   Being had, enjoying it decayes:
        And thence,
What before pleas'd them all, takes but one sense,
And that so lamely, as it leaves behinde
A kinde of sorrowing dulnesse to the minde.   20

    Ah cannot wee,
As well as Cocks and Lyons jocund be,
   After such pleasures? Unlesse wise
   Nature decreed (since each such Act, they say,
Diminisheth the length of life a day)   25
   This; as shee would man should despise
        The sport,
Because that other curse of being short,
And onely for a minute made to be
Eager, desires to raise posterity.   30

    Since so, my minde
Shall not desire what no man else can finde,
   I'll no more dote and runne
To pursue things which had indammag'd me.
And when I come where moving beauties be,   35

   As men doe when the summers Sunne
       Growes great,
Though I admire their greatnesse, shun their heat;
Each place can afford shadowes. If all faile,
'Tis but applying worme-seed to the Taile.[6]   40

Donne's categorical dismissal of love has none of the high passion of the kind, though its terse address and muscular wresting of syntax suggest brusque impatience. The audacious rhetoric of 'Farewell to Love' serves an argument which strains to breaking point the resources of lyric verse.

    The poem follows out a lover's development, taking us through a whole cycle of experience from innocent enthusiasm to disillusioned rejection and its consequences. This lover's case against love is ironically unlike the complaints of the court poet and the moralist, and assumes a quite different kind of ruinous obsession from theirs. We see him wrestling his way to the hard truth about a practice long indulged. He doesn't take love for a state of unrequited servitude; on the contrary, we find him

[6]Text from the 1635 edition save in line 23, where *1635* reads '. . . pleasures, unlesse. . .'.

simply resolving to abandon a repeated indulgence which has never lived up to its promise. He believes that he at last sees through the game of sex, after long proof of it which has left him wiser and warier.

The brusque opening lines of the poem don't so much challenge as contemptuously dismiss the worship of love or a lady; and they make such sententious petrarchism as Thomas Watson's rejection of love look like child's play:

> My Love is past, wherein was no good how'r:
> When others ioy'd, to cares I did encline,
> Whereon I fedde, although the taste were sow'r,
> And still belev'd Love was some pow'r divine,
>   Or some instinct, which could not worke in vaine,
>   Forgetting, Time well spent was double gaine.

Ekatompathia (1582), xciii

Donne's poem assumes as close an experience of sexual life as Shakespeare's Sonnet 129, however unshakespearean its temper; and the two poems have at least their disillusioned candour in common. Yet Donne isn't really arguing something out here, or developing a debate. The logical sequence of the poem follows the stages of a progress which is already complete, and has brought him to a realization he sees no need to question. The argument moves forward only to affirm the resolve that follows the lesson which his long experience has now brought home to him.

Donne ironically plays off his harshness against the very different expectation which the elaborate layout of the poem itself helps to foster. A reader who anticipates Spenserian ceremony, or a grace in the rendering of love, finds himself keenly challenged by those stabbing phrases, and the downright refusal to be fooled. Though this is a poem about love rather than a love poem, its forceful mental life may affront people who think that the heart is entitled to its own reasons.

This first stanza sets out, and accounts for, a man's virgin illusions about love. Its movement has logical form and the appearance of logical sequence, though the several parts claim a more intimate connection. The opening lines proclaim that the worship of a divinity in love is a projection of inexperience, and owes more to the cravings of unfulfilled desire than to the spiritual qualities of its object. The bizarre leap to the dying atheists, which is so ambiguously linked with the opening acknowledgement, leaves us uncertain for a moment how this analogy is to be used; so that the firm resolution in line 6 seems to clinch the connection of two such different conditions, and to suggest that the self-deluding hope which Donne remarks in lovers is a general trait of inexperience. The argument ridicules atheists by simply taking it for granted that their unbelief won't stand up to the final test of their imminent death; but it also reflects upon the reasons for such deathbed conversions, which might be wholly subjective. The lines leave it sceptically open to question whether the atheists' change of heart is justified, or merely mirrors their fear of death. The atheists' case simply instances our tendency to take our inward states for pictures of a reality beyond ourselves. Line 6 gives the argument a thoroughly sceptical twist: 'As ignorantly did I crave'. Atheists at the last really hope that God exists, but are as ignorant of the truth as the rest of us.

The remaining lines of Stanza 1, 7–10, bring us from these particular instances to the way our desires affect our beliefs. We venerate what we least understand, and lose our awe of things as we know them better. Our controlling desires are like appetites, increasing when they are starved and dying with repletion; and our need of the gods they create grows or fades with them. Almost in passing Donne prompts us to ask ourselves what impels us to believe in powers beyond nature; and he coolly accounts for some of our profoundest credences by looking to their motives and causes, rather than to their objects and ends. The difference is enough in itself to separate him from most other love poets. Cavalcanti, Dante, Petrarch, Michelangelo, undeviatingly refer their love to the supernatural qualities of its object, asking themselves how and to what end they admire such beauty of spirit. The Tuscan tradition of intellectual idealism assumes a commitment to love which won't let the lover question its grounds, and prompts him to awestruck admiration; whereas Donne makes a principle of questioning his own motives by the means of his sceptical wit. He holds opposite possibilities in play, keeping passion at a manageable distance and refusing unqualified commitments. 'Farewell to Love' isn't so much as addressed to a particular woman. It only asks us what makes people love, and whether love is worth their devotion.

The argument from causes and motives has a further consequence. If our reverent worship merely projects our innocent expectations, then our spiritual desires and fears must be equally the offspring of innocence, and of ignorance also, since experience isn't likely to justify them. We might draw the deeply sceptical conclusion that we make our gods in the likeness of our untried yearnings rather than our tested experience, if only because our experience never remotely matches expectation. The ribald suggestion of line 10, which the image of desires that rise and fall keeps discreetly distant, is that these unknown gods whom we ignorantly worship are projections of erotic craving, and no more substantial than their cause.

If our desires so radically delude us then our impulse to worship is a poor enough creature of our sexual state, and allows us no more than the bitter wisdom of disillusioned satiety. Such a self-defeating predicament frustrates us with the perverseness of our own nature. Yet our minds seem to be even more desperately self-entangled than this, for we can't know anything with absolute certainty when the propositions which we take for knowledge only mirror the state of our desire at that moment. The inductive form of the argument persuades us that we aren't even able to understand our own condition, or know ourselves at all save by what we can prove in experience. Donne's management of syntax here is a virtuoso feat, yet it follows his attempt to hold together ideas which people commonly take to be separate when they aren't really so.

The second stanza of the poem briskly makes the move from desire to experience which the Florentine tradition never allowed. Donne ironically inverts the neoplatonic hierarchy of the senses, taking sight for an instrument of wondering self-delusion and touch for our means to disillusioned actuality. His opening analogy of the children who become sated with what had previously amazed them pleasantly dismisses five centuries of European love poetry. There's a true lover's progress here, as in Ficino's *Commentarium* and Pico della Mirandola's *Commento;*[7] but this lover has simply matured from childishness to adulthood and exchanged innocence for experience, fancy for reality, illusion for disillusionment.

'His highness' must be a little more than a gilt gingerbread effigy from a recent Bartholomew Fair, for the lines discreetly remind us how rapidly popular feeling for an actual ruler passes from naive anticipation to familiarity and indifference. When we see that children with a fairing, and subjects with a new prince, all behave in the same way as lovers, then we may take love for an instance of a larger human condition. Here Donne does seem to be delineating a general character of human conduct, which not only lands us in various forms of childish fickleness, or gross self-delusion, but accounts for the way people admire and worship, showing us why they submit themselves to authority or rebel against it.

Love is absurdly self-defeating, not least because lovers so blindly admire and pursue something which loses its savour once they have had it. 'Decays' is a strong word, as though the lovers' disillusionment with sex is part of a larger degeneration, which is registered again in the difference between 'pleases' and 'takes'. The anticipatory excitement of all our senses dwindles to a mere dull impression upon one of them, like toothache or nausea. This 'kind of sorrowing dulness' which the mind is left with seems to be more than just a case of *post coitum triste*. The phrasing

[7]M. Ficino, *In Convivium Platonis De Amore, Commentarium*, in *Opera*, Basilaea, 1576, Tom. ii, pp. 1320–61. Italian version, transl. and augmented by Ficino himself, *M. Ficino sopra lo Amore*, Firenze, 1544.

Pico della Mirandola, *Commento Del Illustrissimo Signore Conte Johanni Pico Mirandulano sopra una Canzona de Amore composta da Hieronymo benivieni Cittadino Fiorentino secondo la mente e opinione de Platonici*,? 1519.

Ficino's *Commentary* was written in 1469 and first printed in 1484. According to legend it is the outcome of Lorenzo de' Medici's attempt to renew the ancient neoplatonic custom of a banquet on Plato's anniversary, 7 November, when he invited a company of platonists to Careggi to dine and expound Plato. Pico's *Commento* was written about 1490 and first published with his works in 1495.

is precise, and we may expect to find that such an outcome matters.

The third stanza of 'Farewell to Love' is as intricate a structure of syntax as Donne ever attempted, and it concludes in a textual crux which has provoked much conjecture.[8] The one text which has authority is that given in the edition of 1635. This 1635 reading isn't obviously corrupt, and yields such apt sense that there seems no reason to amend it; yet the difficulty lines 28–30 have given shows us how radically Donne taxes the language in his effort to articulate a very complex idea, and reminds us of the truth Coleridge perceived, that a poem by Donne makes an organism in which the functioning of every part must be referred to the sense of the whole.[9]

From the evidence of spent virility the poem turns to possible reasons for the loss, asking why things should be thus. The question comes in a lamenting outcry, 'Ah cannot we. . .?', whose fine vehemence parodies itself when it intimates that this lover's large speculations may just come down to a worry about his virility. When cocks and lions have the advantage over human lovers we are a long way short of the dignity of man; and 'jocund' and 'pleasures' suggest a lighthearted randiness, or a nice epicureanism of sex, that scoffs at highflown ideas of love. But the biggest irony of all is the implied contraction of our nature. The surmise that our sexual shortcomings only instance a general impoverishment of our humanity, which the rest of the creation hasn't suffered, prompts a search for their cause.

The argument in lines 23–30 follows out a scholastic idea that men drain their virility as they spend their stock of semen, which Donne keeps ironically speculative when he turns it into the old wives' tale that each sexual act shortens life a day. If sex really does abbreviate our lives so, then our impulses are hopelessly self-defeating and we need some imposed check on our indulgence; for the various shortcomings of our present state only drive us to repeat the act so as to repair them; and without restraint we should quickly destroy our lives in striving to prolong ourselves.

Donne offers our sexual inadequacies for like effects of a curse — 'that other curse' — which 'desires to raise posterity'. It is nothing else than this curse, then, whose effects make us so anxious to have children, and to do whatever else 'raising posterity' may suggest.[10] These effects them-

[8]See in particular H.J.C. Grierson, *The Poems of John Donne*, Oxford, 1912, ii, pp. 52–3; J. Hayward, *Donne: Complete Poetry and Selected Prose*, 1929, pp. 766–7; G. Williamson, *Modern Philology*, 1939, pp. 301–3; L. Hotson, *The Times Literary Supplement*, 16 April 1949; Helen Gardner, *The Times Literary Supplement*, 10 June 1949; T. Redpath, *The Songs and Sonnets of John Donne*, 1956, pp. 145–9.

[9]Marginal note in Charles Lamb's copy of Donne, 2 May 1811. See *John Donne: The Critical Heritage*, ed. A.J. Smith, 1975, p. 266.

[10]*OED* Desire: 3. *trans.* Of things: To require, need, demand. 8b. To invite a course of action, etc.
Posterity: 3. Posteriority *Obs. rare.*
Posteriority: 3. The back, the back parts of the body. *Obs. rare.*

selves are resolved into the several disadvantages of our 'being short', and 'only for a minute made to be/Eager'.[11] The elliptical phrasing invites us to gather for ourselves the related meanings which such words as 'short' acquire as the argument unfolds; but there's no doubt that Donne is seeking to account for the wilful self-destructiveness of our sexual drives, and finds the stimulus to sexual acts in our anguished awareness of our own mortality. We are goaded by our consciousness of brevity in every aspect of our sexual lives, and in our existence altogether.

If our brevity is the 'other curse', then the first curse can be no other than the curb which regulates its effects, our loss of zest and pleasure after orgasm. 'Curse' suggests some disastrous disorder of the proper state of things, which all these afflictions exemplify. Indeed, if its effects weren't regulated this 'other curse' would soon send us spiralling to self-ruin; for the shorter we feel ourselves to be the more imperatively we rush to sex, and the faster we undo ourselves in sex the more keenly we feel our brevity. Donne doesn't name this larger curse, or directly say that our sexual acts thus ironically appease the urge to amend the consequences of the Fall. But if it really should be our fearful consciousness of brevity that makes desire so urgent then our entire kind is caught up in this accelerating spiral into ruin; and unless it is checked, the world must soon undo itself.

Fortunately for humanity there is still 'Wise Nature'. This curiously unspiritual entity seems to work for our survival and the continuance of life, much as any living organism will strive to conserve itself by the economy of its own nature. Nature wisely counters our fatal urge to indulge our sexual appetites by taking away our zest after the sport, dulling sentience as well as eagerness so that we are not so desperately haunted by the consciousness of our own predicament. Insensibility enables us to sustain a condition which is so perverse that our best human capacities most damage our humanity, and one curse upon us can be countered only by another curse. When man's life is maintained by the very limitations of his present being, then the force that saves him inflicts as much loss and pain as the force that would destroy him.

However speculatively Donne may propose this argument the idea of self-frustration dominates Stanza 3 of the poem. Our human frailties become instances of a general perversity in nature which drives the natural creation to thwart and even undo itself; so that only some makeshift adjustment, imposed at the expense of the very gratifications that impel creatures to renew their kind, stays the world from grinding itself to dust in ever-increasing frenzy. Our escape from a spiral which is so vicious that we can't even recognize it until we are caught up in it is to

[11]*OED* Eager: a. O.F. aigre sharp, keen, sour. . . . ii 6. Of persons: Full of keen desire or appetite; impatiently longing to do or obtain something. . . . Also of desires or appetites: Intense, impatient.

make the resolve the title of the poem announces. The final stanza puts the lover's grounds for renouncing love, which he simply equates with sex. His chief reason is the pragmatical one that the end of the sport is coitus, which never actually yields the pleasure we anticipate but affords at best only a momentary excitement, soon followed by sorrowing dulness. Experience proves that love just doesn't live up to its promises. Nobody has been able to discover the supposed divinity in love, or even prolong love's delight, which lies rather in the anticipation than the having. Why ever should men desire what they certainly won't find! And why need men's minds seek a divine source for a power which is so essentially mortal, so manifestly subject to time and our general frailty! Still more persuasive than the certainty of disillusionment, and the wish to be undeceived, is the danger to life. Engaging in the sport the lover has pursued his own harm, for he has only doted on things which would damage him if he gained them.[12]

When we say farewell to love we put ourselves beyond the cycle of desire by refusing the initial urge. Yet we can scarcely escape so until disenchanting experience has allowed us to detach ourselves from our desires and see love for what it really is. The lover endeavours to gain a freedom which must be asserted against our own nature. He is far from warning us that the world is to be despised, or that love distracts our minds from God. On the contrary, he discovers in the economy of nature a way to such freedom as we may have. In dismissing love this lover certainly isn't turning back to the Creator from the worship of the creature, as Petrarch did. He is acknowledging that we gain such truth as we may reach by repeated disillusionment, and win our freedom by abnegation. If we have no means of amending our state then at least we may show that we need not be the slaves of blind desire, and can act out of understanding and judgement. He proposes just such a negative freedom from our own frailties as Boethius wins when he stoically gains peace of mind by making himself indifferent to outward fortune.[13]

The final lines of the poem complete the organic image which has shaped the entire argument. When he speaks of the 'heat' of 'moving beauties' which 'Grows great' like the summer sun he reduces the game of courtship to an animal excitement, which is as easily allayed as aroused. The final line offhandedly pricks the illusions of devout lovers. You can collapse the whole empery of love with a little application of

---

[12]Helen Gardner, *John Donne: The Elegies and The Songs and Sonnets*, Oxford, 1965, prints and argues for the reading in one of the manuscripts, S96, 'To pursue things which had, indammage me'. I prefer the reading of 1635 because it gives a sharper sense of a new realization, which does matter here — 'I now see that the consequence of my doting and running would not have been satisfaction but harm; my eyes are at last fully opened, and so I can be free'.

[13]*Consolat. Philosoph.* passim, but esp. iv. vii.

wormseed.[14] A coarse joke brusquely sees off the self-deluding idealism which prompts men to make gods of their unfulfilled desires. The means to a liberating disillusionment is no more than a shrunken penis.

In 'Farewell to Love' Donne tries to the limit the resources of poetic syntax and form so as to hold together a complex of ideas which couldn't otherwise be rendered in their subtle interdependence. This is an impressive piece of thinking in verse, as much in the cut of its argument as in its coherence. A poem which so deflatingly ribalds those who seek something divine in love takes its stand on our natural experience, and even purports to move forward just by pure induction from the encounters our senses have already well proved. Michelangelo's love poetry may resemble this in its muscular force, but its temper is wholly alien to Donne's:

> La forze d'un bel viso a che mi sprona?
> c'altro non é c'al mondo mi diletti:
> ascender vivo fra gli spirti eletti
> per grazia tal, c'ogni altra par men buona.

[To what am I spurred by the power of a beautiful face? — For there is nothing else that delights me in the world: to ascend alive among the elect spirits, by such grace that every other good falls short of it.]

We should look for Donne's kind among the new thinkers of the age, the sectaries of scepticism, empiricism, stoicism, naturalism.[15] Directly, or just by the way they think and proceed, these people challenge the mystical metaphysics which Plotinus and the supposed Dionysius Areopagus had developed out of Plato; and Casaubon's discrediting of hermetic texts in 1614 seemed to justify them finally. The neoplatonic philosophy of love effectively faded away, and it is the sceptic naturalism of 'Farewell to Love' which came home to seventeenth-century love poets:

> Fruition adds no new wealth, but destroys,
> And while it pleaseth much the palate, cloys;

> Suckling, 'Against Fruition'

'Farewell to Love' undermines neoplatonic ideas as much by its naturalistic cast of thought as by a new understanding of love. Yet it doesn't represent the whole body of Donne's love poetry. As it happens, the only evidence that Donne really wrote 'Farewell to Love' is its appearance in the edition of 1635; and one of the Harvard manuscripts

---

[14]Wormseed was not an anaphrodisiac but a popular name for such herbs as fennel, or their dried flowerheads, which were supposed to shrivel up intestinal worms.

[15]See L.I. Bredvold, 'The Naturalism of Donne in Relation to Some Renaissance Traditions', *Journal of English and Germanic Philology* XXII, pp. 471–502.

actually attributes it to a 'Mr An. Saintleger'. Modern editors have confidently accepted it as Donne's because no other poet wrote and thought just like that. The poem proclaims the man who also wrote the *Metempsychosis* and the two *Anniversaries*.

Yet if Donne's love poems figure his own experience in any way then this one must have been written while he had still to prove other possibilities of love which he doesn't glimpse here. The poem invites us to relate it to the rest of the lover's experience; though we can no more take it for the expression of a passing mood of love than for a final dismissal of sense. Donne offers it for a report on experience up till then: 'Whilst yet to prove. . . .' If we take his love poems as we find them in almost all the manuscripts, scattered at hazard among the rest of his writings, we might conclude that they could not have been conceived like Petrarch's, or Sidney's, or Shakespeare's, or even Michelangelo's. They don't tell a story, or form a pattern, because the poet has no such overall design. His poetry just seems unusually open to experience. A poem will refer us not to some goal to be attained, but rather to an experience which it seeks to articulate and to place in the order of all our experiences in the world, including those which seem to belie it. As there can be no finality in our experience, so there is no absolute end against which we can measure the poet's development. Every poem is its own moment; and the differences which unsettle us from poem to poem simply bring home to us the relativeness of all our sexual experience, when love comprehends so many possibilities, and no one of them can be definitive.

We much underrate Donne's positivism if we suppose that 'Farewell to Love' might be just the poet's dismissal of sense, marking the limits of a state which later poems will outgrow. That reading doesn't account for what is there, or do justice to a poem whose truth isn't denied by things Donne wrote elsewhere. The differences between a man's several experiences of love sharpen his understanding of love just to the extent that his mind can gain possession of unlike qualities without submitting them to regularizing norms. Donne's love poetry is held together not by some pattern he imposes upon his sentimental life but by a coherent reading of human nature, and a consistent temper of mind.

These love poems may be occasional, yet the way they relate to one another is a part of what they say. Some of them offer a developed understanding of love in that they build upon other possibilities which Donne entertains. The attitudes he tries in Elegy 1 or 'Woman's Constancy' aren't denied in 'The Good Morrow', 'The Anniversary', or 'The Canonization', even though he may now claim a more singular bond with a woman. The one truth isn't annulled by the other, but may very well hold for the rest of the world, and even for the poet himself in other areas of his life; indeed, the brave vaunt of the lovers' unalterable assurance moves us just because it is made in the face of the common frailty of love, and the frailty of their own natures. Donne's poems remind us that our

lives aren't organized in literary categories, and that a man doesn't need
to sublimate his sensual nature, or undertake a new course of reading, to
develop an idea of a mutual love. When people say that Donne's poems
articulate their own experience of love they tend to have the diversity of
his insights in mind, as well as their complexity. For here too is a truth
about love, and about love's relativeness, which is easily falsified if we
value only what aims at ideal beauty, or at marriage. The poems make
their own categories.

'You (I think) and I am much of one sect in the philosophy of love;
which, though it be directed upon the mind, doth inhere in the body, and
find pretty entertainment there'.[16] Donne proclaims his allegiance in the
philosophy of love by the ideas he spurns as well as by the attitudes he
makes his own. He derides professions which make light of the body:

> That loving wretch that swears,
> 'Tis not the bodies marry, but the minds,
>   Which he in her angelic finds,
>   Would swear as justly, that he hears,
> In that day's rude hoarse minstrelsy, the spheres.

> 'Love's Alchemy'

The sceptical pragmatist of the *Metempsychosis* and *The Second Anniversary* could have had little sympathy with a doctrine which defines love by
an end, according to its place in a universal scheme. That kind of teleo-
logy carries a moral imperative when the consummation proposed for
love is offered as an ideal form which all actual loves must strive to
achieve, and by which they price themselves. Donne judges love by those
qualities he discovers in the relationship itself which fit it for its particular circumstances, and he refuses such definitions as might impose an
external end, or a goal to be attained. Ficino's lovers 'never know what it
is they desire or seek,[17] because they don't yet know God himself. Donne
merely points to a realized condition which he may identify at all only by
remarking what it is not:

> If that be simple perfectest
> Which can by no way be expressed
>   But negatives, my love is so.
>   To all, which all love, I say no.

> 'Negative Love'

A mind which so determinedly refuses the received categories of

[16]Letter to Sir H. Wotton, Amiens, February 1612.
[17]*M. Ficino sopra lo Amore*, Firenze, 1544, pp. 26–7; *In Convivium Platonis de Amore,
Commentarium*, in *Opera*, Basilaea, 1576, p. 1326.

understanding is likely to feel its way forward tentatively, and relatively, using irony and wit as a means of holding in play a number of possible ways of taking things. To be absolute for truth is alien to the temper of Donne's verse, even the religious verse. Within the poems themselves he tries one occurrence by another, one kind of behaviour against another, inviting a relative estimation of both; and he assumes that such effects as love and beauty hold only for the situation which gives them value:

> Therefore I'll give no more; but I'll undo
> The world by dying; because love dies too.
> Then all your beauties will be no more worth
> Than gold in mines, where none doth draw it forth;
> And all your graces no more use shall have
>   Than a sundial in a grave.

'The Will'

The lady's beauty has no other worth than its effect upon the lover while he is receptive to it, a value which he himself bestows upon it then. Voices from the following decades remind us that Donne's admirers saw the drift of his anatomy of love:

> Know, Celia, since thou art so proud,
>   'Twas I that gave thee thy renown;

Carew, 'Ingrateful Beauty Threat'ned'

> Nay, 'tis true: you are no longer handsome when you've lost your lover; your beauty dies upon the instant. For beauty is the lover's gift; 'tis he bestows you charms, your glass is all a cheat. . . .

Congreve, *The Way of the World* II, iv, 354–7

But then a love poet with such a sharp eye for the sleights of sexual skirmish scarcely stood to gain from Plato or Plotinus; and Donne has more in common with Boccaccio and Machiavelli than with the idealists and transcendentalists of an opposing Tuscan tradition. He sought his own way to master the infirmities of our condition, through the senses not in spite of them.

6

Beyond All Date

certain o'er incertainty,

Shakespeare, Sonnet 115

Izaac Walton's diptych of the two Donne's, the rake and the religious, half-persuades us to expect such a division in the poetry. But we scarcely need ask ourselves what strange alchemy of the sentiments metamorphosed the 'great Visitor of Ladies'[1] with his virile imagination and sceptical wit, into a celebrant of mutual love. For the one man may be recognized in the other, however the occasion might change; and the same cast of mind is at work:

> All kings, and all their favourites,
> All glory of honours, beauties, wits,
> The sun itself, which makes times, as they pass,
> Is elder by a year, now, than it was
> When thou and I first one another saw:
> All other things, to their destruction draw,
>   Only our love hath no decay;

'The Anniversary'

Such poems as 'Woman's Constancy', and 'The Indifferent', show us a lover who simply exploits an unstable world of change — 'For by tomorrow, I may think so too'. He seizes delightedly on love's momentariness as the condition of his freedom, assuming with cool assurance that in the game of sex, as in his writing about it, frank fidelity to the real motive is all that matters. 'The Anniversary' doesn't deny our common condition of change, or seek to transcend sense. With 'The Good Morrow', 'The Canonization', 'The Ecstasy', it simply confirms these particular lovers in a condition they have already found, which will not be subject to time

---

[1]Sir Richard Baker, recalling Donne at Lincolns Inn in *A Chronicle of the Kings of England* (1643), 1684, p. 427.

119

and alteration. They don't need to try some neoplatonic ascent to a realm
of universal form beyond the world of sense and particular embodiments.
On the contrary, what distinguishes them is just this unique relationship,
their achieved and embodied mutualness which sets them apart from the
common course of affairs in the world:

> Love, all alike, no season knows, nor clime,
> Nor hours, days, months, which are the rags of time.

'The Sun Rising'

> My face in thine eye, thine in mine appears,
>   And true plain hearts do in the faces rest,
> Where can we find two better hemispheres
>   Without sharp north, without declining west?

'The Good Morrow'

> Call us what you will, we are made such by love;
>   Call her one, me another fly,
> We are tapers too, and at our own cost die,
>   And we in us find the eagle and the dove,
>   The phoenix riddle hath more wit
>   By us; we two being one, are it.
> So to one neutral thing, both sexes fit
>   We die and rise the same, and prove
>   Mysterious by this love.

'The Canonization'

Some of the finest of Donne's love poems speak for lovers who assure
themselves that they are a whole world to each other. We can't take for
casual hyperbole an idea which is so much of a piece with attitudes Donne
consistently assumes. He is firmly, if implicitly, amending accepted
faith. It was scarcely a new conceit that the lover's mistress is his world,
who in his eyes comprehends or far surpasses all the wealth and dignities
of the world about her; and there had been lovers enough who claimed
that their previous tussles with love were only an immature preparation
for the present consummate encounter. Donne makes something
different of these fancies just because he presumes a shared experience.
He transforms an idealizing device of praise into an emblem of a mutual
bond, which attests a real accord between people in the world. On this
understanding a one-sided love can't truly be love at all. The man's
passion won't get beyond admiring adoration if it isn't given active
embodiment, or 'sphere', by her love; and her love remains dormant until
he activates it:

> Just such disparity
> As is 'twixt air and angels' purity,
> 'Twixt women's love, and men's will ever be.

'Air and Angels'

The very boldness with which he urges his argument proclaims this lover's defiance of worldly calculation. He implies his contempt of the courses which advance men's fortunes when he claims that lovers who are wholly sure of each other possess the world, and are the world; or that they are more than the world, since the world outside their love means nothing to them. If the woman and her lover between them sum up in themselves all the true values there may be, then the common traffic in commodities and titles is at best a sham and a self-deceit. Statecraft, commerce, nobility, are alike mere play and mimicry; and the stir of civic aspiration has no value compared to their fruition in bed, which alone enacts the vital business of human kind. Donne never neglects an opportunity to confound orthodox expectations; and here he quietly mocks the solemn wisacres who talk of love as a toy of youth, which a man must leave behind for the serious business of life. Yet defiantly or triumphantly, some of his finest poems proclaim a judgement on such estimations of what truly matters to human kind. It is no mere conceited whimsy which 'The Anniversary' enlarges, but a personal testimony to a substantial creed of love. Their love is uniquely exempt from time, and makes them superior to all the world's honours and riches and the sun itself; indeed their state here on earth now as human lovers must be even better blessed than they will find themselves in the life of thorough but communal bliss to come:

> And then we shall be throughly blessed,
>   But we no more, than all the rest.
> Here upon earth, we are kings, and none but we
> Can be such kings, nor of such subjects be;
> Who is so safe as we? where none can do
> Treason to us, except one of us two.

'The Anniversary'

The colossal hyperbole can't be taken for extravagance. Its triumphant rhetoric proclaims its fidelity to the lovers' feelings, and claims a more general truth.

'The Canonization' confirms that this lover's radical wit effects a considered appraisal of his experience in a world he knows well:

> For God's sake hold your tongue, and let me love,
>   Or chide my palsy, or my gout,
> My five grey hairs, or ruined fortune flout,
>   With wealth your state, your mind with arts improve,
>   Take you a course, get you a place,
>   Observe his Honour, or his Grace,
> Or the King's real, or his stamped face
>   Contemplate; what you will, approve,
>   So you will let me love.

> Alas, alas, who's injured by my love,
>> What merchant's ships have my sighs drowned?
> Who says my tears have overflowed his ground?
>> When did my colds a forward spring remove?
>>> When did the heats which my veins fill
>>> Add one more to the plaguy bill?
> Soldiers find wars, and lawyers find out stil,
>> Litigious men, which quarrels move,
>> Though she and I do love.

The poem opens superbly, yet it is so much more than a fine lamenting outcry. These humorously self-mocking conceits intimate that love is a kind of faith which exacts some sacrifice of its devotees, ruining them in the world only to remake them in another and better sense. True lovers must and do renounce the world for each other, and their own lives as well if need be. Love denies them the prizes of the world, but it gives them another superior world which has its own conditions and laws:

> We die and rise the same, and prove
> Mysterious by this love.

Here is the escape from the dilemma of 'Farewell to Love', which the poet didn't reckon with when he renounced his search for a bliss such as 'no man else can find'. They have realized a condition of love which exempts them from the common process of change in the world, because it isn't committed to the biological cycle. 'The Canonization' shows how this claim may be justified though their bodies aren't denied, revealing a mystery which is nothing more than the human evidence of their own experience. Their miraculous exemption from the common case of alteration after coitus attests both the rarity of their love, and their mutual victory over change and decay.

Donne wittily weaves their sexual valour into an emblematic proof of their mutualness, which epitomizes the wonder of their love:

> We are tapers too, and at our own cost die,
>> And we in us find the eagle and the dove,
>>> The phoenix riddle hath more wit
>>> By us; we two being one, are it.

'The Canonization'

Modern lovers may find such a love more readily intelligible than the transcendentalism of Ficino and the moralism of Petrarch. For there's no doubt of the achievement which assures their heroic triumph over our human frailty and fits them to be love's martyrs and saints, who may even offer less blessed lovers a pattern of consummate love. The poem celebrates their conjugal bond itself, figuring the mutual love of two people whose sexual coupling may ruin them in the world, yet only confirms their oneness.

The proclamation of the last stanza meets the demur which Donne himself might have been the first to make anywhere else, that the triumph the poem claims merely appeases these people's feelings in this situation, as they desperately seek to snatch some advantage from ruin. The conceit of a religion of love is brilliantly brought off. They are love's martyrs and saints, who may therefore intercede with the god himself on behalf of lovers still struggling for the heroic resolution to perfect their love. Yet the witty play itself realizes the claim that the condition they have already proved makes them a paragon of right love. It assures us that a perfected love will be that which is determined and steadfast enough to carry through the conviction that nothing else matters as much as its truth to itself. Such a love makes its devotees martyrs just by giving them the clear-sighted resolution to put their simple human compact before considerations of expediency and worldly success, before even their own lives, and to stand by their commitment to each other come what may.

'The Dream' powerfully defies expediency in a tiny divergence from the conventional decorum of an amorous visitation:

> Coming and staying showed thee, thee,
> But rising makes me doubt, that now,
>   Thou art not thou.
> That love is weak, where fear's as strong as he;
> 'Tis not all spirit, pure, and brave,
> If mixture it of fear, shame, honour, have.

>   21–6

That the visitant might give herself to her lover clandestinely in no way impugns the truth and sincerity he so warmly imputes to her. Yet their love would be belied by her wish to conceal it. 'The Sun Rising' tells us that genuine love pays no more regard to fear, shame, and honour than to the traffic of the world which our civic values serve, or to the seasons and climates that regulate our lives:

> She' is all states, and all princes, I,
>   Nothing else is.
> Princes do but play us; compared to this,
> All honour's mimic; all wealth alchemy.

>   'The Sun Rising'

'Break of Day' confirms that there is a higher honour than reputation, which consists in keeping faith with our own truth at whatever cost:

> Light hath no tongue, but is all eye;
> If it could speak as well as spy,

This were the worst, that it could say,
That being well, I fain would stay,
And that I loved my heart and honour so,
That I would not from him, that had them, go.

'Break of Day'

One lesson of the emblematic shadows in 'A Lecture upon the Shadow' seems to be that it is an immature love which seeks to conceal itself:

> So whilst our infant loves did grow,
> Disguises did, and shadows, flow,
> From us, and our care; but, now 'tis not so.

> That love hath not attained the high' st degree,
> Which is still diligent lest others see.

'A Lecture upon the Shadow'

A mature love bravely eschews such masks, and makes all clear as it sees all clear. Pretence, deceit, disguise, concealment have no place in so absolute a dedication of lovers to one another.

'A Lecture upon the Shadow' prescribes a further condition of mature love. A love which seeks no concealment, and lays itself so vulnerably open, can be upheld only by perfect mutualness. The slightest slackening on either side lets in deceit and falsehood, which will swallow up all. There's a still harder lesson for lovers in this testimony, a stand against a deadlier expediency. The terms may be modest, but the need is imperative. For love is more threatened by the lovers' fear of each other than by their fear of others. Uncertainties and reservations, however, warrantable, no more go with love than does concealment; and mistrust simply has no place in a loving union:

> True and false fears let us refrain,

'The Anniversary'

The ingenious fulfilment of the emblematic design in 'A Lecture upon the Shadow' comes with graphic finality:

> And his first minute, after noon, is night.

Love's absolutists pose themselves on the brink of chaos. We are truly in the world of Troilus and Othello, where the onset of doubt is the instant ruin of bliss. The starkness of that witness of experience admits no compromise.

The mutual trust of the lovers is the condition of a love which is so secure from the alterations of time and place that it 'no season knows, nor clime/Nor hours, days, months':

> What ever dies, was not mixed equally;
> If our two loves be one, or, thou and I
> Love so alike, that none do slacken, none can die.

'The Good Morrow'

While they remain as one they need not fear each other, for their love is not only exempt from the world's vicissitudes but enriched and strengthened by the union; whereas in division their mistrust and concealment would feed upon itself, and undo them. The highest degree of love is a love of souls so complete that it makes a new and superior soul, which is capable of more than either of them might manage singly, and preserves them both from change:

> A single violet transplant,
>   The strength, the colour, and the size,
> (All which before was poor, and scant,)
>   Redoubles still, and multiplies.
>
> When love, with one another so
>   Interinanimates two souls,
> That abler soul, which thence doth flow,
>   Defects of loneliness controls.

'The Ecstasy'

Such a reciprocity of powers keeps them steadfast even in physical separation:

> Thy firmness makes my circle just,
>   And makes me énd, where I begun.

'A Valediction: forbidding Mourning'

Love requires its metaphysics, no less than its natural morality and its psychology. Donne always gives real substance to the courtly commonplaces he takes over. Hearts stolen and strayed, or exchanged, fused, and united, appear in the *Songs and Sonnets* as often as in Serafino d'Aquila or in Sidney. In Donne's poems these figures contribute to an appraisal of love which makes them no extravagant fancy but the realization of a truth, attesting the commerce of mutual lovers. The lovers are so completely one that they sigh one another's breath. They have been wholly interfused by love and no longer have separate existence, but remain one being even when they are apart. The sheer grandeur of the address authenticates the vast hyperbole that the lover is so involved with his mistress that he depends upon her for his understanding, his growth, his very existence; that he dies in absence from her; that his being is violently dissolved, annihilated, made nothing and the quintessence of nothing by her death:

> If I an ordinary nothing were,
> As shadow, a light, and body must be here.
>
> But I am none; nor will my sun renew.
> You lovers, for whose sake, the lesser sun
>   At this time to the Goat is run
>   To fetch new lust, and give it you,
>   Enjoy your summer all;
> Since she enjoys her long night's festival,
> Let me prepare towards her, and let me call
> This hour her vigil, and her eve, since this
>   Both the year's, and the day's deep midnight is.

'A Nocturnal upon S. Lucy's Day'

Donne works out these figures with logical relentlessness, and an intellectual authority which is more than mere rhetoric for the process may genuinely analyse, clarify, define. He is preoccupied with the need to discriminate the several kinds of love which his own acquaintance brings home to him, and questions his experience with wondering honesty, pragmatically refusing to commit himself to any prescriptive limitation of motives and ends. The lover of 'The Paradox' discovers that the very attempt to prescribe for love is as misguided as it is self-defeating. Love can't be defined, for it would be vain to attempt such a task without experience of the state itself; yet the experienced lover is by definition already beyond need of speech, and insensible to worldly reason. There is more in this parody of mystical experience than a casual twist of wit. 'A Valediction: forbidding Mourning' assures the lovers that even they themselves don't know, and can't define, the essence of a love which has reached the highest degree; and 'The Ecstasy' makes it a mark of such a love that it escapes our humdrum categories:

> We see by this, it was not sex,
>   We see, we saw not what did move:

We can say what isn't truly love, or what other amorous attitudes are to be distinguished from the perfected sexual union the poet has proved. The *Songs and Sonnets* themselves try out many kinds of sexual encounter. We may gather by these divertingly various versions that the bond he

speaks of in the poems of mutual love no more consists in a pure marriage
of minds than a mere coupling of bodies; nor is it sealed by so cool an
affection as a disinterested love of inward virtue, such as the brave spirits
of 'The Undertaking' consciously propose for their object, in miraculous
despite of their senses. When people can't point to some overall design or
end to justify what they do then the logical consequence is plain. If their
behaviour has meaning at all we must value it in its own right; or it may
even stand altogether beyond definition, as divine mysteries do.
'Negative Love' turns precisely on the lover's search for the ends and
motives of his love, and shows why they can't be found. Love is fixed
neither in sense nor in a disembodied admiration of virtue or the mind,
for both sense and understanding know their proper end, and the way to
satisfy it; whereas lovers must define their love by negatives, since they
don't know what they seek, and propose no object which would fulfil
their endeavour and conclude their dealings with one another. They
know what their love is not, but they don't know what it is. Donne makes
it a proof of a mature love that the lovers have no end to attain but are
content simply to exist as one being. The human substance of his inquiry
brings life to the arid scholastic processes, letting us see the habit of a
sceptical mind which tests its positive assurance by rejections and
negations. These lovers have proved a condition which is no more a
simple motion of sense than a contemplative bliss of the spirit. The
appeal from absolute categories to the unresolved particularity of what
they prove in themselves shows us a lover who resists definition of his
love on principle, not only because he won't compromise experience for a
falsifying categoricalness, but because a condition which may be defined
by motive and end must be finite.

'The Undertaking' and 'The Relic' selfconsciously proclaim a
different kind of bond with a woman, which has its own claim to
singularity:

> First, we loved well and faithfully,
> Yet knew not what we loved, nor why,
> Difference of sex no more we knew,
> Than our guardian angels do;
>   Coming and going, we
> Perchance might kiss, but not between those meals;
>   Our hands ne'er touched the seals,
> Which nature, injured by late law, sets free;
> These miracles we did;. . . .

'The Relic'

> If, as I have, you also do
>   Virtue attired in woman see,

> And dare love that, and say so too,
>   And forget the He and She;

'The Undertaking'

These lines bring Donne as near as he gets to the manner of Michelangelo's admiration for Vittoria Colonna. Yet they are quite unlike Michelangelo's sonnets and madrigals:

> Tanto sopra me stesso
> Mi fai, Donna, salire,

[Lady, you make me ascend so far beyond myself . . .]

'The Relic' and 'The Undertaking' don't hint at such a self-transcendence, or celebrate an ideal beauty. If they pose an ideal for lovers it is decidedly not disembodied. 'The Undertaking', which some manuscripts entitle 'Platonic Love', does claim that in this unique instance the poet has got beyond the outside appearance to the beauty of the virtue within, and loves that quality for its own sake, regardless of the difference of sex. 'The Relic' describes a strong mutual affection, possibly the same one, which is miraculous just because it is wholly unsexual. 'Platonic love' seems apt, in the popular sense of the term which implies no metaphysical aspiration or heroic self-denial.

Yet these people too are good and faithful lovers, though they may even recognize what it is and why they love. The difference between them and the lovers 'The Canonization' and 'The Ecstasy' show us is that this state imposes its own restraints. They make no use of the difference of sex, kissing only in salutation, and willingly eschewing the freedom which nature originally gave people to enjoy physical love. It isn't because they condemn sense that they go against nature so; quite the contrary, for the lover doesn't propose that theirs is the best condition of love, or that it transcends the love which heeds the senses. He claims only that they have achieved something unique by their willing abstinence from what is allowable, or what ought to be allowed. The laws now governing sexual conduct can't be natural, since nature didn't impose them on the first men; they are later arbitrary creations which injure nature. These lovers who willingly abstain from sex prove a miracle of love by the canons of this natural morality; and strictly so, for a miracle confirms the order of nature by the inexplicable departure from it. Donne is a poet who remains true to the unprescribed inflections of living, even when they cause him to qualify his conviction that love inheres in the body no less than the mind. His fine self-surprise as a celebrant of sexless love makes still more cogent his different understanding of love everywhere else.

There seems particular point in the way that Donne's poems move from idea to body. In 'The Dream', the mere apparition of his mistress has to give way in the end to the better reality of bodily love. 'Air and Angels' figures a lover's progress, following his advance from an unlocalized idea of love to a particular embodiment, and then from the admiration of physical beauty to a more inward regard; and the movement flowers in his new understanding that love is neither a worship of an idea nor an admiration of beauty, but an impulse that needs an answering love to give it substance:

> For, nor in nothing, nor in things
> Extreme, and scatt'ring bright, can love inhere;
>   Then as an angel, face and wings
> Of air, not pure as it, yet pure doth wear,
>   So thy love may be my love's sphere;

The poem quite beautifully proposes that the proper object of love is not disembodied form but another human being, and persuades us that love is not truly love, even when it has an object of flesh and blood, until it is returned and mutual.

In the poems which assume a mutual love the lover's progress from fantasy to reality, intelligible idea to sensible actuality, marks his discovery of a state in which mind and body aren't separate. Donne insists that a mature love brings sense and spirit into one. When we separate mind from body we don't always kill love but we do diminish it, as 'The Blossom' lightly suggests when its lover proposes to abandon a mistress who isn't 'As glad to have my body, as my mind'. The relation of body to mind in love is finely observed. When the lover of 'A Valediction: forbidding Mourning' consoles his mistress with the assurance that separation won't divide them he might well have been content to fall back on the canonical assumption that love consists in a pure union of minds. Donne carefully sets out the articles of a love which has 'attained the high'st degree'. Theirs is a highly refined state of love which has its arcana and priesthood, and sustains itself by an absolute interassurance of minds; all the lovers themselves may know for certain about it is that the body is important to it, though its essence isn't sense. Love can survive the physical separation; yet Donne won't let the lovers console themselves with the easy assurance that sense has no place at all in their love. He writes 'Care less, eyes, lips, and hands to miss', where the 'less' seems delicately true to what parting lovers would really feel, and takes care not to concede something that matters.

'Love's Growth' marvellously realises the perfected state of love which 'The Ecstasy' so carefully anatomizes:

> I scarce believe my love to be so pure
>   As I had thought it was,
>   Because it doth endure
> Vicissitude, and season, as the grass;

Methinks I lied all winter, when I swore,
My love was infinite, if spring make it more.
But if this medicine, love, which cures all sorrow
With more, not only be no quintessence,
But mixed of all stuffs, paining soul, or sense,
And of the sun his working vigour borrow,
Love's not so pure, and abstract, as they use
To say, which have no mistress but their Muse,
But as all else, being elemented too,
Love sometimes would contemplate, sometimes do.

And yet not greater, but more eminent,
    Love by the spring is grown;
    As, in the firmament,
Stars by the sun are not enlarged, but shown,
Gentle love deeds, as blossoms on a bough,
From love's awakened root do bud out now.
If, as in water stirred more circles be
Produced by one, love such additions take,
Those like so many spheres, but one heaven make,
For, they are all concentric unto thee,
And though each spring do add to love new heat,
As princes do in times of action get
New taxes, and remit them not in peace,
No winter shall abate the spring's increase.

In this poem love enlarges itself from winter to spring precisely by its progress from one-sided adoration to the quickening of mutual affection. Love's winter is contemplation, love's spring stirs up desire and action. Love must be deficient while it is purely contemplative and concerns only the mind or soul, for its nature requires a reinforcing of wonder with 'Gentle love deeds' and 'heat', in which the soul and body work together. Love is not pure but a mixed state of spirit and sense; and once passion and loving acts have been added to admiration to make up love they will not be revoked again but endure as a permanent again, preserving the love they perfect from any return of winter. Literally, a love which is entirely mutual, and yet so essentially human, will be proof against frailty and decay.

7

Drawing to Destruction

> a lust of the blood, and a permission of the will.
>
> *Othello* I, iii, 333–4

John Webster's *The White Devil* was first put on within six years of *Antony and Cleopatra* but its opening speeches take us into a different world from Shakespeare's, which will offer us little prospect of moral reassurance:

> *Lodovico:* Banish'd?
> *Antonelli:*   It griev'd me much to hear the sentence.
> *Lodovico:* Ha, ha, O Democritus thy gods
> That govern the whole world! Courtly reward,
> And punishment! Fortune's a right whore.
> If she gives ought, she deals it in small parcels,
> That she may take away all at one swoop.
> This 'tis to have great enemies, God quite them:
> Your wolf no longer seems to be a wolf
> Than when she's hungry.
> *Gasparo:*   You term those enemies
> Are men of princely rank.

This strange eruption of noble desperadoes which begins the play in a manner so unlike the Shakespearean lead-in unsettles us at once by catching in its language the temper of a man of drastic habit of life, one of those perverse wills who 'rather than be less/Car'd not to be at all' (*Paradise Lost* ii, 44–5):

> *Lodovico:*   Oh I pray for them.
> The violent thunder is adored by those
> Are pash'd in pieces by it.
> *Antonelli:*   Come my lord,
> You are justly doom'd; look but a little back
> Into your former life: you have in three years
> Ruin'd the noblest earldom —

Gasparo:	Your followers
	Have swallowed you like mummia, and being sick
	With such unnatural and horrid physic
	Vomit you up i'th' kennel—
Antonelli:	All the damnable degrees
	Of drinkings have you stagger'd through; one citizen
	Is lord of two fair manors, call'd you master
	Only for caviare.
Gasparo:	Those noblemen
	Which were invited to your prodigal feasts,
	Wherein the Phoenix scarce could scape your throats,
	Laugh at your misery, as fore-deeming you
	An idle meteor which drawn forth the earth
	Would be soon lost i'th' air.
Antonelli:	Jest upon you,
	And say you were begotten in an earthquake,
	You have ruin'd such fair lordships.
Lodovico:	Very good,
	This well goes with two buckets, I must tend
	The pouring out of either.
Gasparo:	Worse than these,
	You have acted certain murders here in Rome,
	Bloody and full of horror.
Lodovico:	'Las they were flea-bitings:
	Why took they not my head then?

'Who cares not to turn back, may any wither come' (Donne, *Metempsychosis*, line 400). This tearaway Count Lodovico, whom Webster realizes so tellingly from a few grim details in the sources, takes us into the main action of the play in a style that opens the way to dispositions as inordinate as his own:

Lodovico:	So; but I wonder then some great men scape
	This banishment; there's Paulo Giordano Orsini,
	The Duke of Brachiano, now lives in Rome,
	And by close panderism seeks to prostitute
	The honour of Vittoria Corombona:
	Vittoria, she that might have got my pardon
	For one kiss to the Duke.
Antonelli:	Have a full man within you.
	We see that trees bear no such pleasant fruit
	There where they grew first, as where they are new set . . .
Lodovico:	Leave your painted comforts.
	I'll make Italian cut-works in their guts
	If ever I return.

The mocking reversal of roles puts a cut-throat in the scales with his condemners, and denies us a sure moral perspective. Love first emerges as a lust of the blood and a permission of the will in a realm where will is law, and death the only sure constraint upon it.

Webster's choice of a 25-year-old European *cause célèbre* to dramatize shows a keen eye for extreme states of spirit, and some alertness to the temper of his own times in an era which had cause to be preoccupied with mortality, and the degeneracy of courts. The Duke of Bracciano's affair with La Accoromboni isn't the stuff of romantic legend. But its bloody outcome in Padua in December 1585 coloured a tale of family turmoil which quickly travelled around Europe in lurid circumstance, and in various forms.[1] Essentially this was the old story, as pathetic as it is squalid, of a middle-aged widower's fatal obsession with a woman 20 years younger than he, which prompted him to get her husband out of the way and defy the opposition of his family and the Church. The lovers' clandestine attempts at marriage, and their pretences and concealments as they sought to evade the menaces of Pope and kinsmen, weren't crowned with much bliss. They snatched a few years together, much troubled by the Duke's ill-health yet still in some hope that their marriage might be recognized when a new pope came in. But events cruelly betrayed them, for Gregory xiii was succeeded as pope by Cardinal Montalto, an uncle of one of the murdered spouses. Bracciano died in his late forties, barely five years after the affair began, leaving a young son by his first marriage; and his own family joined with the boy's protectors to prevent La Accoromboni from inheriting the duke's possessions, or at least from marrying again. When she continued to outface and outwit them they put a murderous Orsini cousin up to avenging the stain upon the family honour, which he arranged, by all accounts, pretty barbarously.

Webster doesn't even try to arrive at a lifelike rendering of what really happened. He simply uses the people and events in a design of his own, inventing dispositions and motives, arranging characters in a strange symmetry of parallels and contrasts, patterning the action itself so that the incidents always seem to be part of a larger structure of meaning, enlarging instrumental manners into a mordant vision of the world. The ordering of episodes is particularly striking. The entire first part of the play turns on a counterposing of scenes which sets the adulterous coupling of Brachiano and Vittoria against its drastic outcome in Brachiano's repudiation of Isabella, Vittoria's rejection of Camillo, and the ingenious dumbshow murders of the superfluous spouses. Stated that way round, Brachiano's inhuman misprizing of his devoted wife becomes more than the mere indifference of a stale marriage which drives him to seek his pleasure elsewhere, as his chroniclers say he did; rather, he suddenly hates his wife because he is obsessed with Corombona. Then both the

[1] The reports are summarized in G. Boklund, *The Sources of The White Devil*, New York, 1966.

love-scene and the dumbshow poisoning of Isabella rehearse the unstable passions of IV, ii, and Brachiano's own death by poison in V, iii at the height of his wedding festivities. Webster's curious art proposes a shape in the events which the sprawl of casual contingency doesn't disclose, and challenges us to make what we can of it.

Webster's patterning is often ironic, and works quite intimately within the episodes themselves. I, ii is a key scene, coming so early in the action and opening up all that follows. This is a big ensemble whose placing, arrangement and effect make a nice contrast with *Troilus and Cressida* V, ii. Like that scene it is conceived in terms of theatrical effect rather than verisimilitude, but the playwright is so little concerned with simulating actuality that we have to work to infer the situation from circumstances the characters take for granted. We may gather that Duke Brachiano has been visiting Camillo and Vittoria at their house in Rome, and is just leaving as the scene opens; but by prior contrivance of Vittoria's brother, and Vittoria herself, he doubles back, dismisses his coach and torches, and conceals himself in the house until Camillo can be got out of the way and Vittoria is free to come to him. The plotters don't know that Vittoria's widowed mother is on the alert, and lurking to mar her daughter's snatched liaison with the Duke. Such an account of what is happening scarcely conveys the effect of a scene which works by keeping practical circumstances menacingly undefined. The characters address each other in brief discontinuities as though they are scarcely contributing to a mutual discourse at all:

Brachiano: Your best of rest.
Vittoria: Unto my lord the Duke,
               The best of welcome. More lights, attend the Duke.
                                   [*Exeunt* Vittoria and Camillo]

Brachiano: Flamineo.
Flamineo: My lord.
Brachiano: Quite lost Flamineo.
Flamineo: Pursue your noble wishes, I am prompt
               As lightning to your service, O my lord!
               The fair Vittoria, my happy sister
               Shall give you present audience. Gentlemen
               Let the caroche go on, and 'tis his pleasure
               You put out all your torches and depart.
Brachiano: Are we so happy?

Cornelia: O that this fair garden,
               Had with all poison'd herbs of Thessaly,
               At first been planted, made a nursery
               For witchcraft; rather than a burial plot
               For both your honours.
Vittoria: Dearest mother hear me.

Cornelia:	O thou dost make my brow bend to the earth,
	Sooner than nature; see the curse of children:
	In life they keep us frequently in tears,
	And in the cold grave leave us in pale fears.
Brachiano:	Come, come, I will not hear you.
Vittoria:	Dear my lord.
Cornelia:	Where is thy Duchess now adulterous Duke?
	Thou little dream'd'st this night she is come to Rome.
Flamineo:	How? Come to Rome,—
Vittoria:	The Duchess,—
Brachiano:	She had been better,—
Cornelia:	The lives of princes should like dials move,
	Whose regular example is so strong,
	They make the times by them go right or wrong.
Flamineo:	So, have you done?
Cornelia:	Unfortunate Camillo.

There's no doubt that a literal explicitness simply isn't Webster's concern, and that his bizarre mode of theatrical ellipsis has its effect in this scene. The characters whizz around intensely in their void, going their own ways without common order or stable point of reference. They move in paths such as some inner impulse prescribes and their wills carve out for them, beyond the regulation of their own understanding.

The congress of the adulterous couple is prepared by intrigue, and farcically engineered by Flamineo's gulling of Camillo, which offsets the exchanges of the lovers with a grim mockery of sexual life. Their colloquy is quite formally arranged as a theatrical rite. Zanche spreads the carpet and cushions, the lovers slip in and lie down, Flamineo stands by as mediating master of ceremonies, Cornelia takes up her station of covert commentary; and off they go with a curious courtly formality, as of people who naturally bring their settled order of greatness into their intimate lives:

Brachiano:	. . . Let me into your bosom happy lady,
	Pour out instead of eloquence my vows;
	Loose me not madam, for if you forgo me
	I am lost eternally.
Vittoria:	Sir in the way of pity
	I wish you heart-whole.
Brachiano:	You are a sweet physician.
Vittoria:	Sure sir a loathed cruelty in ladies
	Is as to doctors many funerals.
	It takes away their credit.
Brachiano:	Excellent creature.
	We call the cruel fair, what name for you
	That are so merciful?
Zanche:	See now they close.
Flamineo:	Most happy union.

These commentating voices haven't much in common with the *obbligati* of *Troilus and Cressida* V, ii. Here they don't so much undercut the lovers' attitudes as frame and point them:

Brachiano:	What value is this jewel?
Vittoria:	'Tis the ornament Of a weak fortune.
Brachiano:	In sooth I'll have it; nay I will but change My jewel for your jewel.
Flamineo:	Excellent, His jewel for her jewel; well put in Duke.
Brachiano:	Nay let me see you wear it.
Vittoria:	Here sir.
Brachiano:	Nay lower, you shall wear my jewel lower.
Flamineo:	That's better; she must wear his jewel lower.

Flamineo's interventions follow out his stream of worldly scepticism throughout the earlier part of the scene, looking to the actualities of obsessive sexual desire behind the veiled courtesies, and pointing the consequences of ardour when to will is to act:

> *Flamineo*:   'Bove merit! We may now talk freely: 'bove merit; what is't you doubt? her coyness? That's but the superficies of lust most women have; yet why should ladies blush to hear that nam'd, which they do not fear to handle? O they are politic! They know our desire is increas'd by the difficulty of enjoying; whereas satiety is a blunt, weary and drowsy passion; if the buttery-hatch at court stood continually open there would be nothing so passionate crowding, nor hot suit after the beverage,—

'Past reason hunted. . . . past reason hated' is a settled irony of the play, but it is taken for ironic truism rather than as bitter home truth. Flamineo's dialogue with Camillo earlier on, which equates love with sexual appetite as a matter of course, and takes lack of virility to justify aversion, offsets with farce the pathetic irony of Brachiano's confrontation with his wife in II, i. Brachiano's heartless behaviour there, to a woman most sympathetically presented who is devoutly loyal to him, makes a pretty harsh contrast with his vows to Vittoria in I, ii, and with his former passion for Isabella as she touchingly reveals it:

> *Isabella*:   O my loved lord,
I do not come to chide; my jealousy?
I am to learn what that Italian means;
You are as welcome to these longing arms,
As I to you a virgin.

Brachiano:	O your breath!
	Out upon sweetmeats, and continued physic!
	The plague is in them.
Isabella:	You have oft for these two lips
	Neglected cassia or the natural sweets
	Of the spring violet; they are not yet much withered.
	My lord I should be merry; these your frowns
	Show in a helmet lovely, but on me,
	In such a peaceful interview methinks
	They are too too roughly knit.

For Brachiano now 'the plague is in' the lips he formerly desired, love has turned to its poisonous opposite with a violence he scarcely seems aware of. The dumbshow murder of Isabella which he watches so callously — 'Good, then she's dead' — confirms the monstrous change, with a shock to our sense of justice and of the domestic pieties when she dies by religiously kissing the poisoned lips of Brachiano's own portrait. Brachiano stands outside the frame of the show and observes its inevitable course with satisfaction; we stand beyond the artifice that frames him and dispassionately watch him destroy his own peace, and lay up a raving ruin for his mind.

The scene in the House of Convertites compounds the irony of staled and sated love with an abrupt turnabout which isn't far from farce, and would be intolerably audacious in a playwright who couldn't count on the ready assent of his audience. Brachiano's sudden jealous rounding upon Vittoria, brought on by the fake love letter she receives from the Duke of Florence, prompts a fit of Antony-like raging in which he can find only terms of disgusted revulsion for the erstwhile object of his appetite, and at once jumps back to love of the dead Isabella:

Brachiano:	That hand, that cursed hand, which I have wearied
	With doting kisses! O my sweetest Duchess
	How lovely art thou now! . . . I was bewitch'd;

Then this mood too is reversed almost at once as Vittoria turns to the counterattack, and Brachiano's frenzy cools:

Brachiano:	I have drunk Lethe. Vittoria?
	My dearest happiness! Vittoria!
	What do you ail my love? Why do you weep?

'I was bewitch'd. . . . I have drunk Lethe', the classic posture of the blind slave of his own appetites — 'Galetto fu'l libro e chi lo scrisse'.[2] It is all the more ironic here because the two supposed self-realizations are quite

---

[2] *Inferno* 5, 137.

opposite in their effect. We see the absurd instability of lives so lived at the mercy of wilful desire, which are subject not only to the consequences of their actions in the world but to the arbitrary compulsions of desire itself. This is a shaping vision which is already built into the big colloquy of love in I, ii, with its exchange of courtesies and gifts pointed by Flamineo, even though the love between Brachiano and Vittoria isn't to be tested in conjugal use:

well put in Duke.

That's better; she must wear his jewel lower.

I, ii threatens the lovers with a still more disturbing instability in fact:

Cornelia: My fears are fall'n upon me, oh my heart!
My son the pander: now I find our house
Sinking to ruin. Earthquakes leave behind,
Where they have tyrannized, iron or lead, or stone,
But, woe to ruin! violent lust leaves none.

Here is the other commentating voice in the scene, which doesn't so much counter Flamineo's sardonic intimations of love's self-ruin as open an abyss beneath the lovers' assurances. The curious ceremony of this first coming together of the Duke and his dependent, the elliptical courtesies of exchanges which nonetheless figure copulation, may be partly accounted for by the playwright's need to keep his characters at a distance from us and make us ironic observers rather than participants. The absoluteness of such lovers as these carries its own rich irony:

Quite lost Flamineo (I, ii, 3)

Loose me not madam, for if you forgo me
I am lost eternally (I, ii, 197–8)

I am lost for ever (V, iii, 35)

Indeed death and ruin heavily overhang this bizarre consummation of love.

Vittoria's dream, which pointedly prepares the way for their marriage, no less effectively puts their love in a context of demonic haunting, graveyards, bones, casual desecration, not to say murder.

Methought I walk'd about the mid of night,
Into a church-yard, where a goodly yew-tree
Spread her large root in ground; under that yew,
As I sat sadly leaning on a grave,

```
                 Checkered with cross-sticks, there came stealing in
                 Your Duchess and my husband; one of them
                 A pick-axe bore, th'other a rusty spade,
                 And in rough terms they gan to challenge me,
                 About this yew.
Brachiano:                    That tree.
Vittoria:                           This harmless yew.
                 They told me my intent was to root up
                 That well-grown yew, and plant i'th stead of it
                 A withered blackthorn, and for that they vow'd
                 To bury me alive: my husband straight
                 With pick-axe gan to dig, and your fell Duchess
                 With shovel, like a fury, voided out
                 The earth and scattered bones. Lord how methought
                 I trembled, and yet for all this terror
                 I could not pray.
Flamineo:                       No the devil was in your dream.
Vittoria:        When to my rescue there arose methought
                 A whirlwind, which let fall a massy arm
                 From that strong plant,
                 And both were struck dead by that sacred yew
                 In that base shallow grave that was their due.
Flamineo:        Excellent devil.
                 She hath taught him in a dream
                 To make away his Duchess and her husband.
```

The power of the sacred yew seems decidedly ambiguous when it centres their love so intimately upon death. What settles the direction of the scene though is the way that Brachiano's interpretation of the dream, with its extraordinary swerve of syntax into a headlong assertion of self-will, is at once shatteringly negated by Cornelia's interruption and the cursings and confusions which that apocalyptic outburst brings on:

```
Brachiano:       Sweetly shall I interpret this your dream:
                 You are lodged within his arms who shall protect you,
                 From all the fevers of a jealous husband,
                 From the poor envy of our phlegmatic Duchess;
                 I'll seat you above law and above scandal,
                 Give to your thoughts the invention of delight
                 And the fruition; nor shall government
                 Divide me from you longer than a care
                 To keep you great: you shall to me at once
                 Be dukedom, health, wife, children friends and all.
Cornelia:        Woe to light hearts, they still forerun our fall.
```

Cornelia's bitter prayer over Vittoria

If thou dishonour thus thy husband's bed

> Be thy life short as are the funeral tears
> In great men's.

expresses a settled attitude of the play, such as puts a pretty short term to men's dignity and standing altogether:

> May'st thou be envied during his short breath,
> And pitied like a wretch after his death.

>   O yes, yes;
> Had women navigable rivers in their eyes
> They would dispend them all;. . . .
> There's nothing sooner dry than women's tears.

>   O men
> That lie upon your deathbeds, and are haunted
> With howling wives, ne'er trust them; they'll remarry
> Ere the worm pierce your winding sheet; ere the spider
> Make a thin curtain for your epitaphs.

> Trust a woman? Never, never; Brachiano be my president:
> we lay our souls to pawn to the devil for a little pleasure,
> and a woman makes the bill of sale. That ever man should marry!

If this is to be put down to the scepticism of the malcontent then it is an attitude to human nature which much else in the play confirms, not least Vittoria's ruthless self-seeking after Brachiano's death. Webster's lines discover a dreadful world in which any consolations the characters may cling to seem merely pathetic when they are so ironically mocked in the consequence.

The temper of the play is set by the way all its characters entertain death so readily. 'Send Dr Julio to me presently' mutters Brachiano as the great love scene breaks up, ironically emerging straight from his sexual fruition to the thought of grim devices of murder. Isabella's response to her husband when he dramatically forswears her bed is no less drastic in its immediate transformation of the trappings of love into the habit of death:

>   O my winding sheet
>   Now shall I need thee shortly. . . .
>   Never?

Brachiano: Never!

We see all their urges in a prospect of certain ruin, sudden and total negation by death in the end, if not by satiety earlier. Those intense and consuming drives become so many blind precipitations of their own inescapable decay, headlong charges upon nothingness which may take them now this way and now quite the opposite way, but always bring them back to the same end:

> The intense atom glows
> A moment, then is quench'd in a most cold repose.

Shelley, Adonais

The play consistently treats love so, negating proud will with sudden arbitrary reversal, belittling human attachments with the squalid nullity of death, poising the whole consequence of wilful passion over an abyss. It projects a dramatic double vision, letting us simultaneously see the imperatives of will, and their likely outcome. Brachiano's undoing at the height of his wedding feast is only the culminating emblem of a vision which closes in on the ironic mortality of his passion itself:

> This is a true-love knot
> Sent from the Duke of Florence.

Yet there's more in the play than wilful desire and its consequences, Webster really does create a world, with a power of dramatic language which renders vivid and credible his disorienting version of life. The dramatic style so vividly hit at the start persists through the play, in a curious intertwining of the wills of subsidiary beings with the wills of great men. Sharp little scenes and episodes engage people suddenly in actions which have their own thrust and force, as if life drives on around the main events in ways that pointedly set them off.

Act III scene ii is a case in point. This is a passage between Flamineo and Lodovico, the hatchet-men of the opposing factions in the play. It's a chance encounter, but it's loaded from the start by the situation that puts them in hostility to each other, most of all by the recent death of Isabella. And that's how it is introduced: either of them has a carefully placed aside, contemptuous of the other, which sets them to use the meeting for intelligence or some factional end:

> *Lodovico* [*aside*]: This was Brachiano's pander, and 'tis strange
> That in such open and apparent guilt
> Of his adulterous sister, he dare utter
> So scandalous a passion. I must wind him.
> *Flamineo* [*aside*]: How dares this banish'd count return to Rome,
> His pardon not yet purchas'd? I have heard
> The deceas'd Duchess gave him pension,
> And that he came along from Padua
> I'th' train of the young prince. There's somewhat in't.
> Physicians, that cure poisons, still do work
> With counterpoisons.

These opposite statements of the same intent neatly balance each other, and set a pattern of tension which the scene will ironically modulate. Moreover the episode itself is offered as a kind of theatrical flourish:

> *Marcello*:   Mark this strange encounter.

Flamineo's brother Marcello, who points the prodigy for us thus, is planted to oversee events and to intervene and arrest things once the immediate effect is made.

The encounter opens in abrasive antagonism, with the two men striving to outdo each other in grotesquely hyperbolic ill-will:

> *Flamineo*:   The god of melancholy turn thy gall to poison,
> And let the stigmatic wrinkles in thy face,
> Like to the boisterous waves in a rough tide
> One still overtake another.
> *Lodovico*:   I do thank thee
> And I do wish ingeniously for thy sake
> The dog-days all year long.

Then a bizarre convergence of style brings them together, and they drift into a brotherly pact of melancholy:

> *Flamineo*:   How croaks the raven?
> Is our good Duchess dead?
> *Lodovico*:   Dead.
> *Flamineo*:   O fate!
> Misfortune comes like the crowner's business.
> Huddle upon huddle.
> *Lodovico*:   Shalt thou and I join housekeeping?
> *Flamineo*:   Yes, content.
> Let's be unsociably sociable.
> *Lodovico*:   Sit some three days together, and discourse.
> *Flamineo*:   Only with making faces;
> Lie in our clothes.
> *Lodovico*:   With faggots for our pillows.
> *Flamineo*:   And be lousy.
> *Lodovico*:   In taffeta linings; that's gentle melancholy;
> Sleep all day.
> *Flamineo*:   Yes: and like your melancholic hare
> Feed after midnight.

They don't so much come to an agreement as discover a shared temper, for no issues have been canvassed. The entry of Antonelli and Gasparo, laughing, confirms the bizarre *rapport*, binding the two malcontents together in common derision of the kind of world that reacts thus to Isabella's death — 'We are observed; see how yon couple grieve'. For them, it seems, it is this same heartless world which has kicked them around and kept them down, even set them at odds by making them creatures of the great adversaries who control the hemispheres of the play. They take themselves for fellow-victims, who have turned fellow-scourges:

Lodovico:	Precious girn, rogue,
	We'll never part.
Flamineo:	Never: till the beggary of courtiers,
	The discontent of churchmen, want of soldiers,
	And all the creatures that hang manacled,
	Worse than strappado'd, on the lowest felly
	Of Fortune's wheel be taught in our two lives
	To scorn that world which life of means deprives.

There's a good deal of skill, as well as theatrical life, in the way the broken dialogue sweeps us through this strange accord of humours.

Then quite abruptly comes news of Lodovico's pardon at the hand of the dying pope; and it produces an immediate convulsion. Lodovico reverses his attitude as suddenly as the news arrives. He laughs, turns on Flamineo's objections with blunt and mocking insults, and in a mounting flurry of slighting exchanges incites Flamineo to strike him. Marcello steps in to drag his brother off and end the episode; and the two desperadoes don't come face to face again until the final showdown.

The scene shows the liveliest sense of theatre, though we may not see what it has to do with the plot. An audience will be struck with its clear-cut movement of reversal, which turns on the abrupt shock of that unmotivated announcement. They start off hostile, draw together, and end with blows in an explosive revel of sardonic railing.

We aren't asked to take sides or adjudicate between the two men, least of all to apportion the guilt of Isabella's murder. It would seem that Webster aims to play off the adversaries in the audience's judgement, so that we don't commit ourselves to either but are forced to take a relative view of them. It is particularly hard to judge them because their motives aren't apparent. The characters don't tell us why they behave as they do; they merely follow out arbitrary attitudes and whims, and seek to uphold their will to please themselves. The pact of melancholy, so rudely reversed, seems to be based on nothing more substantial than a shared sense of general grievance. Then the attitudes they strike are comically posed, like grotesque play-acting. The moment Lodovico hears of the pardon he drops his contempt of the world altogether, and swings to the other extreme; no doubt Flamineo would have done the same had his fortune suddenly improved thus. But then the issue itself is trivial. We take it that the characters are simply determined to act out, with grotesque ferocity, the humour of the moment; they show their will at random, and impose it if they can.

There's no questioning the dexterity of the writing, or the sheer sense of the stage it shows. Yet the episode is hardly important to the plot in the end, and only marginally relevant. The insulting blow leads on to Lodovico's later butchery of Flamineo; but Francisco's gold is a wholly adequate motive for that. And if the quarrel here is supposed to prepare the later bloodshed then it is another such *ad hoc* stroke as Lodovico has to carry off when he tells us, just once in a casual afterthought, of his thwarted lust for the poisoned Isabella.

Overall the scene makes a curious impact of randomness, momentary force. Its vivid complex life comes out of nowhere, is abruptly broken off, and then sinks back into unimportance. We might think it a gimmick or a mere *coup de théâtre*. But even if there were no more to it than that, then the evidence is that it has been carefully plotted as such. We have to reckon with the force of a calculated randomness.

The scenes which open Act V are no less strikingly odd. In the midst of the preparation for the ceremonial barriers, under cover of which the plot to poison Brachiano is working up, there are some ironical broken exchanges between Brachiano's courtiers and the feigned foreigners who are plotting to murder Brachiano. A little action develops, and drifts in and out of the confused stir, between Flamineo, Marcello and the Moorish courtesan Zanche. This brisk exchange concerns the way Zanche hangs amorously about Flamineo, a pursuit which prompts him to a good deal of sceptical comment on the lascivious nature of women, delivered in a spirit of cold clinical reductiveness.

Flamineo's family now try to force Zanche away from him for the sake of the family honour, which we might think has already been too deeply compromised to be much affected by her small slight to it. Cornelia finds her with Flamineo and beats her away; Marcello kicks her. A quarrel suddenly flares up between the two brothers, abruptly transforming their previous attitudes to each other. They exchange savage words, and Flamineo leaves; Marcello draws his sword and sends it after his brother by way of challenge.

Zanche now sets herself amorously at the disguised Francisco whom she takes to be a Moor like herself, boldly protesting love and desire for him. Cornelia enters with Marcello, having heard news of a fight he is to have with some unnamed adversary. As they talk, Flamineo comes in briskly with Marcello's sword and runs Marcello through —

I have brought your weapon backe.

The quarrel itself seems trivial. Indeed the episode is elaborately arranged to let us see that while Flamineo doesn't give a damn about Zanche (or about any kind of enslavement to a woman) and seeks to shake her off, Zanche herself has no great care for Flamineo either beyond the immediate prospect of pleasure, and at once offers herself to Francisco. The issue for Flamineo is plainly not love or solicitude for Zanche, but self-will — he won't be dictated to. And the peculiar irony of the incident, carefully set up around the conflicting reactions of Cornelia, is that these are brothers. We see that the ostensible warrant of an action may matter less than a man's arbitrary and indifferent will to pursue it; he does what expresses his humour (and therefore his will) for the moment. The episode puts human attachments in a relative light when brotherly regard is so subject to whim, and love so easily transferred. But then every gesture in this scene stands in pawn to the ironies that run right through and mock the wanton will, as when Zanche offers love to the disguised Duke of Florence, the plotter who will ultimately have her killed.

Above all though it's the way the episode moves that gives it force. The sudden act of violence arrests and points the drifting casual action between which this little plot interweaves itself, coming as if at random, suddenly out of nowhere. It isn't the craftsmanship that's casual. The theatrical point of the action seems to be just this unmotivated abruptness, or convulsive spasm: not here — *here* — gone, and Marcello lies dying. Such a stroke sustains the mode of a play in which a breach between brothers raises no issues of consequence, invites no appeal to imperatives of kin. Their family tie only harshens the ironies, which are so brutally exploited in the talk of the crucifix Flamineo broke as a baby, and the quick exchange of the momentary scuffle. Shock is the effect of the event in the theatre, if only at the sheer physical impact of the explosive entry and blow, Cornelia's scream, Marcello's retching, the blood; but the shock is quickened with a kind of wit. The special quality of the scene comes from the way it combines an assault on the sensibilities with a sharp mental life, which puts this revelation of the instantaneous onset of death in a wider context of understanding, opening a prospect of arbitrary horror.

Here again we might ask how the episode is relevant to the plot. Nothing in the action turns on it. It leads to Cornelia's lament over Marcello's corpse, and the picture that passage presents of the world we live and die in; it gets Marcello himself conveniently out of the way, if that matters; it gives an extra turn of irony or so to Brachiano's poisoning which immediately follows — 'The last good deed hee did, he pardon'd murther'. Why shouldn't we write it down as a random, if pungent, theatrical *coup*?

But if these scenes are mere sensation-mongering then it's the play itself that stands in question, for they are wholly typical of the way the action moves. What makes *The White Devil* more than a disjointed sequence of theatrical effects? To attempt to meet that challenge is to seek the real power of a play which is more in the end than the sum of its oddly diverse parts. Those who feel that power may be confident of their judgement without any prior assurance of their ability to substantiate it. The proof is the single impact the play makes where it matters, in the theatre. To think of staging it is to see how much the effects are of a piece, and how far they grow out of a consistent imaginative apprehension of our human state.

The White Devil is inherently elusive not least because the speeches themselves, pungent as they are, offer us so little to grip on. To try some reading of a character or motive against the lines themselves is to see how little they actually show us of inner life. For one thing, they never offer us a coherent line of reasoning, any more than the action overall develops a consistent argument. We can find passages that seem to carry on a debate:

> Pray what means have you
> To keep me from the galleys, or the gallows?
> My father prov'd himself a gentleman,
> Sold all's land, and like a fortunate fellow,
> Died ere the money was spent. You brought me up,
> At Padua I confess, where, I protest,
> For want of means, (the university judge me,)
> I have been fain to heel my tutor's stockings
> At least seven years. Conspiring with a beard
> Made me a graduate, then to this Duke's service;
> I visited the court, where I return'd —
> More courteous, more lecherous by far,
> But not a suit the richer; and shall I,
> Having a path so open and so free
> To my preferment, still retain your milk
> In my pale forehead? No, this face of mine
> I'll arm and fortify with lusty wine
> 'Gainst shame and blushing.

Yet this is no more than the delineation of a set character, and a mode of life in the world. There's no genuine deliberation because nothing is put in question. Such principles as are invoked don't imply an order of values, which a man might test in his life.

Our most basic concern with the play is to see what the speeches actually do say, and how they work. It seems that far from building an argument they tend to put one thing by another in a kind of gnomic discontinuity, heaping up adages and likenesses:

> Oh my lord,
> The drunkard after all his lavish cups,
> Is dry, and then is sober; so at length,
> When you awake from this lascivious dream,
> Repentance then will follow; like the sting
> Plac'd in the adder's tail: wretched are princes
> When fortune blasteth but a petty flower
> Of their unwieldy crowns;

Such language works rather to distance people than to take us into a speaker's consciousness. It partly accounts for the impression we get that the characters resist our attempts to pin them down:

O gold, what a god art thou! and O man, what a devil art thou to be tempted by that cursed mineral! Yon diversivolent lawyer; mark him; knaves turn informers, as maggots turn to flies; you may catch gudgeons with either. A cardinal; — I would he would hear me, — there's nothing so holy but money will corrupt and putrify it, like victual under the line.

The violent energy of the writing doesn't simulate the life of a working mind; the lines point outward to the world, often by some relatively impersonal and public manner of reference such as proverbial lore. These speeches work above all to offer a context of reference and action, present a certain account of the world; through them the characters of the play are always offering to define the kind of world they inhabit, or the kind of world they think they know and can manipulate. The discontinuity of the movement argues that the only coherence most of them can hit on is the settled attitude of sceptical mistrust itself, a sense enforced by the steadily reductive tendency of the language and assumptions as they play upon the common motives of the world and men's actions. Webster's supposed method of commonplace composition follows out this disposition. But it vastly overdoes the case to speak of *The White Devil* as a work of imitative art like Tasso's *Aminta*, that delicate *cento* of other men's splendours marvellously rewoven into a novel texture.[3] Reweaving of that kind isn't Webster's interest. The common matter lies about here and there in nuggets, enlarging our sense of an atomized world:

> We see that undermining more prevails
> Than doth the cannon. Bear your wrongs conceal'd,
> And, patient as the tortoise, let this camel
> Stalk o'er your back unbruis'd: sleep with the lion,
> And let this brood of secure foolish mice
> Play with your nostrils; till the time be ripe
> For th'bloody audit, and the fatal gripe:
> Aim like a cunning fowler, close one eye,
> That you the better may your game espy.

Webster's borrowings in this play present themselves in random effects and sentences, all his people can offer us by way of developed thought or sustained moral purpose. They allow the characters a pungent local life without tying them down to settled principles, or at any rate without making their principles explicit. We can speak only of attitudes people strike.

The notorious ambiguity of the motives and characters of *The White Devil* comes back to the language and the way it pushes us away; we can't

---

[3] See R.W. Dent's illuminating account of the use Webster makes of other men's flowers, *John Webster's Borrowing*, Berkeley and Los Angeles, 1960. Some of Webster's critics have supposed that such borrowing amounts to plagiarism, and betrays a lack of originality.

place these people because they don't tell us about themselves. Critical readings of the play amply demonstrate the difficulties we get into if we try at all coolly to get at the real motives on which the main characters act. Webster himself seems less concerned with motives — which he takes for granted — than with conduct and its consequences, or with humours strikingly assumed. What does Brachiano amount to? How indeed do we fathom him? His language offers us no play of mind or consciousness, but only a series of impulses. We mark his love for Vittoria — 'Quite lost Flamineo'; his barbaric rejection of Isabella yet willingness to use her; his sponsoring of the murders and relish for them; his boldness, and sharpness too, in the arraignment of Vittoria; his statesmanlike courtesy in welcoming the 'foreign' visitors; his wild misery and emptiness at the last; and so on. The character is nothing more than the sum of the various scenes in which he appears, the several attitudes he strikes. The same holds for Vittoria, and we waste time as literary critics speculating about what the play itself pointedly withholds. These characters are not given to scrutinizing their own impulses; they are viewed from the outside, and Webster seems no more interested in moral discrimination than in psychological exposure. Whatever we make of *The White Devil*, it is no drama of consciousness.

What then moves the characters to action? Love and hate are the poles on which revenge plays turn, and *The White Devil* starts in an amorous enslavement. Family love gets a distinct showing here, which we need to reckon with. Hate is another matter, and this play simply doesn't allow human indifference that moral dignity. Yet what do we really see even of the sexual love which sets the plot going? Several modes of erotic life are put before us, for not only does Brachiano follow out to the ruinous end his obsession with Vittoria (whatever she really feels for him) but he loathes Isabella just because he formerly doted on her, and seems repelled by those charms which are still quite fetching enough to stir Lodovico's lust. But no episode opens the passion itself to us, and the love dialogue in Act I quite pointedly keeps our attention on other matters than mutual feeling.

The bond of kin is more poignantly expressed in the play, and to that extent seems still more cavalierly handled. Webster sets up his domestic episodes with elaborate care for their effect, which usually blends irony with pathos. These homely affections are all that stand against the callous self-will of the world, and their ineffectualness excites only our pity; indeed they emerge just in reaction to the shaping events, as Isabella's loyal response to her husband's aversion, Cornelia's mourning over Marcello and divided feelings towards his murderous brother, Giovanni's inquiries after the condition of the dead when his mother has just been poisoned. It's especially striking that the one such sentiment which leads to important action, Francisco's care for his sister, isn't displayed pathetically at all after she is poisoned but assumed, just at the moment when the scene is set up for its expression. Francisco himself brusquely brushes aside any expression of regard for his sister as an obstacle to his witty revenge:

> Remove this object,
> Out of my brain with't: what have I to do
> With tombs, or death-beds, funerals, or tears,
> That have to meditate upon revenge?

None of these pathetic attitudes is developed in itself; they are all simply displayed for an immediate stage effect, leading nowhere but always painfully vulnerable. Isabella is poisoned by the loving kiss she gives Brachiano's portrait, Cornelia torn apart by love of all three of her dissident children, Marcello stabbed unarmed by his brother over his care for their family honour. It is the victims alone who act out of unselfish concern for others; and that is what makes them victims.

Are we to see these people as expendable pawns of the policies of great men? The world the play offers us revolves round the corrupting whims of men of power, and its malcontent characters tend to see themselves as betrayed to it by their poverty. The condition of late Renaissance courts defines if it doesn't limit an action which persistently reminds us that this is what happens in such places, and with such people; this is the fate of princes as well as their parasites:

> To see what solitariness is about dying princes. As heretofore they have unpeopled towns; divorc'd friends, and made great houses unhospitable: so now O justice! where are their flatterers now? Flatterers are but the shadows of princes' bodies, the least thick cloud makes them invisible.

Yet the piece is no more a mirror for magistrates than a warning to aspiring courtiers. Nor does it play up such forms of greatness as political power, and an etiquette of honour, so much as it brings out a great man's freedom from external constraint, and the larger scope which that immunity gives to free will. If Webster had a point to make about courts and great men then he has taken care to let us see that this world of power is a special case only in its writing large of human will, more particularly, in the freedom it gives some men to do as we would.

The instability of such a world must have some bearing on the unorthodox articulation of the play. Webster seems to have conceived the work less as an organic development than as a series of set pieces. The supposed short-comings of construction themselves partly account for our sense that events and occasions simply emerge. Instead of controlling climaxes we get only a mounting succession of *coups*. Motivation seems contemptuously sketchy even when we know that the originals of Webster's characters really had behaved so, as when Monticelso nurtures such animosity towards Vittoria and Brachiano just because his nephew is Vittoria's wronged husband. Striking theatrical effects seem incidental to the thrust of the action, depending upon contrivances that get nowhere, episodes that come to nothing, characters who peter out. Why the elaborate plot between Monticelso and Francisco to get Camillo out of the way, so that Brachiano may dishonour himself publicly with Vittoria? Its pointlessness is built in since Camillo gets his neck wrung before he can even set foot outside Rome. Why the dumbshows, and the comic flummery of the conjuror and poisoning doctor? Why the culinary arrangements at papal elections? And why the election itself? What of Cornelia's curse upon Vittoria and Branchiano when she finds them together? of Monticelso's book of all the villains in Rome? of Monticelso himself after he's elected pope and dissuades Lodovico from the revenge to which he himself had earlier prompted Francisco? These scenes are effective in themselves, and they are of a piece in their variously ironic commentary on men's actions. Indeed the surprises and the ironies are so carefully plotted, so dexterously contrived to shock, that we might suspect Webster of erecting theatrical effect into a dramatic principle, and of seeking no more in his source material than a bagful of opportunities for sheer stage tricks (as Shaw thought Shakespeare did).[4] One thing these contrivances don't suggest is that the characters are in full command of their affairs, or of the outcome of the acts they will; they are all flashing around in the dark, to some little purpose or none.

If their scattered professions suggest motives which the action itself makes nothing of, that needn't impugn Webster's craftsmanship. It might show his cool concern to frustrate our rage for motives, and to keep us outside them. The *ad hoc* motivation even seems to be a condition of the peculiar power of the play in the way it exploits the sudden unexpectedness, and violent randomness of events in a world of dislocated energies. We see something of the special character of the tragedy by the inappropriateness to it of such orthodox categories of Aristotelean criticism as heroic steadfastness and tragic choice. This is scarcely a play in which a hero elects to press through with things to the end by adherence to some principle or driving design. What it shows us instead are characters who move by emergent expedients to self-regarding ends, and whose tragedy lies just in their inevitable collisions with the emergent wills of others. The singularity of this view of greatness is that in the end it allows men freedom of choice only in their response to infringements of their own will. For the paradox of the movement is the way that a sense of the inevitable pulls the very randomness into coherence.

If this is gimmickry there's a consistent method in it, and a consistent apprehension of life. One noted feature of the play is the relativeness of its

---

[4] Shaw's notices of productions of Shakespeare in *The Saturday Review* repeatedly express this view. See *Our Theatres in the Nineties*, passim.

values and attitudes, an equivocalness which is so persistently plotted that it looks like a leading principle of the construction. Nothing is ever allowed to stand absolutely, or unquestioned. Vittoria's accusers are themselves viciously tainted. Monticelso's catalogue of criminals was compiled to a dubious end and is used to a corrupt one. Francisco puts the right pious objections to Monticelso's promptings to revenge but discloses his own sinister designs the moment Monticelso goes.

Every moral posture is undermined, if not in our regard then in the eyes of the characters themselves. At Monticelso's dreadful admonition Lodovico forswears his revenge, but is immediately pulled back to it again with double resolve by the arrival of Francisco's gold, sent as from Monticelso:

> Why now 'tis come about. He rail'd upon me;
> And yet these crowns were told out and laid ready,
> Before he knew my voyage. O the art,
> The modest form of greatness! that do sit
> Like brides at wedding dinners, with their looks turn'd
> From the least wanton jests, their puling stomach
> Sick of the modesty, when their thoughts are loose,
> Even acting of those hot and lustful sports
> Are to ensue about midnight: such his cunning!
> He sounds my depth thus with a golden plummet;
> I am doubly arm'd now. Now to th'act of blood;

Above all there's the sequence of violence that clinches the action, which enacts no effective morality but unfolds, one behind the other, a series of relative gains. Brachiano poisons Isabella, and Francisco has him poisoned; Flamineo goes to kill Vittoria and Zanche, who then think they have killed him; Flamineo, Vittoria and Zanche are butchered by Lodovico and his crew, criminal assassins in the pay of Francisco, who are shot down by the guards under Francisco's young nephew Giovanni; Francisco himself is roundly condemned as a murderer by Giovanni. Is it the condemnation that's in question here, or is revenge itself wrong? Or who is wronged and who justified in this action? And if we think to take Giovanni himself for a juvenile Fortinbras, who will restore right order, then we recall that his brave innocence has already been undermined by Flamineo's pointed delineation of the selfseekers great men inevitably grow to be when they feel their power secure. In the end it is only the passive victims who have an unequivocal claim on our esteem.

If relativeness is one principle of the arrangement, then another seems to be shock. The very succession of scenes has a startling discontinuity which the theatre ought to bring up. Repeatedly a situation develops in which easy assurance is abruptly shattered by sudden violent action. Not only the main events but quite incidental effects work in this way, such as Cornelia's interruption of the love dialogue in Act I, and the brusque cataclysmic announcement of Monticelso's election to the papacy, and the turnabout shifts of the several quarrels. These sudden reversals, violent swings from extreme to opposite extreme, give the unstable world of the play its most alarming aspect.

The long final episode is a virtuoso exercise in ironic undercutting which opens when Flamineo's assault on the women is so startlingly countered by their turn on him and his feigned death, and then wittily carried off after all by his confounding of their triumph, as well as our expectation, when he rises so blandly:

> O cunning devils! now I have try'd your love,
> And doubled all your reaches. I am not wounded:
> The pistols held no bullets: 'Twas a plot
> To prove your kindness to me;

The delayed horror of the knifings is itself shatteringly outgone as the guards rush in to shoot down the murderers in their turn. There's an accelerating tempo of incident and riposte, a mounting series of assaults on our nerves and senses, the discomforting exhilaration of ironic twist upon twist in the unresolved mutations of this play.

Yet the scene which most shocks us with an ironic reversal of fortunes is the one that presents Brachiano's dying and death, V, iii. Webster seizes his chance of a real theatrical *tour de force* such as his sources don't prescribe for, the enactment of a man's moral disintegration by degrees as he slowly dies of poison. In an action that continually asks the spectator to keep opposite extremes in view together the supreme irony is the transformation of life itself into the state of not being, a cataclysm which makes nonsense of our erstwhile state.

The fearful world of this vision presents itself in theatrical terms, and we must encounter it imaginatively there. The action gradually resolves out of the scattered preliminaries for the tournament, with the preparations for the murder, the conspiratorial side-mutterings and embracings, the sense of wire-taut peril more finely drawn with every fresh move (the plotting has an odd kinship with Jonson's *Alchemist*). Lodovico's sprinkling the beaver with poison comes as a casual parenthesis in the sequel of Marcello's murder, though it is pointed out by Francisco's melodramatically sinister aside — 'He calls for his destruction.' Then out of the random confusion of the barriers there's the Oedipus-like entry itself, a sudden eruption of shrieking agony, 'An armourer! Ud's death, an armourer!', that at once transforms the scene into one of those images of hysterical disorientation which Webster felt with such force and controlled so brilliantly. The effect is sustained in this mood of panic, even extended over an arbitrary stage-exit; so that we get the further shock of the rapid degeneration at the re-entry — 'There's death in's face already' — as well as the multiple ironies of Flamineo's conversation with the disguised Francisco about the deaths of great men:

O speak well of the Duke.

It is characteristic of the play to shift the moral perspective so startlingly as the avenger sees his own condition in the fate of his victim, and to leave us uncertain whether he means it or is just acting out his role.

An ironic reversal is implicit in the fearsome vision of misery caught so vividly in this staging of a lonely death amid a collapsing world. In the coming and going of physicians and holy men, the howling of women off-stage, the dying man's delirious visions of horror, the muttered gibes of courtiers which are already emboldening into open detraction, we apprehend the total overthrow of everything that gave sense to the man's life. There's little to console us here; and the deathbed scene itself enacts a grotesque parody of pious consolation with its picture of the last rites thus turned into a fiendish mockery of the dying man and of death, a farce which keeps before him as he dies the fearful indignity of his own dissolution, and the absurdity it makes of his existence. Brachiano's last shriek of 'Vittoria! Vittoria!' terrifies more than all, bringing it home to us that he has grasped this ultimate vision of horror, his secular hell and final human degradation. The clinching irony comes pat:

Lodovico:	My lords he's dead.
Omnes:	Rest to his soul.

It is a piety which Vittoria's aside savagely places — 'O me! this place is hell!'

If such an account of Webster's art has force then it is clear that *The White Devil* isn't a play of the order of *The Spanish Tragedy* or *The Revenger's Tragedy*, where the moral alignment follows the obligation of revenge and allows us to talk of heroes, Machiavellian villains, avenging justice, and the like. Nor has it anything in common with such a work as *Hamlet*, whose action develops moral outrage into a sifting of human nature and existence to which every speech indispensably contributes. The counterpointing of scenes in *Troilus and Cressida* and *Henry IV* may be the nearest thing Shakespeare affords to the relativism of *The White Devil*; but Webster's play has little in common with a movement which allows as much scope to the heart's drastic gestures as to the world that keeps giving them the lie. Webster's far more limited sense of human possibility allows no such insights as Troilus, or Hector or old Shallow incarnate, and consequently no such effective moral scourges as Thersites and Falstaff. Donne's work makes a closer comparison. The *Metempsychosis*, written some years before *The White Devil*, is an exuberant attempt to carry through a thoroughgoing sceptical relativism in an account of the economy of fallen nature. But its vision of the civic jungle has, and assumes, an assured purposefulness that is quite missing from Webster's play; and we simply can't take the action of *The White Devil* for a demonstration of man's rapacity, or the relativeness of our judgements in respect of absolute truth. Even Donne's *Anniversaries*, which are exactly contemporary with this play and share its apprehension of a collapsing civil order, offer an absolute refuge to the mind from the spreading ruin:

> The world is but a carcase; thou art fed
> By it, but as a worm, that carcase bred;
> And why shouldst thou, poor worm, consider more,
> When this world will grow better than before,
> Than those thy fellow worms do think upon
> That carcase's last resurrection.
> Forget this world, and scarce think of it so,
> As of cold clothes, cast off a year ago.
> To be thus stupid is alacrity;
> Men thus lethargic have best memory.
> Look upward; that's towards her, whose happy state
> We now lament not, but congratulate.

The Second Anniversary, 55–66

Donne's is a fearful world, but we know just where we stand in it. Webster's world is desperate because that is just what no one who inhabits it can know.

We must ask what its inhabitants make of their world, and what they don't or can't make of it. For all the furniture of counter-reforming zeal, inquisitions of moral included, the characters themselves don't effectively admit any metaphysical dimension in their lives at all. There's only the here and now, which death simple negates:

> On pain of death, let no man name death to me,
> It is a word infinitely terrible.

Turn this horror from me:

What then do they live by? Nothing in the play warrants our speaking of 'a world of evil', or even of anything so resolved as Machiavellism. Only the successful working of Francisco's plot suggests that people's actions aren't all blind self-will and momentary expediency, mocked by ironic circumstance. Even Francisco's devious control is pointedly casual, and limited, so that however Webster meant it we see him not as a Machiavellian but simply as the least vulnerable performer in a game of pride, a self-justifying avenger whose justice is itself wholly in question. The absence of a central moral focus makes it meaningless to place him in relation to Brachiano, or Vittoria, or Flamineo, for all their impulses present themselves as arbitrary attitudes and choices. If we look for settled motives or principles we find only local values, wifely loyalty, motherly love, family solicitude, the motions of the victim in the world of this play. But the submissive virtues themselves aren't so much coldly exploited as simply over-vulnerable in a world where men are seeking to impose their wills at random, moving dimly round each other like self-enclosed atoms whose only check is the reaction they provoke in others.

Whether designedly or not the action moves to fix our minds on the kind of world these people face up to so confidently, with its inherent relativeness, ironic reversals and persistent unsettling of assurances, annihilating shocks and debacles. The most frightful thing about it is its denial of human dignity. This does seem pointed. We hear much of the politic statesmanship of both Brachiano and Francisco but we don't for a moment see them engaged in some public concern beyond their own self-willed ends, never meet them in any aspect that might seem to give their lives stature, point, settled sense. What we do understand is that syco-phancy is the due of power, and the moment power is lost, as in death, then derisive indifference is all that naked humanity can claim. The speeches themselves, which offer us so little of the speaker, continually tell us about the world he apprehends. They point to a condition of petty corruptness in which humanity is prey, but prey less to calculated evil than to man's own animal status, squalid and debasing cankers, poisons, decay, maggots, wolves:

> They are first
> Sweetmeats which rot the eater: in man's nostril
> Poison'd perfumes. They are coz'ning alchemy,
> Shipwrecks in calmest weather! What are whores?

If the tone and texture of discourse steadily hold life cheap, so do most of the characters in their actions, ironically enough when they set such store by their own lives:

> Excellent, then she's dead, —

The chilling disparity between the value people put upon the lives of others and their concern for their own lives, the monstrosity of their affront to human kind, comes out most starkly in the circumstances of Brachiano's death. Hamlet's graveyard democracy of dust is a benign vision compared to this grim levelling of men's lives and impostures in the degradation of dying. Any man alive may feel himself superior to a dying prince and feed his pride that he has won the game. If the reduction of life to absurdity makes nonsense of tragic choice, then it also negates tragic heroism. Webster offers us an unheroic tragedy which moves by expediency, protagonists who act on no other principle than the gratifica-tion of pride and will. The tragic attitude stands, if at all, in the teeth of men's self-concern. Vittoria faces up to her death so bravely only when she sees that she has no choice. Until then she wriggles, craftily and deviously with shameless unheroism, to evade Flamineo's threats; and

even when the assassins rush in she offers herself to them or their master
to save her skin:

> O your gentle pity!
> I have seen a blackbird that would sooner fly
> To a man's bosom, than to stay the gripe
> Of the fierce sparrow-hawk.

The bizarre irony of her clutching now at Francisco's feigned offer of
love to confirm her power over men, pointedly lets us see that we aren't
here dealing with a Cleopatra or a Beatrice Cenci. The passing self-
disclosure scarcely holds Vittoria up to our contempt, but it does put her
concern with her own skin in a light of grim farce.

Elements of farce intermittently burlesque the traffic of lust and blood,
and not only because so much of it is mediated to us by sceptical malcontents. Repeatedly episodes assume aspects that bring into derision the
moral and human issues, as do Brachiano's lovemaking, the gulling of
Camillo, the dumb-show murders and the passages with the poisoning
doctor, the arraignment of Vittoria, Brachiano's deathbed, the final kill-
ings. But ironic mockery is itself a moral posture in this play. Brachiano
mocks Monticelso; the diversivolent lawyer, grotesquely parodying the
law, makes a charade of the inquisition of morals before it starts;
Francisco's concern with the wit of his revenge marks a desire to make
much of his adversaries; Vittoria and Zanche turn to easy mockery of
Flamineo when they think they have him down; he turns the mock
against them when he rises. The urge to belittle their fellows shows them
uneasily aware how suddenly they themselves may be reduced to
grotesque objects of derision:

> O thou cursed antipathy to nature! Look his eye's bloodshed like a needle a
> chirurgeon stitcheth a wound with. Let me embrace thee toad, and love thee,
> O thou abominable loathsome gargarism, that will fetch up lungs, lights,
> heart, and liver by scruples.

For there is something inherently farcical both in the view that characters
take to each other, and in the playwright's attitude to all of them. We see
them struggling to control their world by deriding it, while he persistently betrays their assurance with his ironies. Brachiano jests coarsely
with Flamineo and the poisoner over the dumb-show murders, and
himself dies horribly of poison; Flamineo acts out a grotesque parody of
facing death, and of death itself, to heighten the wit of his gulling of
Vittoria and Zanche, and is at once confronted with the actuality.

In a world where people respect each other so little our pity finds no
assurance. The characters rarely claim as much as our respect. For most
of its course the play seems arranged to resist our sympathies, opposing

intolerance and deviousness on the one hand with effrontery and head-strong self-will on the other, qualities which are striking enough but not especially admirable. If we feel that it does nonetheless allow people a kind of grandeur in the end it can only be the final episode which sublimes their scattered powers, and at last offers us something in human nature to esteem. All the play allows us for our unreserved respect is the way that the three meet their deaths when they see that they have to; and they invite our approval themselves by their fine acknowledgement of each other's defiant pride:

Gasparo:	Are you so brave?
Vittoria:	Yes I shall welcome death
	As princes do some great ambassadors;
	I'll meet thy weapon half way.

Flamineo:	Th' art a noble sister,
	I love thee now; if woman do breed man
	She ought to teach him manhood. Fare thee well.

Circumstances are arranged so that we see them caught up in play-acting, half menacing, half absurd, right up to the moment when they recognize that there's no evading death. From then on we are concerned only with what comes out of this narrowing down of their wills on their inevitable undoing.

The catastrophe offers us two drawn-out enactments of dying which seem to set each other off, so that we try the deaths of Vittoria and Flamineo against the death of Brachiano. The truly singular feature of the management of the plot is the way that everything is brought back to the frontier between life and death:

Lodovico:	What does think on?
Flamineo:	Nothing; of nothing: leave thy idle questions;
	I am i'th'way to study a long silence
	To prate were idle; I remember nothing.

The violent abruptness of the turn of fortunes which is so chillingly realized in Brachiano's screaming metamorphosis from vigour to dying torment, in the entry of the murderers to Vittoria and the others, in the moment of the dagger-thrust, throws back on all the passions of the play to show the utter precariousness of our affairs. The frenzied energy the characters display expresses for us the lurking apprehension of people who live wholly for this world, in an action that never remotely proposes a surer way of making sense of our lives. The power of Brachiano's death scene is that it so devastatingly shows us all that frenzy of will and pride coming to senseless nothing. The death it offers is the ultimate horror, which mocks our lives and dignity by reducing them to meaninglessness before we even cease to be aware.

It is the intimate apprehension of ruin within the sexual impulse itself that distinguishes this play's rendering of love, and gives the action its peculiar metaphysical substance. Donne's sardonic dismissal of love, and Vendice's shuddering fascination with his mistress's skull, precisely catch the mode:

> And now methinks I could e'en chide myself . . .
> For doting on her beauty, though her death
> Shall be revenged after no common action.
> Does the silkworm expend her yellow labours
> For thee? For thee does she undo herself?
> Are lordships sold to maintain ladyships,
> For the poor benefit of a bewildering minute?
> Why does yon fellow falsify highways,
> And put his life between the judge's lips
> To refine such a thing . . .?
>
> *The Revenger's Tragedy*, III, iv, 68–77

We might count it more than bizarre coincidence that the same year, 1612, saw the appearance of works by Donne and by Webster which so persistently and radically put our worldly lusts in pawn to change and death, and leave love no hold upon the world at all:

> what essential joy canst thou expect
> Here upon earth? what permanent effect
> Of transitory causes? Dost thou love
> Beauty? . . .
> Poor cozened cozener, that she, and that thou,
> Which did begin to love, are neither now;
> You are both fluid, changed since yesterday;
> Next day repairs, (but ill) last day's decay.
>
> Donne, *The Second Anniversary*, 387–94

The deaths of Vittoria and Flamineo might have offered no less belittling a prospect of horror. Webster sets up his dramatic inquisition as rigorously as for Brachiano, holding the scene there frame by frame right up to the blow, and then beyond it, to take the victims' responses at each step:

> I do not look
> Who went before, nor who shall follow me;
> No, at myself I will begin and end.
> *While we look up to heaven we confound*
> *Knowledge with knowledge. O I am in a mist.*

The sheer blindness of self-assertive will makes this tragedy a study of comportment in extremities which men aren't capable of avoiding. It is here that the deaths of Vittoria and Flamineo and Zanche pull the whole action into perspective, suggesting a possible human sublimity for the first time, where the earlier deaths only negated life and dignity. This shared confrontation of death (shared with the assassins too, in the end) gives us the one stable point of reference the play affords, an absolute human attitude which is wholly worthy of admiration and love and has nothing in it of pathetic self-delusion. Only here, when it is thus narrowly constrained and concentrated, do we see human will take on an ennobling dignity and reach out in true fellow feeling; and here, also, intelligence finds some better employment than in preying on its own humanity. For the only heroism the play allows is the refusal to capitulate in the face of inevitable death, when there is nothing to lose, or gain, or hold on to at all save self-respect and pride. They are exalted by their self-conceit, which nothing further can impugn:

> Let no harsh flattering bells resound my knell,
> Strike thunder, and strike loud to my farewell.

Lodovico, when his turn comes, sustains a heroic pride which defies his captor's invocation of heavenly justice:

> I do glory yet
> That I can call this act mine own. For my part,
> The rack, the gallows, and the torturing wheel
> Shall be but sound sleeps to me; here's my rest:
> *I limb'd this night-piece and it was my best.*

A proud self-will is the condition of this limited grandeur, as it is the agent of the moral wilderness love makes in the play. Love itself offers nothing here to live by; and men's capacity to make their wills prevail gives their lives a sense only in their unwillingness to let even death defeat them. The prospect of the world Webster holds out to us may be bleak, even desperate, but it isn't in the end mean.

8

Manhood Recovered

> What hate could hurt our bodies like our love?
>
> Donne, *To the Countess of Bedford*, 'To have written then', 53

The Samson of *Judges* xiii–xvi presents an extraordinary picture of self-reliant, not to say self-willed masculinity. Here is a champion so confident in his manhood that he shows zest in exercises of it which seem to put it at risk, casually scourging the oppressors of his nation, openly swaggering into the tyrants' stronghold to enjoy their women, relishing his virile prowess the more because he knows that every woman he takes only seeks her chance to rob him of his strength, and betray him to the lurking ambush of those who would have him dead. *Judges* unfolds a mounting series of risks, which culminates in the posing of the riddle and his perilous conduct of the interrogations and responses it begets, but then takes him just too far in his hubris so that he himself prompts the right answer. To his own vast astonishment he suddenly finds himself impotent, taken, blinded, enslaved. He comes before us as the very type of the fallen hero of romance, who is frustrated of his heroic end by a woman because he has let himself become the slave of his own senses:

> To follow nothing but the eye in the choice of his wife, was a lust unworthy of a Nazarite: this is to make the sense not a counsellor but a tyrant. . . . I cannot wonder more at Samson's strength than his weakness. He, that began to cast away his love upon a wife of the Philistines, goes on to mispend himself upon the harlots of the Philistines: he did not so much overcome the men, as the women overcame him. His affections blinded him first, ere the Philistines could do it: would he else, after the effusion of so much of their blood, have suffered his lust to carry him within their walls, as one that cared more for his pleasure than his life? O strange debauchedness and presumption of a Nazarite! I would have looked to have seen him betake himself to his stronger rock than that of Etam, and, by his austere devotion, to seek protection of Him of whom he received strength: but now, as if he had forgotten his consecration, I find him turned Philistine for his bed, and of a Nazarite scarce a man. In vain

doth he nourish his hair, while he feeds these passions . . . . Samson's victories have subdued him, and have made him first a slave to lewd desires, and then to the Philistines. . . .[1]

That is how Rembrandt depicts him, in an astonishing series of paintings and drawings which span the artist's career;[2] and it is decidedly how Goethe took his attachment to Dalila:

A thoroughly bestial passion of a hero supreme in strength and gifted by God for the most despicable wretch on the face of the earth; this devouring lust, which drives him back to her over again, even though he knows by her repeated treachery the danger he runs every time; this lust springing from the danger itself. . . .[3]

Whether we see him as an enervate sensualist, or as romantic self-victim of desire, Samson defines a predicament of sexual life. He might have made fit fellow to Hercules and Antony on that fatal gate of gold at the entrance to Armida's garden:

Mirasi qui fra le meonie ancelle
favoleggiar con la conocchia Alcide.
Se l'inferno espugnò, resse le stelle,
or torce il fuso; Amor sel guarda, e ride.
Mirasi Iole con la destra imbelle
per ischerno trattar l'armi omicide;
e 'n dosso ha il cuoio del leon, che sembra
ruvido troppo a sì tenere membra.

D'in contra è un mare; e di canuto flutto
vedi spumanti i suoi cerulei campi.
Vedi nel mezzo un doppio ordine instrutto
di navi e d'arme, e uscir da l'arme i lampi.
D'oro fiammeggia l'onda; e par che tutto
d'incendio marzïal Leucate avvampi.
Quinci Augusto i Romani, Antonio quindi
trae l'Oriente, Egizii, Arabi ed Indi.

Svelte notar le Cicladi diresti
per l'onde, e i monti co i gran monti urtarsi.
l'impeto è tanto, onde quei vanno e questi

---

[1] Joseph Hall, *Contemplations on the Historical Passages of the Holy Scriptures* (1612–26), Edinburgh, 1837, pp. 127b, 134a.

[2] Some nine drawings and five paintings depict scenes of Samson's life, and centre on the affair with Dalila. They date from 1628 to 1656; though the major paintings seem to have been done in 1635/6.

[3] Letter to C.F. Zelter, 19 May 1812.

co' legni torreggianti ad incontrarsi.
Già volâr faci e dardi, e già funesti
sono di nova strage i mari sparsi.
Ecco (né punto ancor la pugna inchina)
ecco fuggir la barbara reina.

E fugge Antonio; e lasciar può la speme
de l'imperio del mondo, ov'egli aspira.
Non fugge no, non teme il fier, non teme;
ma segue lei che fugge e seco il tira.
Vedresti lui, simil ad uom che freme
d'amore a un tempo e di vergogna e d'ira,
mirar alternamente or la crudele
pugna ch'è in dubbio, or le fuggenti vele.

Ne le latebre poi del Nilo accolto
attender par in grembo a lei la morte;
e nel piacer d'un bel leggiadro vólto
sembra che il duro fato egli conforte.

Tasso, *La Gerusalemme Liberata* xvi, 3–7

[Here you might see Alcides among the Maeonian serving-maids, gossiping over the distaff. Though he had stormed hell, controlled the stars, now he turns the spindle; Love looks on at him and laughs. You might see Iole mockingly wield his murderous weapons with her weak right arm; and on her back she wears the lionskin, which seems too rough for so soft a body.

On the other side is a sea; and you see its blue fields foam with white surges. You see in the midst of it ships and arms drawn up in double rank, and the guns flashing. The waves flame with gold; and it seems as if Leucothea herself bursts into martial conflagration. Here Augustus marshals the Romans, there Antony draws together the East, Egyptians, Arabs and Indians.

You might say that the Cyclades have been plucked up to swim through the waves, and that mountains crash against great mountains, so great is the impetus with which this navy and that rush together to encounter each other with towering timbers. Already torches and darts fly; and already the seas are devastatingly spread with slaughter. Here — while the battle still rages at its height — here the pagan queen takes to flight.

And Antony flees; and he chooses to abandon the hope of ruling the world, to which he aspires. No, no, he doesn't flee, he doesn't fear the broil, it isn't fear; but he follows her who flees and draws him with her. You may see him, like a man who at one and the same moment quivers with love and with shame and rage, looking alternately now to the fierce fight which stands in doubt, now to the fleeing sail.

Then sheltered in the recesses of the Nile he seems to wait in her lap for death; and in the pleasure of a fair comely face it appears that he consoles himself against his hard fate.]

But if Samson is an exemplary faller, he is a no less exemplary recoverer. The bizarre paradox is that this Old Testament tearaway, whose abiding virtue seems to be that he drinks only purest water, figures in Christian exegesis as a third Adam, the type of the regenerate man and even a formal type of Christ. Samson came to mean so much to the exegetes simply because he rises from the depths as by miracle to triumph over himself, vindicating and fulfilling himself like a godly Antony in the apparent ruin of his death:

> Samson abides to be tied by his own countrymen, that he may have the glory of freeing himself victoriously. Even so, O Saviour! our better Nazarite! thou which couldst have called to thy Father, and have had twelve legions of angels for thy rescue, wouldst be bound voluntarily, that thou mightest triumph. . . .

> Thus didst thou, O blessed Saviour, when thou wert fastened to the cross, when thou layest bound in the grave with the cords of death — thus didst thou miraculously raise up thyself, vanquish thine enemies, and lead captivity captive! . . .

> It is no marvel, if he were thus admirably strong and victorious, whose bodily strength God meant to make a type of the spiritual power of Christ.[4]

There's a fruitful tension in the Christian view that Samson was a great sinner yet a great champion of God; and the rich dramatic promise of the material itself was much exploited in Europe from the fifteenth century to the seventeenth century. We know of upwards of 20 European plays about Samson in that period.[5] A sense of possibility unfulfilled may account for the disappointment many readers seem to feel when they turn from the imaginative grandeur of *Paradise Lost* to the low-spirited bleakness of the opening of *Samson Agonistes*.

Samson can't be said to have recovered its reputation in the general revival of interest in Milton, if only because it has never had much reputation to recover. For Milton's last masterpiece the deadliest of literary fates has been reserved, to be sadly dismissed by successive generations of critics and mugged up by successive generations of examination candidates, almost as if the one affliction followed from the other. Johnson found the work still more defective as a drama than he had found *Comus*:

> . . . it is only by a blind confidence in the reputation of Milton that a drama can be praised in which the intermediate parts have neither cause nor

[4] Hall, *op. cit.* p. 133a–b.
[5] They are listed in F.M. Krause, *Milton's Samson and the Christian Tradition*, Princeton, 1949, pp. 85–7.

consequence, neither hasten nor retard the catastrophe . . . it wants that power of attracting the attention which a well-connected plan produces.[6]

Mark Pattison, no detractor of Milton, wrote more in sorrow than in censure when he put the case against *Samson Agonistes* which has since become standard:

> It must be felt that as a composition the drama is languid, nerveless, occasionally halting, never brilliant . . . . If this drama were composed in 1667, it would be the author's last poetical effort, and the natural explanation would then be that his power over languages was failing. The power of metaphor, i.e. of indirect expression, is, according to Aristotle, the characteristic of genius . . . . It is evident that this intense action of the presentative faculty is no longer at the disposal of the writer of *Samson*. . . . The simplicity of *Samson Agonistes* is a flagging of the forces, a drying up of the rich sources from which once flowed the golden stream of suggestive phrase which makes *Paradise Lost* a unique monument of the English language.[7]

These are reasonable opinions which one might dissent from and pass on. F.R. Leavis, however, challenges an admirer of the work more directly:

> How many cultivated adults could honestly swear that they had ever read it through with enjoyment?[8]

Well, some of us may care to own up, even if it means confessing ourselves something short of cultivated adulthood by Dr Leavis's standards. But surely there are adult readers enough who do enjoy *Samson Agonistes*, and can't accept an account of it which speaks of its 'factitious, mechanical life' and 'rhythmic deadness'. Their experience of the work might be better described by de Quincey's account of rhetoric.

> . . . an exhibition which presupposes a state of tense exertion on the part of auditor and performer.[9]

They might justly add that Milton's dramatic poem is a thoroughly purposeful exhibition, which many people have found not only imaginatively exciting but deeply satisfying in the resolved account of human experience it yields. So possibly the quarrel lies between those who find themselves unable to respond to a work of art as consciously wrought as

---

[6] *John Milton*, in *Lives of the English Poets*, ed. G. Birkbeck Hill, Oxford 1905, I, p. 189.

[7] *English Men of Letters: Milton*, (1879), 1896, p. 197.

[8] *Revaluation, Tradition and Development in English Poetry*, London 1962, p. 67.

[9] *Works*, ed. D. Masson, Edinburgh 1889–90, x, p. 35.

Samson Agonistes, and those who find such conscious artistry exhilarating. For there can be no doubt that *Samson Agonistes* is calculated down to the intimate detail in terms of the precise effect and end proposed for the whole.

Plainly Milton was limited by the end he proposed. He denied himself the opportunity to dramatize directly any of the material he found in his sacred source, Judges xiii–xvi, though those chapters are singularly rich in dramatic incident and situation. Still more cramping, he seems to have refused to allow himself a concern with human motives for their own sake. If you turn back to Judges from *Samson* you may well find Milton's choice of events, and his arrangement of them, very curious. It's not difficult to imagine what Shakespeare might have made of such narrative material, which would so readily lend itself to the kind of epic treatment he gave to the history of Antony and Cleopatra, and afford no less apt a study in human self-squandering and self-realization. Milton cuts off these possibilities at once by opening his play at such a late moment in Samson's career, and allowing himself only the last crowded hours of his protagonist's life to work upon, a choice which also commits him to launching the action with Samson's inconsolable self-reproaches rather than with some more stirring motive. Yet, having discarded so much promising material from the Judges narrative he proceeds to inflate a quite minor figure in that story, Manoah, and to supply another character who doesn't appear in it at all, the Philistian champion Harapha. Then he forgoes the interest of a narrative plot by arranging his play as a series of parallel episodes linked by choruses, in which characters keep going back in retrospect over the events of Samson's career.

The Old Testament story is thus oddly recast in a Greek dramatic form, or at least, in the version of classical form which had been popular in Italy at the time of Milton's visits some 30 years before he wrote this play.[10] Readers brought up on Shakespeare may well feel that so inherently un-Shakespearean an approach to an epic story must be misguided in itself, but they should reflect that the formal arrangement of a plot is itself a function of the artist's vision and aim. Milton's aim here isn't as remote as it seems. Ibsen has made us familiar with plots which move forward through people's repeated attempts to reappraise their past, so as to expiate or exorcize it. More recently we have had the theatre of Piscator and Brecht, which forbids us to indulge our humane interest in character for its own sake and offers us instead the hard objective reality of an embodied argument:

> . . . all the responses of the characters, whether inner or outer, are related to the theme of the play as tactics primarily, rather than as mental attributes.[11]

[10] See G. L. Finney, *Chorus in Samson Agonistes*, *PMLA*, LXIII, 1943, pp. 649–664.
[11] M. Gorelik, *New Theatres for Old*, London 1947, p. 418.

I take this to mean that the play aims to objectify a truth which lies beyond the wills or characters of particular people, whose responses are important just as far as they help to bring it out. Certainly *Samson Agonistes* seems to be a dialectical play in the sense that clashes of opposite attitudes compose its action, and develop a running argument upon whose outcome all the outside events depend. Its characters are important to us not so much because we feel for their human sufferings as because they make us recognize something about people, about ourselves, and about the creation we live in. They are types, rather than individuals.

Milton's commentators sometimes give us the impression that even professional Miltonists have long abandoned *Samson* entirely to the luckless school pupils who still find it set for their Advanced Level examination. Yet the work makes admirers of those very pupils; and I believe it merits the attention of all serious readers. In the first place its subject is important, or Milton makes it so. Adam–Christ–Samson: *Paradise Lost, Paradise Regained, Samson Agonistes*. This may seem a strange transformation of the Old Testament strong man, that creature of impulse, lust and blood who ultimately did something to redeem a headstrong life by bringing the roof down on his country's enemies, and perishing with them. But in Christian tradition Samson meant much more than that, and in fact he supplies a necessary term to the account of man's standing. Like Spenser's Red Cross Knight he becomes the type of frail humanity, the would-be just man who has inevitably fallen, and whose struggles to recover are limed by the consciousness of his sin:

> Thus his immoderate affections toward a wicked woman caused him to lose Gods excellent gifts, and become slave unto them, whom he should have ruled.[12]

Penitent, and restored to physical strength, he still has to recover enough confidence in his own deserving to save him from despair in further trials, and to justify his continuing the struggle at all. Yet his actions execute God's secret will even when they appear most arbitrary: 'Though his parents did justly reprove him yet it appeareth that this was the secret work of the Lord' is the Geneva Bible's gloss on the marriage at Timnah.

Milton had given his account of our fall from the first state of innocent love, and of Christ's redeeming care for us. What remained for him to explore is the most urgent human predicament of all, the unregenerate condition of us human beings in a creation already lapsed. That he picked on so notorious a sinner as Samson, who lived long before Christ's coming and prefigured Christ by his resurgence, suggests that he was concerned with what we may do unaided to recover ourselves, or perhaps

---

[12] Geneva Bible, gloss on Judges, xvi, 17.

with what we must do for ourselves before Christ's blood and God's grace may avail us. He could scarcely have been concerned here with redemptive love. The love which looms large in the Judges story is just the debilitating sensual affection that all but unfits God's champion for his elected duty. In choosing Samson for his emblem of moral life in the fallen world Milton allowed humane compassion no saving scope.

In a lapsed creation we will certainly fall. Samson enacts the process of moral regeneration after inevitable default. True his prescribed error is peculiar to himself, but Milton had the authority of the Fathers for generalizing it and didn't need to go beyond the traditional understanding such as we might find in a popular gloss on the scriptures. In Samson we see a typical example of the way a due pride degenerates into undue self-conceit, and that into a self-indulgent laxity which soon causes a man to betray God's trust. Samson's manhood undoes itself when sense brings him down and so abjectly effeminates him. In the fallen world even God's champion is easily vulnerable to the perversion and debasement of sense which Adam observed from the high mount, and to the self-tormenting remorse that follows. The extreme degradation of the hero at the opening of the play is comment enough on a pride in one's manhood which blinds one to its origin; and it is the more striking here just because Samson had counted himself elect of God:

> Thus by Gods just judgements they are made slaves to infidels which neglect their vocation, in defending the faithful.[13]

Yet Samson's blindness is more than an appropriate humbling of his pride:

> It is better for Samson to be blind in prison, than to abuse his eyes in Sorek: yea, I may safely say, he was more blind when he saw licentiously, than now that he sees not; he was a greater slave when he served his affections, than now in grinding for the Philistines. The loss of his eyes shows him his sin; neither could he see how ill he had done, till he saw not.[14]

Milton plays off Samson's physical blindness against the moral blindness around him so that the action of the play repeatedly puts a question to us: Who is really blind here? At the opening Samson has lost his moral vision as well as his eyes. He is in the state of desolation which devotional writers often speak of as an inner darkness, whose particular anguish is brought on by a sense that God has irrevocably withdrawn from us in just punishment of our transgressions:

---

[13] Geneva Bible, gloss on Judges, xvi, 25.
[14] J. Hall, op. cit. p. 136a.

Not for the losse of his haire, but for the contempt of the ordinance of God, which was the cause that God departed from him.[15]

Milton shows him, in fact, still in the grip of error. He has just such a wrong understanding of his own condition as nearly undoes the Red Cross Knight in the Cave of Despair, and finally cuts Faustus off from salvation in his last agony. In effect, his full recognition of one error has landed him in another; manly pride has given way to a hopelessness not far short of despair.

Milton's Samson isn't really the Old Testament wild man at all. He is much more like Spenser's Red Cross Knight, a just and temperate man, God's elect minister at that, who has transgressed once and now thinks the worse of himself just because he is still righteous. But his case raises issues that go beyond his unfulfilled vocation. Where is the justice, let alone providence, in a creation which lets God's sworn enemies triumph so completely over his champion!. *Quare via impiorum prosperatur?* Suppose that our universe is, after all, indifferent to our fate, or wayward, or actually hostile to goodness. Samson's fortunes, as Boethius's, invite him and us to call God in question. Does God provide for his people? Is he the one just and true God? Can we be sure there is a God at all? Alongside such questions the political issue the play poses seems small beer, that is, whether a man can be more free in heroic imprisonment than in pusillanimous liberty; but it really comes back to the same thing, for unless we live in a universe where justice has meaning we might as well settle for our own ease, and forget the question of right and wrong. In its scope, at least, *Samson Agonistes* is not minor work.

Milton has arranged his action so that it continually raises these questions. Each of Samson's three main confrontations, with Manoah, Dalila, and Harapha, brings him to a fresh decision and sets the ensuing action upon a different course. These episodes are quite sharply defined, and they complement each other. Manoah presents Samson with that cruellest emblem of his mortality, the contrast between his former self and what he is now. Dalila puts his past more starkly before him, re-enacting the fatal temptation and unwittingly trying his penitence. Harapha simply permits him the ease of uncomplicated defiance, which resolves his will so that he can re-emerge regenerate as God's champion. These encounters successively limit the prospect of doubt and guilt which had at first seemed to leave Samson with nothing more than a choice between comfortable ignominy and despair. His forfeiture of manhood in sensual slavery is not excused or expunged, but the spurning of Dalila exorcises the power that sense has over him:

Even yet, still the God of mercy looked upon the blindness of Samson, and in

[15] Geneva Bible, gloss on Judges, xvi, 19.

these fetters enlarged his heart from the worst prison of his sin: his hair grew, together with his repentance, and his strength with his hair.[16]

Yet had he not his strength againe, till he had called upon God, and reconciled himself.[17]

The drama turns upon the episode with Dalila, and the decisive offer and rebuff of physical contact fall exactly in the middle of the play. From this point on Samson is no longer shackled by his own guilt, and the turn upward begins. Finding himself firm in the face of such provocations he can put his former lapses behind him, and have less fear of his own frailty. The pattern of the drama closely follows out the stages of his new understanding; for only when he begins to see things clearly again, not blinded by self-concern, can the action at last resolve into the old straight encounter between slave and oppressor, godly and ungodly, God and anti-God. One of the broader ironies of a play which seems all irony is that Samson's friends, like Job's, pull him further down, while his avowed enemies help his recovery by their open hostility.

Each episode has its own kind of life. The dialogue with Harapha is cast in the terms of chivalry, and evokes the great heroic encounters as well as some thrasonical episodes:

O Baal-zabub! can my ears unused
Hear these dishonours, and not render death?

Here Samson quite expressly comes before us as the hero of a romance, a champion held back from his saving vocation by a seductress's guile; and the ease with which he meets the martial challenge shows that this time the blandishments of sense have not sapped his strength. Yet his encounter with Dalila goes beyond sexual manoeuvre, and the seductions it offers are as much of the mind as the flesh. Now it is truth itself which is threatened as the woman shifts her ground, and subtly confuses plain reason with sophistries; indeed Milton seems to invite our sympathetic half-assent to her plausible sleights just so that Samson can jolt us the more salutarily when he reaffirms the moral law by which each fresh equivocation stands condemned. She excuses herself by allowing her proneness to such venial frailties of her sex as mere curiosity and tattling; puts the fault on him for trusting such a secret to a woman; urges that she acted only out of love for him, to secure him to herself; pleads her debt of patriotic loyalty, which the importunities of her people's bigwigs had brought home to her; claims that her intention was good, even though events fell out so unfortunately. The self-justifications roll out pat as politicians' cliches.

16 Hall, op. cit. p. 136a.
17 Geneva Bible, gloss on Judges xvi, 22.

Renaissance audiences were accustomed to read a man's real motives in the style of his rhetoric and the subtle speciousness of his arguments, as in Leander's attempt on Hero, Iago's corruption of Roderigo and Othello, Comus's assault on the Lady, Satan's seduction of Eve; and as in the scriptural rendering of Dalila's cajolement of Samson:

> Againe she said unto him, How canst thou say, I love thee, when thine heart is not with me? Thou hast mocked me these three times, and hast not told mee wherein thy great strength lieth.
> And because shee was importunate upon him with her wordes continually, and vexed him, his soule was pained unto the death.
> Therefore hee told her all his heart . . . .[18]

Dalila's rhetoric piquantly betrays her mind behind her protestations, and that isn't a pretty picture; her private reason for wanting Samson out of prison, and unmindful of his destiny, seems to be that she fancies him as a tame stallion:

> Here I should still enjoy thee, day and night,
> Mine and love's prisoner, not the Philistines',
> Whole to myself, unhazarded abroad,
> Fearless at home of partners in my love.
> These reasons in Love's law have passed for good . . .

Samson Agonistes is intellectually exciting, rather than theatrically powerful, because it invites its readers to take part in an urgent search for truth. The drama grips us, or ought to grip us, because the search matters so much, and because it always seems unlikely that there can be any way out for Samson which will redeem him and confirm God's justice. Milton makes the most of the irony on which the whole story turns. Not only is his title ironically equivocal — in what sense is Samson 'agonistes'? — but he repeatedly involves the reader in the ironic misjudgments of the characters themselves. At each stage we are offered a fresh way of looking at Samson and invited to dispose of him summarily; which would also be to answer prematurely, and every time in fresh error, the universal questions that depend upon his fate.

A reader who enters imaginatively into this taxing movement is liable to find himself repeatedly revising his idea of the way it was going, and so progressively deepening his understanding of such a case as Samson's. The very first chorus proffers Samson as a simple example, *de casibus virorum illustrium*:

> O mirror of our fickle state,
> Since man on earth, unparalleled!

[18] *Judges* xvi, 15–17, Geneva text.

The rarer thy example stands,
By how much from the top of wondrous glory,
Strongest of mortal men,
To lowest pitch of abject fortune thou art fallen.

The judgment seems definitive, as if there is no more left to do but lament his fate and draw the moral lesson from it. When we see that such an account of this particular tragic hero won't stand up to events we move on to a better one, which is again tested and found too simple; and so on until it becomes clear that Samson's situation can only be resolved when it is adequately understood. Milton has him glimpse that understanding well before we are allowed to reach it. We are still kept guessing even when there aren't many possibilities left and the bold alternatives of the chorus 'Oh, how comely it is' have indicated the way out, leaving Samson only the choice of martyrdom by heroic action or a kind of sainthood by patient resignation. Indeed the climax of the drama isn't even the catastrophe itself, though we hear the noise of that even in the distance and have the shock of it thrust before us; for we are still kept waiting through the eyewitness's account until Samson's deed is at last revealed. In that artfully mounting crisis all the issues of the play hang still unresolved; the denoument comes in a moment, and there is no spectacular stage show to divert our minds from its meaning.

The drama is in the mind because its subject is mental life. Like George Herbert's *Affliction* poems it invites us to seek point in human suffering and to reason our way through doubt to reassurance. We are put in the place of the poet of 'Affliction 1', whose mind struggles to make sense of a cruel alteration of fortunes and is repeatedly misled or frustrated by it, always tempted to choose wrong, and abandon the effort in despair. If we then find something satisfyingly right, indeed inevitable, about the way the issues are resolved in the end it is because we can recognise in retrospect that the answer was there all the time. The trouble was that our human minds hadn't courage to credit, or faith to accept, the way in which God's providence takes our frailty into account, and operates through it. Thus we as readers are invited to rehearse Samson's *agon* in our minds, and to see for ourselves that we need not despair. It is a taxing task, and a reader who really lived it through might come to the end with drained but reconciled will, needing no talk of catharsis to show him why the celebrated closing line falls so aptly:

And calm of mind, all passion spent.

Like some poems by Donne and Herbert, the play gives imaginative life to a tough argument. Like a radio drama, it doesn't depend for its sense upon a particular embodiment but appeals through the ear to the mind and imagination; and it makes exacting demands on a reader's sensitivity.

There's a symphonic splendour in the way speeches are arranged so that one movement stands against another; and the mood modulates through the whole range of poetic expression from lyric plangency to something near prose:

> O dark, dark, dark, amid the blaze of noon,
> Irrecoverably dark, total eclipse
> Without all hope of day! . . .
> The Sun to me is dark
> And silent as the Moon,
> When she deserts the night,
> Hid in her vacant interlunar cave.
> Since light so necessary is to life,
> And almost life itself, if it be true
> That light is in the soul,
> She all in every part, why was the sight
> To such a tender ball as the eye confined,
> So obvious and so easy to be quenched,
> And not, as feeling, through all parts diffused,
> That she might look at will through every pore?

The setting isn't concretely realized at all at first but lightly sketched in as the action develops, so that we sense it with Samson rather than have it put concretely before us. Yet in the end it has quite enough particular presence to weigh, where it is needed:

> Occasions drew me early to this city;
> And, as the gates I entered with sun-rise
> The morning trumpets festival proclaimed
> Through each high street.

The sense of morning stir in an excited city, as of the Philistines' flushed revelry at their games, is evoked for its irony — God is not mocked. Such real dramatic skill as Milton had at his command is powerfully deployed in the sequence of events after Samson's exit, which amount to an authentic *coup de théâtre*. As in the first big dialogue of *Julius Caesar* the audience is deliberately thwarted, compelled to put up with wrongheaded chatter while the real action is audibly going on somewhere else. It has to endure its drawn-out uncertainty, searching this way and that for an explanation while the clamour in the distance gives way to the sound of debacle, and the fleeing Messenger's terror subsides enough for him to begin his graphic story. Yet we recognize that this prolonged screwing up of tension isn't done just for a dramatic effect, powerfully as the climax hits us when it comes at last. It is essential to Milton's design that his audience should come to see how its own uncertainties and anxieties might thus be brought to their extreme pitch, and providentially resolved at a stroke.

Here indeed Milton and Shakespeare stand at opposite removes. Shakespeare deals in particulars, always inviting us to see the common case in the individual instance. Milton has evidently judged that his account of experience in this work demands the widest generality, and exemplary postures akin to those of Greek myth. The scale of the drama is vast. Samson's lines demand a huge voice to fill them and a huge labour — as well as a sensitive ear — to set them working. Episodes and characters are repeatedly presented in the aspects of the great epic situations, as if Samson's story brings together and consummates all that poets have severally said of Job, blind Oedipus, Prometheus bound, Philoctetes, Aeneas, Helen of Troy, Ajax, Achilles, Thraso, and a whole gallimaufry of enslaved warriors and enslaving beauties. Milton was a very old hand at the Renaissance game of ingeniously reworking established matter into surprising new forms. Drawing in all these characters here, he lets the reader's startled recognition of them suggest an ever-widening application of the events, until Samson comes to comprehend in himself a recurrent experience of heroic suffering and recovery.

Undoubtedly Milton did seek to enlarge Samson's story into a map of the moral universe, as Hanford suggested.[19] Whether this is an adequate map he provides is something one must judge for oneself. To my mind his picture is limited but not obviously deficient. It takes memorable account of suffering; indeed I have known readers complain that we are left with so strong an impression of pain as to overshadow any triumph there might be. It reckons with several kinds of folly, frailty, viciousness. No one could say of this revenge that the hero's triumph in death is an easy consolation, or a victory too easily gained. A triumph achieved at the expense of so many lives is another matter, and we may sense the unease of the commentators on Judges at this point:

> I never read that Samson slew any but by the motion and assistance of the Spirit of God: and the divine wisdom hath reserved these offenders to another revenge .... Now he to whom vengeance belongs, sets him on work, and makes the act justice: when he commands, even every cruelty is obedience
> ....
>
> As one, therefore, that had yet eyes enough to see him that was invisible, and whose faith was recovered before his strength, he sues to that God, which was a party in this indignity, for power to revenge his wrongs, more than his own. It is zeal that moves him, and not malice. His renewed faith tells him, that he was destined to plague the Philistines; and reason tells him, that his blindness put him out of the hope of such another opportunity. Knowing, therefore, that this play of the Philistines must end in his death, he re-collects all the forces of his soul and body, that his death may be a punishment, instead of a disport,

[19] J. H. Hanford, *Samson Agonistes and Milton in Old Age*, in *Studies in Shakespeare, Milton, and Donne*, Michigan 1925, p. 171.

and that his soul may be more victorious in the parting, than in the animation; and so addresses himself, both to die and kill, as one whose soul shall not feel his own dissolution, while it shall carry so many thousand Philistines with it to the pit. All the acts of Samson are for wonder, not for imitation.[20]

Milton's human compassion evidently stops short of the Philistines here. Yet they have properly asked for what they get, not only by the bullying way they exult over helpless Samson but by making their quarrel with him a straight issue between God and Dagon, so that he has no means to make truth prevail save by destroying God's foes at the height of their arrogant pride. Milton is by no means the only Christian writer who tells us that our pity had better not extend to the devil or his minions. Like Dante, he had won his wisdom in the school of a brutal world. He had good reason to know that the truth admits no compromise, and may be very unpleasant.

Samson Agonistes has been so often pronounced deficient in its poetry that one can scarcely speak of the vivid and sometimes violent life of the writing without seeming perverse. Yet the verse is continually exciting, in its own way. 'For we are not to seek for every sort of pleasure . . . but for that only which is proper to the kind.'[21] Milton was a European artist who took decorum seriously. He certainly knew Tasso's refined analysis of the verse-textures which are appropriate to each poetic mode or kind.[22] In this distinctive kind he seems to have decided to work primarily through the formal properties of syntax, subordinating figure and image to the argument as it develops. When he does put something before our eyes, as in the vivid little cameo of Dalila's first entry, or the contrasting emblems of Samson past and Samson present, it is to enforce a point which may be best brought home by such a single sharp impact. But the verse really lives because of the marvellous virtuosity of the rhetoric, which is as unaustere in its way as the style of the *Gerusalemme Liberata*. Milton's extraordinary sensitivity to the placing of words gave him an instrument of great expressive power, which he uses with the utmost art. He works English syntax as Michelangelo worked the living marble, making it yield powerful effects of imitation, contrast and emphasis. We might take these speeches for little dramas in themselves, which vibrate with ever-changing life as the formal elements ceaselessly vary, as if word-order, stress, tempo, attack, phrasing, climax have been fashioned into a sensitive register of the mind. It is through such subtle modulations of syntax that Milton brings out the play of ideas and feeling which constitutes the inner life of his characters. He is our one great dramatic poet who attempts this formal way of displaying motives, perhaps the only one who might warrantably attempt it; and the irony is that critics

[20] Hall, *op. cit.* pp. 131a–b, 136b.
[21] Aristotle, *Poetics*, Oxford 1907, xiii.
[22] T. Tasso, *Discorsi del Poema Eroico*, Napoli 1597, iv–vi.

have gone on condemning him because he didn't write like Shakespeare. But then anyone who finds this poetry lifeless is scarcely qualified to read Milton.

Some of the writing undoubtedly expresses desolation, and worse states too; but such utterances are as carefully placed as Macbeth's 'Tomorrow, and tomorrow' speech:

> O miserable change! Is this the man,
> That invincible Samson, far renowned,
> The dread of Israel's foes, who with a strength
> Equivalent to Angels' walked their streets,
> None offering fight; who, single combatant,
> Duelled their armies ranked in proud array,
> Himself an army — now unequal match
> To save himself against a coward armed
> At one spear's length? O ever-failing trust
> In mortal strength! and, oh, what not in man
> Deceivable and vain?

Manoah's heavy baffled misgiving can be felt in the movement of the verse, as clause-structure and sense weigh down the rising voice of the repeated questions. The contrast with the resolved confidence of his valediction could scarcely be more forcible:

> Come, come; no time for lamentation now,
> Nor much more cause. Samson hath quit himself
> Like Samson, and heroicly hath finished
> A life heroic, on his enemies
> Fully revenged . . .

Samson's inner renewal is more elaborately plotted through the work. The tortuous schemes and leaden cadences of his early speeches show us a mind in a trap, wearily returning upon itself for the thousandth time:

> hence, with leave
> Retiring from the popular noise, I seek
> This unfrequented place, to find some ease —
> Ease to the body some, none to the mind
> From restless thoughts, that, like a deadly swarm
> Of hornets armed, no sooner found alone
> But rush upon me thronging, and present
> Times past, what once I was, and what am now.

By the Dalila episode the self-questioning mood has quite given way to driving imperatives and certainties:

> Out, out, hyaena! These are thy wonted arts,
> And arts of every woman false like thee —

Then these in their turn modulate to a manner more steadfastly resolute, which the brisk self-assuredness of the last passages with the Chorus confirms:

> Be of good courage; I begin to feel
> Some rousing motions in me, which dispose
> To something extraordinary my thoughts.

Dalila's speeches offer the subtlest example of this kind of inner plotting. Her shifts of ground from wheedling importunity to brazen self-righteousness are delicately signalled in the rhetoric, which always lets us see the tendency of her circling wiles:

> But I to enemies revealed, and should not!
> Nor should'st thou have trusted that to woman's frailty:
> Ere I to thee, thou to thyself wast cruel.
> Let weakness, then, with weakness come to parle,
> So near related, or the same of kind;
> Thine forgive mine, that men many censure thine
> The gentler, if severely thou exact not
> More strength from me than in thyself was found.

'I/thou', 'I/thou', 'This/mine/thine', 'thou/me/thyself'. She plays on Samson's remorse with consummate rhetorical guile, juggling pronouns and chopping logic until she settles the married couple comfortably in the same boat, with nothing to do but solace each other in weakness and forgo the great public issue between them.

The verse sometimes imitates motives more directly. Nothing more vividly sums up the division between Harapha and Samson than the abrupt shift from the irresolute self-involved syntax of Harapha's speech at line 1130:

> Thou durst not thus disparage glorious arms,

to the driving nakedness of Samson's reply:

> I know no spells, use no forbidden arts;

Repeatedly, an arrangement of syntax conveys a state of spirit. Harapha's speech 'Presume not on thy God' exhibits a sustained effect of imitative rhetoric, running on and on, persistently hanging over the line-end, so that the reader feels himself uttering a brash mouthful which is articulated only by gulps for breath:

> Whate'er he be,
> Thee he regards not, owns not, hath cut off
> Quite from his people, and delivered up

Into thy enemies' hand; permitted them
To put out both thine eyes, and fettered send thee
Into the common prison, there to grind
Among the slaves and asses, thy comrades,
As good for nothing else, no better service
With those thy boisterous locks; no worthy match
For valour to assail, nor by the sword
Of noble warrior, so to stain his honour,
But by the barber's razor best subdued.

Milton controls such effects minutely:

Immeasurable strength they might behold
In me; of wisdom nothing more than mean.

Samson's early lines evidence impeded power. Here we are made to see how a huge labour, heave, prolonged effort, topples over into curtly contemptuous self-dismissal. Even the unbalanced phrasing, which makes the lines so laborious to read, shows us how Samson sees his own moral nature and God's seeming maldisposition of things.

Milton's rhetoric, in sum, is no mere accessory to his meaning but an integral part of it. By dislocating the normal order of words and phrases, sometimes quite radically, he vastly widens the range of expressive emphasis:

                                        Of what now I suffer
She was not the prime cause, but I myself
Who, vanquished with a peal of words (O weakness!).
Gave up my fort of silence to a woman.

This is quite pungently brief, for the *contrapposto* stressing, 'She . . . I myself', precisely brings home the irony of Samson's case. Milton often starts a sentence up again with a relative after what appeared to be a closing cadence; here the tagged-on clause 'Who, vanquished . . .' hangs from its subject like a label of self-contempt. There seems little point in our going on about Milton's un-English idiom, latinate constructions and the like, when his manner is so evidently an effect of art directed to dramatic ends. In the language of *Samson Agonistes* we have the most thorough going attempt our literature can show us to exploit the dramatic possibilities of English syntax itself. Milton was one English writer who followed his European mentors in treating a language as the raw material of art. Yet artifice and conscious artistry were taken for granted in the continental discussions of the day. When Dr Leavis fails to find in Milton 'the achieved naturalness of a great English poet'[2] he condemns the

---

[23] F. R. Leavis, *Revaluation*, p. 66.

poetry by a criterion the poet would have flatly repudiated. Leavis may be right to think that naturalness, not artifice, is the proper end of art; and he is certainly very English in assuming so without question. But Michelangelo and Tasso are just two great artists who would not have agreed with him.

In the end there is very much more to Milton's verse than a few local effects. It's not easy to say why reading *Samson Agonistes* can be so peculiarly exacting, and exciting. Milton treats language like music, setting up patterns of tension and release by the way he disposes his words, so that we pursue the meaning with a kind of fugal exhilaration:

> To hang upon one's own thoughts as an object of conscious interest, to play with them, to watch and pursue them through a maze of inversions, evolutions, and harlequin changes. . . . . .[24]

de Quincey was speaking here of the excitements of rhetoric, but he might have added anyway that what matters in the end is the sense the thoughts make. Milton's rhetoric is dramatically alive because it is infinitely varied from moment to moment, yet always wholly expressive; it has meaning because, like baroque music, it builds up ideas architecturally, assembling bars into phrases and phrases into large patterns which hold many distinct apprehensions together in a tense complexity. Each sentence or movement is a little world of meaning in itself. What Milton demands of his reader is no more than Bach demands of his hearer, that he should hold the parts of the movement in his head as they come if he wants to feel the full power of the thought, and see the whole sense:

> Shall I abuse this consecrated gift
> Of strength, again returning with my hair
> After my great transgression — so requite
> Favour renewed, and add a greater sin
> By prostituting holy things to idols,
> A Nazarite, in place abominable,
> Vaunting my strength in honour to their Dagon?

The forward impulse is what matters. Milton repeatedly launches these incredible arches of meaning, continually drawing one on through the artful mazes of the syntax to the hoped-for-key. But in this movement the poetry only mirrors the economy of the whole action, which invites the reader to puzzle his way through the play in just Samson's state of urgent insecurity, thwarted, baffled, tempted to settle for an easy way out, and at last illuminated in an instant. Milton is one of those truly great artists whose work from first to last develops a single, ever more inclusive

---

[24] de Quincey, *Works*, p. 97.

vision. *Samson Agonistes* shows that he also had the Shakespearean 'faculty of realizing the whole locally',[25] though he thinks in terms of movement to an end where Shakespeare creates a texture of images. To have conceived and contrived so intimate a fusion of means and end as we find in this work is hardly evidence of declining powers. For all its austerity of effect, *Samson Agonistes* is in many ways a consummation of Milton's artistic career. It brings us through the extremities of a world to which frail sense betrays us, inviting us to see how disorder itself has place in a final order of providence; and it demonstrates the achieved artistry of a great English poet.

'*In Samsone figuratus Christus. Uxor Samsonis,* . . . Video fortitudinem Filii Dei, video infirmitatem filii hominis.'[26] Samson is another Adam because he uxoriously let his wife's importunities vanquish his manhood, and subject him to wills which worked against God's providence. He is another Christ because he overcame his human weakness to rise again from the depths in triumph, and vindicate God's justice upon his enemies. But Dalila is not another Eve. Milton insists upon the sanctity of the bond between them only to show us how far short of grace this marriage falls. When sexuality becomes a means to gain advantage there can be no mutualness in their intimacies, or mutual consolation in their frailty, whatever affection is offered. We may not sentimentalize the pair into tragic victims of circumstance, or accept Dalila's plea that her ensnaring of Samson was a heroic sacrifice of love to duty. She is starkly shown up for a seducer and a betrayer, whose appeals to the weakness of kind must be flatly rebutted. Such an inveterate corrupter of truth becomes her husband's most poisonous enemy, who is dismissed from the action with such absolute contempt that her fate concerns us no further. Milton's Samson cautions us fallen creatures that we need not look to draw saving strength from each other. His recovery of manhood is the dismissal of love.

---

[25] F.R. Leavis, *Revaluation*, p. 60.
[26] St Augustine of Hippo, *Sermo CCCLXLV. De Samsone*, Sermones Dubii, Migne, P. L.xxxix, col. 1640.

The Thinking Body

A naked thinking heart, that makes no show,
   Is to a woman, but a kind of ghost;

                                        Donne, 'The Blossom'

Never go about to separate the thoughts of the heart, from the colledge, from
the fellowship of the body. . . . All that the soule does, it does in, and with, and
by the body.

         Donne, Sermon at St Paul's, Easter-day 1923 (*Sermons* iv, 14, p. 358)

The Person, the whole man, not taken in pieces, soule alone, or body alone,
but both.

         Donne, Sermon at St Paul's, Easter-day 1626 (*Sermons* vii, 3, p. 103)

All the writings examined in this book were shaped by the assumption
that the mind realizes itself in the body. The opposition between flesh
and spirit was an old story. In the debate about love which had started
with St Augustine platonic idealism loomed so large because it offered a
way of reconciling sexual passion with the providence that sustains the
entire creation. From Dante to Michelangelo votaries found themselves
caught between conflicting imperatives of love, and strove to accommodate them by rising beyond sense to a pure spiritual apprehension of
beauty such as the body could at best shadow.

By the sixteenth century the Aristotelean notion was gaining ground
that soul and body aren't opposed elements but may be in some way inter-
dependent. Commentators on love, not all of them Christian, proposed
that human nature is one entity in which sense and intelligence aren't
separable in effect. English sacramentalists tried the idea that spiritual
being isn't disjoined from natural being but discovers itself in temporal
events, which may thus assume a double status when they simultaneously
have consequence in the sensible order and the intelligible order.

Donne was one English writer who took a deliberate stand for the integ-

rity of our experience in love. Yet the telling evidence of a special direction of concern in England is the working assumption that action fulfils
thought. The attempt to show the mind's construction in the senses
marks off English dramatic poetry down to the 1650s. Ideas contend in
the language of feeling and gesture because the physical dispositions are
taken to substantiate metaphysical causes. An impulse of passion
becomes a direction of intelligence, and thinking itself implies an ordering of sense and affection which the body must prove.

The tension between flesh and spirit isn't abated when a categorical
choice between the diverse promptings of our nature seems no longer
possible. If anything, the paradox of our condition comes home all the
more intimately to lovers who must struggle to vindicate in the momentary and corruptible their rage for the absolute, and seek a completeness
in natural life. Love becomes a condition of radical self-frustration when
the lover can do nothing but follow out the contradictory ends proposed
by his whole nature, betraying his hunger for stability in his commitment
to the present bliss, seeking a spiritual fulfilment in the gratification of
sense, entertaining as vivid sensation even the prospect of not being.
Suitors of God no less than sexual lovers express the anguish of a double
heart, which belies in very sentience its yearning for a pure incorruptible
union of love.

That such a divided enterprise should bring some uncompromising
spirits to ruin seems less remarkable than the refusal of all these lovers to
let the limitations of their state diminish them. They will their apotheosis, not by seeking to rise above their senses but by committing themselves to their humanity and triumphing in the doomed body. Whether
we take them for self-martyrs or love's heroes they live out our human
affirmations, surprising us with the vitality of natural intelligence as with
the prospect of an enduring splendour in the flesh. There may be little
enough to console us in the consummation they wring for themselves
from the extremities to which their own nature brings them, whose
power to redeem love's frailty lies wholly in conceit. Disdaining as much
as the hope of a renewal in offspring they proclaim the inextinguishable
sublimity of their whole being, whether they seek it by the
transformation into timeless glory of the here and now, the indomitable
defiance of mortality, or the realization of a providential calling against
all the odds. In seventeenth-century English writing such promises have
their irony, if only because they must always abide the sceptical whisper
that shrivels men's dignities to pathetic self-delusion, and a handful of
dust. Yet the art which discovers such a rage to perpetuate what dies
offers at least some prospect that a quality of present being may outbrave
the wastes of time.

Index